Acknowledgements

My interest in property was first inspired by an extraordinary undergraduate law course designed and taught by Kathy Bowrey and Valerie Kerruish. I am grateful to Kathy and to Valerie for their intellectual and pedagogical gifts and would like to acknowledge their deep influence on my own thinking about law, property and education. I thank Kathy in particular for her ongoing and exceptional generosity, kindness and encouragement over many years.

My doctoral research at the Faculty of Law, University of Sydney, formed the basis of the enquiry of this book. At Sydney, I enjoyed the enthusiastic support of Hilary Astor, Terry Carney, Julie Stubbs, Jeremy Webber and my indefatigable supervisor, Desmond Manderson for which I am very grateful. I am grateful also to the examiners of my dissertation, Brendan Edgeworth, Alain Pottage and Terry Threadgold for their generous and enthusiastic responses to that work. I would like to acknowledge also the influence of Alain's own work and thank him for the questions he's encouraged me to ask, for the directions he's encouraged me to pursue and for writing the Foreword for this book.

Work on the book began at Macquarie University and I thank my colleagues there for their interest and support in my research, especially Andrew Buck, Rosalind Croucher, Shayne Davenport, Richie Howitt, Edwin Judge, Bruce Kercher, Lawrence McNamara, Denise Meyerson, Sandy Noakes, Peter Radan, Alex Reilly, Simon Rice, Meg Sherval, Cameron Stewart, Sandie Suchet-Pearson and my excellent research assistants, Louise Dargan, Jonathan Light and Sacha Peldova-McLelland. The book was completed at the University of Technology Sydney with the generous and concrete support of Katherine Biber, Tracey Booth, Lesley Hitchens, Isabel Karpin, Jill McKeough, Jenni Milbank, Bronwyn Olliffe and my research assistant Nathania Nero.

At Routledge, I found an enthusiastic editor in Colin Perrin whose engagement with and encouragement of the project was pivotal to its development. I thank Holly Davis for her kindness, patience and precision in organising the project and keeping it on track and Rhona Carroll and Helen

Baxter for their production and copyediting support. The generous reports of the two referees of my book proposal encouraged and challenged my arguments in important ways and I thank them both. I thank Belinda Allen, the artist of the extraordinarily powerful and beautiful photograph of Murray River country used for the cover of this book, for her kind permission to do so. I thank Tom Kristensen for introducing me to Belinda Allen's work and showing me how her photograph connected with the themes of *Lawscape*. The author and publisher are grateful to Hart Publishing for their kind permission to reproduce parts of the chapter: 'Restoring the 'Real' to Real Property Law' in *Blackstone and His Commentaries: Biography, Law, History*, Prest, Wilfred (Ed) (Oxford: Hart Publishing, 2009) in Chapter 5 of this book.

For their feedback on my ideas and my writing in important and practical ways I thank my friends, particularly Kirsten Anker, Andrew Baron, Katherine Biber, Margaret Farmer, Lici Inge, James Ley and James Rose. To Margaret I owe special thanks for her generous, detailed and extremely helpful comments on the entire manuscript. For rainchecks and moral support along the way I thank Donna Mosford, Lorraine Rose, Madeleine King and Tom Kristensen. For important lessons in the significance of home, connectivity and place I thank my unfailingly supportive and loving family, Geoff Graham, Bronwyn Graham, Leigh Graham, Catherine George and Alex Cuadra. For detailed feedback on the manuscript, understanding, support, encouragement, inspiration and love, I thank Stuart Khan.

Finally, I acknowledge Ruby Langford Ginibi. Ruby's writing and her love of country have long been a source of inspiration to me. I am grateful to Ruby for sowing the seeds of my curiosity in these ideas by asking me, over a decade ago, 'what is the whitefella's relationship to land?' Without her intellectual generosity and kindness of spirit, this work would not exist. I dedicate this book to Ruby.

Foreword

Alain Pottage

In *Lawscape* Nicole Graham develops a rich, timely and (in more senses than one) radical critique of orthodox and critical perspectives on property. After reading this critique, many theorists of property who imagine themselves to be innovative deconstructionists of orthodoxy will have to give serious consideration to the question whether they are not instead on the trailing edge of an ideological current whose origins lie in the middle of the last millennium, if not earlier. The basic premise of this ideology is the property lawyer's belief that property 'is not about real things but about abstract rights'. Taking on this premise is no small task, and in *Lawscape* Graham works through a challenging agenda that spans a broad range of disciplines and idioms: history, economics, geography, environmental studies, legal theory and, of course, legal doctrine. The project is ambitious, but it delivers a challenge that will compel property theorists of all kinds to rethink the premises of property analysis.

Lawscape retraces the irony that has shaped legal doctrines and theories of property from the early modern period onwards. The ironic form of property is expressed in the legal figure of 'real property'. Historically, this figure originated in the distinction that Roman lawyers drew between rights and objects. Both rights and objects were things: rights were incorporeal things (*res incorporales*) and the objects to which they referred were corporeal things (*res corporales*). In the language of science studies one might say that at this point the common thingness of rights and objects made them symmetrical, not yet invested with the polarities of law and fact, or law and land, whose emergence and entrenchment Graham so carefully recounts. Roman law imagined rights as external or incidental attributes of their corporeal referents. Rights were attached to corporeal things rather than compounded into them. The exception was property: a property right was treated as a 'real right' (*ius reale*) because the right was so tightly implicated in its material object that the one merged into the other. Right and thing formed a single *corporale*. To transfer the object was to transfer the right, and the modalities of the right were directly conditioned by the material properties of the thing. This gave rise to the mediaeval sense of land as real property. The rights that persons might have in relation to land were supposed to be inscribed or rooted in the land itself. The German historian Heinrich Brunner characterized the relation as one of 'racination' (*Radizierung*). The basic irony is expressed in this metaphor of racination.

Graham describes how the old doctrinal language of racination has become a warrant for the abstraction of property laws from the landscape or lawscape in which their effects are materialized; and abstraction has become a movement of involution in which property law increasingly refers to itself rather than to the environments it shapes. Things themselves have been dematerialized and denatured by historical and social processes that are critically described in Marxist accounts of property and commodity and (re)naturalized in economic theories of property rights. Graham gets at this process by way of an intensive analysis of 'person-person' theories of property, exemplified by the writings of Bentham, Mill and Hohfeld, and 'thing-thing' theories, exemplified by Marx's analysis of commodity fetishism. And, in one of the most innovative parts of her analysis, Graham shifts from the canonical texts to the practices of teaching property; she explores the role that the teaching of property law, both traditional and progressive, plays in fostering the sense of property as a placeless institution. This is the lesson that even the most progressive of academic property lawyers teach their students. The lawyer and anthropologist Annelise Riles observes similar phenomena through the lens of 'instrumentality'; the instrumentality of property law is itself instrumentalized as the pedagogic means by which property law is taught in the form of problem scenarios that compel students to assume the role of the skilled user of property-instruments. Conceived and practised as an instrument, property law can appear as a means of intervening in the world in more or less redemptive ways, but what ultimately counts is mastery of means that can be turned to any end. Both of these perspectives on the teaching and practice of property law reveal the sense in which property has become a weightless institution: things are fungible, rights are tradable, and the effects of the institution are eclipsed by a fetishism of its technicalities.

This is the background against which Graham calls for a 'paradigm shift' in our thinking about property. This intervention is timely because it draws on the experience of a context in which the old paradigm of placeless property has been exposed to geographical facts that expose its partiality. The history of native title jurisprudence in Australia is a tributary of the history of one universal localism: 'real property' as it was imagined by the English common law. If one were to ascribe a motto to the common law in the period of colonial expansion it might be Gertrude Stein's response to the question whether forty years of life in France had caused her to lose her American roots: 'what good are roots if you can't take them with you?' According to William Blackstone the English settlers of a new colony would bring so much of the content of the common law as was 'adapted' to the terrain of the new land: 'if an uninhabited country be discovered and planted by English subjects, all the English laws then in being, which are the birthright of every subject, are immediately there in force. But this must be understood with very many and very great restrictions. Such colonists carry with them only so much of the English law, as is applicable to their own situation and the condition of an infant colony'. This line of argument was, infamously, taken to its furthest (further than Blackstone himself might have prepared to go) in the judicial theory that the land of Australia was *terra nullius* at the moment of colonization. Although this legal fiction was formally repudiated in the decision of the High Court of Australia in *Mabo* v *Queensland* (1992) the landscape made by the fiction cannot be unmade.

Graham is especially interested in the physical – or 'biogeographical' – effects of the expansion of the English law of real property in Australia in the nineteenth century. What was in question was not simply the expansion of a technique or a set of concepts: the effect of putting those concepts to work was to change the biogeographical matrices of place in Australia. An example is the effect of the grants of land made to pastoralists in the nineteenth-century: 'Once colonists in Australia rejected the land laws and economies of local indigenous peoples, then abandoned early hybrid economies that combined food production with hunting, and then embraced completely surplus agricultural, pastoral and forestry production – the physical consequences were impossible to undo'. The legal landscape that had these quite simply left no 'ground' for the continued practice and existence of indigenous customs. As Elizabeth Povinelli observes, the decision in *Mabo* v *Queensland* effectively revitalized the engine of the 'placeless' theory of property, namely, the 'abstract machine' of the common law. In such circumstances, property became, as Graham puts it, 'maladapted': 'the law was not adapted to the land, rather, the land was adapted to the law'. Or, to make the same point in other language, it was and is essential to property law's performativity that it should be blind to its own environmental effects. Property law, true to the idiom of inscription or racination, 'describes, prescribes and explains unsustainable people-place relations' in such a way as to obscure its own effects.

The answer does not lie in an unmediated return to land or place itself. There is no such thing. Etymologically, the term landscape equivocates between representation and territory. The landscape is a reflex of the means and idioms in which it is represented: there is no territory without the map, no *paysage* without the *tableau*. Graham addresses the implications of this relation of intermediation by, for example, turning to critical geographical theories of landscape, notably Jessica Weir's theory of 'landscape connectivity', which draws on Bruno Latour's scenography of networks, actants, and hybrids. The point is to get away from the divisions that shape modern property thinking – persons and things, persons and place, propositions and things – and to think instead in terms of relations of hybridization, or connections whose terms are not persons and things but agents that 'exchange competences'. Interestingly, Latour has characterized this kind of connectivity in terms of the figure of property, or possession. In a gloss on Gabriel Tarde's remarks on 'having', Latour takes property (or possession) as a formula for a kind of unbinding bond. In his *Monadologie et sociologie* Tarde observed that philosophers would have done better to take having rather than being as their basic premise: whereas philosophy as a whole seemed to be based on the verb *to be*, a lot of sterile debate would have been avoided if it had instead based itself on the verb *to have*. This is not property in the sense of rights but property in the sense of predicates. Philosophically, Tarde's sense of 'having' turns on the question of what it means for a subject to have predicates. Predicates are verbs rather than qualities: that is, a predicate is not an attribute that inheres in the subject so much as it is a verb – a doing – that includes or absorbs the subject in a process of variation and transformation. Having is a mode of exposure: to 'have' properties is to be exposed to the effects of inflection or irritation that are prompted by the predicates that one attaches to oneself. These effects of irritation and inflection are reciprocal. As Latour puts it, 'possession is another way of talking about translation' (in a specific theoretical sense); or, there are always 'two-way connections between the having and the had'.

Graham takes up the question of how to rethink the relation of property in terms of this kind of two-way connectivity by way of an extraordinarily rich historical and conceptual analysis. In an expansive and incisive critique, she explores how the basic division between persons and things that is held in the notion of inscription or racination has been reinvented – or rather, ongoingly involuted – by a long succession of doctrinal and theoretical accounts of property. *Lawscape* – both the analysis and the word itself – opens out a way of thinking about the environment of property that does start from a division that has already simplified and obscured the workings of the institution. In so doing, it sets a challenge that will prove compelling to a diversity of teachers, theorists and philosophers of property.

Preface

The research that led to this book initially began as an examination of Indigenous Australian laws about 'country'. Not long into my research author and historian, Bundjalong woman, Ruby Langford Ginibi said to me that it seemed to her that while white researchers were curious about blackfellas' laws about country, too often they were ignorant of the relationship between law and land *in their own culture*. It was a point well made, and well taken. The work for this book started from there. It had to ask: what *is* the relationship between property law and Anglo-centric culture? And, what *is* the relationship between property law and the land itself?

The specific conditions of British climate and geography supported a specific kind of economy and land law which was exported across the globe to places with entirely different climatic and geographical conditions. The material consequences of this process are evident in England's former colonies. These consequences present urgent questions regarding the suitability of English land law to regulate land use practice and ownership in parts of the world with utterly different physical conditions. The most important of these questions is, what can we do about the mismatch? To be in a position to do anything at all, we must be equipped with a deeper knowledge of the complex circumstances from which modern 'whitefella' property law emerged.

As the title suggests, *Lawscape* explores the relationship between the abstractness of property law and the physical materiality of place. The central theme of the book is that the law can, should and does have a direct relationship to land and natural resources through its property regime – regardless of whether it acknowledges this relationship. As such, the book explores the ways in which the vocabulary and practices of ownership in property law transform natural environments. *Lawscape* contends that the agency of property law in anthropogenic environmental change must be acknowledged and included in the endeavour to better adapt cultural and economic practices to the actual capacities and limits of the physical world in which it operates and on which it ultimately depends.

Chapter 1

Introduction

> Revolutions are inaugurated by a growing sense . . . that existing institutions have ceased adequately to meet the problems posed by an environment that they have in part created.
>
> (Kuhn 1996: 92)

> The devil is not in the detail but in the framework within which the detail is perceived. That is not something you can set out to look for; and if you stumble upon it, because distracted by incongruities when working within the received framework, you must resign yourself to being a heretic.
>
> (Milsom 2003: 107)

1.1 Paradigm, property, place

Peter Spencer is a farmer in New South Wales, Australia. In 2007 he organised National Chop down a Tree Day. For almost 50 days from late 2009 to January 2010, he protested against NSW laws that regulate and prohibit the felling of trees and clearing of vegetation on private land by occupying a platform 10 metres up a wind-monitoring tower on his property and refusing to eat. His 'hunger strike' made national headlines and attracted attention to the tension between property rights and environmental values in contemporary law. High-profile Senator Barnaby Joyce addressed farmers who subsequently marched on Parliament House, Canberra to demonstrate their support of Spencer and their opposition to native vegetation laws saying:

> [T]he Australian people are starting to say we've had enough of being signed up to these agreements, where you get the kudos, or the happy clapping in Bali or some conference, but the bill goes home to working families, the bill goes home to the family farm.
>
> (Senator Joyce cited in Harrison and Cubby 2010)

The point he makes resonates with many farmers and articulates the equation of property rights with liberty and environmental law with its deprivation.

The central issue in the debate is compensation and whether it is the 'solution' to the tension depends on how property is defined and whether the environment is external that definition:

> That no one has a property right to destroy the benefits of a natural system ... may seem obvious, yet its opposite has been the (unarticulated) watchword of the developmental economy's property system.
>
> (Sax 2008: 16)

This book explores the meaning of property in legal and cultural discourse and practice. It contends that the dominant meaning of property, that property is not about real things but abstract rights, can be linked directly to maladapted land use practices and their ecological consequences. As the title of the book suggests, what we see when we look at a landscape is a series of legally prescribed land use practices in action. The point is not that the landscape could or should be devoid of evidence of human interaction with the earth's systems. The economic base of human life can only be the environment. Consequently, the human occupation of any area of land can result in the exploitation or degradation of that environment for a period of time until lessons are learned and management practices and land laws eventually sustain that society's occupation of that area (Kohen 1995). The point is: when we look at our landscapes and we see our land use practices and law system in action, what does the landscape tell us about their interaction with the earth's systems? *Lawscape* asks what landscapes reveal about law. The answer is that the necessary lessons are yet to be learned and that is due to a particular mindset, a paradigm that detaches people from place, viewing the world not as a network of relationships, but as two separate spheres: culture and nature. This paradigm is, however, in crisis, and this book attempts to weave together the histories, philosophies and geographies of property to find out why.

The source of the paradigm of the contemporary property system can be traced back hundreds of years. American geographer, David Harvey, said: '[W]e are, whether we like it or not, inheritors of the Enlightenment tradition and the only interesting question is what we make of it and what we do with it' (Harvey 2000: 149). The Enlightenment tradition that Harvey refers to is a paradigm, a framework of ideas, values and expectations that both creates and is created by a particular economy. Referring to an economy and its ideological framework in terms of tradition locates the culture of a particular society within the nature of a particular place. Paradigms (or traditions) develop over time with successful cultural adaptation to particular conditions and thus describe not only social relationships but also ecological relationships. Paradigms are the result of an accumulation of knowledge that works in its specific time and place. Thus while paradigms are not universal truths, they are true in a given time and place under a set of particular conditions. Traditions become traditions, they succeed as prescriptions of social order and economy, because they are useful and viable as knowledge and practice. As French sociologist Pierre Bourdieu argued: '[T]he rule is not automatically effective by itself . . . it obliges us to ask under what conditions a rule can operate' (1990: 76). The conditions under which a tradition or paradigm operate are actual as well as abstract. That traditions are grounded in particular realities suggests that they are not simply inherited – they are made (Kerruish 1999). The paradigms that inform our culture today are not only legacies of the past, they explain the practices of *today* in terms of time and place. The conditions under which a rule, or paradigm can operate are not just historical conditions, they are ecological conditions, as such they are particular not universal, temporary, not eternal.

American scientist, Thomas Kuhn, argues that paradigms enable and inhibit social and intellectual development in certain directions. He acknowledges the role of nature, the physical world, in the development and crisis of any given paradigm (1996: 69), but his focus is predominantly the intellectual and ideological function of paradigms in science. Kuhn's theory of paradigm shift argues that one paradigm ends and another begins when the prior paradigm becomes dysfunctional. The function of a paradigm is to be meaningful and practical, to describe, explain and prescribe activity. When the usefulness of a paradigm has, for whatever reason, diminished and another practice or theory seems more useful, the latter may replace the former and become a new paradigm. Again, Kuhn emphasises the role of nature or the physical world in reaching that moment:

> The decision to reject one paradigm is always simultaneously the decision to accept another, and the judgment leading to that decision involves the comparison of both paradigms with nature *and* with each other.
>
> (1996: 77)

A paradigm shift, the conception and creation of a new economy or relation in or to the world, is supported by that world, by its material, environmental conditions. Kuhn's philosophy of paradigms and paradigm shift is a useful way of thinking about the frameworks that govern legal development and practice, such as property law. In addition to considering the social and intellectual conditions of the paradigm of property law, it is important to consider the physical and environmental conditions of that paradigm. The Enlightenment tradition that we have 'inherited' was made and succeeded not just under specific historical conditions but in the specific environmental conditions of a particular place: Europe. The gradual emergence of the modern European tradition of land use and the 'enlightened' modern paradigm of property law were neither solely cultural nor solely natural events, but rather ecological events that were made possible by particular climatic, geological, biological, social and technological conditions. Europe is an environment that receives high rainfall and in which 'vegetation regrows quickly':

> Much of northern and western Europe is still able to support productive intensive agriculture today, 7000 years after the arrival of food production. In effect, Europe received its crops, livestock, technology, and writing systems from the Fertile Crescent, which then gradually eliminated itself as a major centre of power and innovation.
>
> (Diamond 1997: 411)

The paradigm of modern European property relations is anthropocentric. It is a dichotomous model of the world that separates people from everything else, placing people in an imagined centre, their environment literally surrounds and is peripheral to them. Kuhn's theory of paradigm crisis and paradigm shift allows us to consider the separation of people and place in this anthropocentric model as particular to a specific time and place, developed in and for modern western science, philosophy, economy and law and so, its truths are not universal, eternal or transcendent but historicised and placed. The feature of any given paradigm that makes it successful as a paradigm, but that inhibits self-critique, is that it makes alternatives unthinkable. The current anthropocentric model of the world insists that people are culture and everything else is nature. It becomes difficult if not impossible to critique this model without recourse to external or alternative models or positions and yet these are explained according to the logic and language they attempt to approach from a position of exteriority:

> For several millennia now, the western tradition has been dominated by various human-centred views of the cosmos. Nature has progressively been defined as ever more distant from human culture . . . (In) spite of . . . many eloquent statements by American Indians, Aboriginal Australians and others, we have very little idea of what a non-human-centred cosmos looks like and how it can be thought to work.
>
> (Rose 1988: 379)

Nevertheless, the current paradigm, like any other, is inevitably subverted by its own failure to describe, prescribe and explain a world that it partly created: 'Nature itself must first undermine professional security by making prior achievements seem problematic' (Kuhn 1996: 169). Using Kuhn's theory, and emphasising the significance of physical conditions in the production and crisis of paradigms, this book attempts to present the 'achievements' of modern property law as 'problematic' with regard to its material conditions in place:

> With legal history, as sometimes with the natural sciences, truly elementary propositions may stand or fall not with evidence of particular facts but with their power to explain all the facts.
>
> (Milsom 2003: xvii)

The paradigm of modern property law describes, prescribes and explains unsustainable people–place relations because it does not situate itself in place. The dysfunction of its propositions is evident in landscapes across the world. When we look at an image of a cattle ranch, a multi-storey carpark or an enclosed and irrigated field of crops, we are seeing the world we have made by our land use practices, which are, in turn, informed by the concepts and norms that facilitate and protect them. The paradigm of placelessness is apparent in landscapes that are not local but 'can be had anywhere in the world' (Newsome, cited in Neumann, Thomas and Eriksen 1999: 160). The universalism of modern law is materialised by land use practices. In effect, what we see in a landscape is not a detached and separated physical realm, 'the land', but ourselves, our practices and our law – a lawscape.

1.1.1 The paradigm of placelessness

If we wish to have a land that is truly Australian restore we must; for we have custody of an extraordinary assemblage of plants and animals. The converse is that otherwise, as a nation, we will be left to identify with a land that is one giant sheep walk, cattle ranch, mining quarry, farm, or tree-felling operation. Such a land can be had anywhere in the world.
                            (Newsome, cited in Neumann et al. 1999: 160)

It's everything. You just can't pick it up and plonk it down somewhere else.
                            (*The Castle* 1997)

Place, or the physical, 'natural' world, is predominantly conceived, experienced and articulated anthropocentrically, as something separable and 'other' to human subjectivity. Until recently, this dichotomous paradigm has meant that people are seen either as dominated by nature, chained to the physical world or as dominating and transcending it. 'Western discourses regarding the relation to nature have frequently swung on a pendulum between cornucopian optimism and triumphalism at one pole and unrelieved pessimism . . . at the other pole' (Harvey 2000: 149). Despite these evaluative swings, anthropocentrism is commonly associated with an instrumentalist evaluation of the things in the world, that is, solely in terms of their use within the processes and products of human life (Smith 1998: 4).[1]

Anthropocentrism characterises modern property law according to which place, in itself, is meaningless. Indeed, the foundational history of modern England and her former colonies depended on an anthropocentric philosophy and practice that made possible the imposition of English law in foreign countries, which principally operates via the notion of the alienability

---

1 For detailed critiques of anthropocentrism, see Garner (1997); Midgley (1996); Sterba (1998).

of places and things. This concept or philosophy of place presents no obstacle to the satisfactory resolution of disputes over property in which the philosophy is shared and uncontested. However, when cultural experiences or philosophies of place are in dispute, a satisfactory resolution is 'problematic'.

The anthropocentric paradigm of modern property law creates and is created by theory, education and legal and cultural practices. Property law scholar, Kevin Gray, concluded in 1991 that property 'does not really exist: it is mere illusion' (1991: 252). Law teachers and practitioners agree with Gray and repeat the time-honoured Hohfeldian concept of 'dephysicalised' property: that property is not about things but about people or, rather, about relations between persons. Consequently, the questions that modern property law excludes are ones that concern materiality. 'There is a long-standing and understandable reluctance to think about property in material terms' (Blomley 1998: 572). This is one of the reasons why modern property law struggles to address adequately the claims of dispossessed Indigenous peoples. How would Australian native title claimants, for example, respond to Gray's conclusion that property is an illusion? This book does not set out to answer this question; its concern is twofold: to ask how property came to be regarded as 'illusory' and to suggest that this conception indicates that the validity and utility of the dominant paradigm of property are 'manifestly running out' (Brady 1991: 9). Why does this matter? Because property law is more than a regulation of abstract relations between people and place, property law is a regulation of real and particular uses of land and non-human things.

The economic significance of property law is well appreciated in commercial terms, but it is less well appreciated in terms of its ecological base. In other words, property law is not usually considered a major determinant of the ecological economy. This is a strange view of the world because the economy of any species is contained within the larger economy of the earth's systems. The words economy and ecology have a shared etymology in their root 'eco-' from the Greek word *oikos*, meaning 'home'. The *logos* of 'ecology' means 'knowledge' and the *nomos* of 'economy' means management or regulation. Ecology means knowledge of the home and economy means the regulation or management of it. 'If we do not know our home we cannot manage it? If there is no healthy Earth community, there can be no healthy human community. If there is no ecological capital, there can be no financial capital' (Kumar 2007).

Viewing property law in the broader framework of economy and ecology, it is apparent that property is at the heart of the environmental changes that it originally presented as the legitimate basis for entitlement to property when the English commons were enclosed and the lands and peoples of foreign countries were appropriated. Thinking and rethinking the paradigm of modern property law in terms of its material application and consequences is important because it has not been sufficiently undertaken to keep the questions that should be unthinkable from being asked. And, because ' "reality" is not in the habit of offering up its meanings already clarified, with a set of instructions for use attached' (Muecke 1992: 4) an effort is required to understand the relationship between law and place and to better align the two.

Lawscape does not advocate a reversal of the hierarchy of the paradigmatic categories nature/culture neither does it advocate a 'harmonious' combination of the twin realms. Rather, through an analysis of modern property law, its origins, developments and consequences, the book argues that because the categories of nature and culture do not exist in reality, they should not serve as the foundation of property relations. Indeed, it is precisely because there is no neat split or separation of nature and culture in the world, that the concept of land-as-commodity fails to make sense. What is needed is nothing short of a paradigm shift. Precisely such a shift was foreshadowed and is required by the land claims of dispossessed Indigenous peoples and environmentalist critiques of property. Is property an illusion? Property is what the law says it is. But, as Indigenous peoples, farmers and scientists have learned, the law is also, partly, what the land says it can be. In other words, the particularities of land, of place, determine the material limits of what is ultimately, authoritatively and sustainably local law and economy.

The inadequacy of the paradigm of modern property law is considered here in terms of the adaptation and maladaptation of people to place. Placing property law, making it responsive to the material conditions of its possibility means critiquing its anthropocentrism both from within that paradigm and with a view to an alternative paradigm. While the idea of biodiversity is not explicitly theorised here, the arguments advanced in the following chapters are imbued with an interest in the possibility of law's connection with place not dichotomously, but as part of an ecological network.

The law's insistence that property is not about things, that property is not really 'real', that property is 'dephysicalised', render the definition of property lofty and elusive because definitions necessarily draw limits and edges, observe finiteness. The trouble with defining property as 'dephysicalised' is that it is not – property relations, by which I mean the relationships between people and place, are *material* relations – something the law finds deeply problematic. The dominant value of property in contemporary legal practice and culture is as a commodity. As such, property has the indefinite quality of being fungible: infinitely tradeable, limited neither spatially nor temporally. But the physical 'things' that are traded and owned as property are physically definable and specific, they have limits. Land, for example, conceived not as a commodity but as part of a particular place, is radical to property law. The limits of land, its qualities and conditions are definable things. Yet, property law insists that place is irrelevant to property law. The universality of the modern law and economic commodification of property can function only on the basis that both law and property are general not particular, global not placed. Specifically, the placelessness or atopia of law was the ideological condition of the colonisation of the world and the imposition of alien regimes of property.

The absence of place is the condition of the possibility of a universal and universalising law that extended 'across the whole globe, like a coinage reducing all things to a common measure' (Thompson 1991: 164). In many ways, the problem of defining property can be related to the problem of defining anything universal: being neither particular nor contextual, it lacks bearings. Lacking or refusing the sense of its locality, property would logically prove difficult to find.

Modern property law is not, of course, universal, but it is universalising. Different historical developments of English property law in foreign countries notwithstanding, these local manifestations of modern law should not be confused as local origins. This is important because if the paradigm of modern property law is to remain, or rather, become functional, as a paradigm of people–place relations, it needs to acknowledge that its placelessness and atopic basis is maladapted to diverse and specific places.

For modern property law to be meaningful and functional, to sustain people–place relations, it must be cognisant of the necessary and inevitable connection between law and place. That relationship has been abstracted by the theory and practice of 'dephysicalisation', which maintains that place is irrelevant to property law and that property is always and already about things that lack any specific and particular value, which can be readily alienated, transferred and exchanged between persons. The Australian film *The Castle* is an excellent illustration of this relationship and how notions of place are radical and nonsensical to the paradigm of modern property law.

1.1.2 The Castle

The 1997 film *The Castle* is often cited in Australian law schools, not least with reference to the law of property. It is one of the first things property students learn, to leave any sense of place in property behind. The film was written and produced by television comedy veterans who had worked collaboratively for the public national broadcaster, the ABC.[2] The team, Working Dog, enjoyed an established reputation in Australian popular culture as political satirists. Their film was a timely and critical commentary on the legal and cultural values of property debated since the controversial recognition of native title in Australian property law in 1992.

---

2 The *ABC* is the national non-commercial television and radio broadcaster in Australia. The television comedy *The Late Show* presented satirical political and social commentary to popular success from 1992–1995.

'I don't want to be compensated. You can't buy what I've got', retorts Daryl Kerrigan to the Judge of the Administrative Appeals Tribunal in the film. Several days earlier, Daryl Kerrigan and his family had been issued 'a kick-out notice' in which the Kerrigan family were offered monetary compensation from Airlink for the compulsory acquisition of their property. Airlink, a federal authority, is a consortium of local, state and federal governments and the Airport Commission, which together seek to expand the airport as part of a multibillion dollar investment. The Kerrigan's chances of keeping their home against the power and interests of Airlink are slim. In the words of Dennis Denuto, Daryl's lawyer and a family friend, Airlink 'write the rules – they own the game'. The film follows the legal battle of the Kerrigan family to keep their home against the interests of Airlink and thus canvasses dominant and marginal ideas of place and property in contemporary Australian law and culture. Produced and screened in Australia at the time of the parliamentary and very public debate of the Native Title Amendment Bill, the rise of Independent MP, Pauline Hanson, and the formation of the One Nation party, the film wove its seductively simple narrative into the fabric of social controversy.[3]

The debate about the value and meaning of property, stimulated in Australia by the native title cases of *Mabo*[4] and *Wik*[5] and subsequent native title legislation,[6] was not the backdrop for the film's narrative, rather it was its focus. Issues of sovereignty, citizenship, dispossession, indigenous land rights, private property rights, classical liberal economy, housing and value conflict are all represented in this film. The structure of the film's narrative follows the legal process of adjudication and appeal from the AAT to the full court of the High Court of Australia. The ideas of improvement and dispossession, against which the Kerrigan family find themselves under the jargoned guise of compulsory acquisition, articulates the core principle of private property law administered in Australia. Together, this narrative structure and ideology connect the design of the film to its subject: the value of place in modern property law.

The Castle presents the dominant value of property in modern law and culture – the alienability of property. Indeed, the vocabulary of contemporary property law is peppered with the notion of alienability: alienation, transferability, acquisition, compensation and exchange. This concept of property is articulated in the film by the interests and actions of Airlink. For Airlink, property is valued as a tradeable commodity or object of ownership. The

---

3 For a discussion of the racism expressed in the controversy over native title and the rise of Pauline Hanson, see Hage (1998) and Manne et al. (1998).
4 *Mabo v Queensland* (1992) 175 CLR 1.
5 *Wik Peoples v Queensland* (1996) 187 CLR 1.
6 *Native Title Act* 1993 (Cth) and *Native Title Amendment Act* 1998 (Cth).

concept of place is absent from this evaluation of property. Thus, in modern property law, if place could be said to exist, it is as land, which is deemed a tradeable commodity. While land owners relate to each other via the value of the object of ownership, that value is determined not by the relationship between the owner and the land, rather by its function as a commodity between landowners. Airlink seeks to acquire the property of the Kerrigan family not for its value to the owner, but for its value as a commodity. Therefore, when Daryl disputes the compulsory acquisition of his property he is asked routinely whether the monetary compensation figure for his property-as-commodity is acceptable. An officer at his local council tries to explain the elementary principle of Daryl's private property rights: 'That's why you'll be duly compensated.' The judge at the AAT hearing repeats this apparently basic connection between property and alienability: 'Are you disputing the amount of compensation?' If all property is always a commodity, such questions make sense. The question does not make sense, however, to Daryl and his family. The Kerrigans express a value of inalienable property precisely because their value of property includes a concept of place. Their value exceeds the dominant value of property as expressed by Airlink, the Anglo-Australian legal system and Anglo-Australian culture – it is radical.

The Kerrigans regard the compulsory acquisition of their property as theft. Devastated by the idea, Daryl says to the AAT: 'You just can't walk in and steal our home.' Later, while packing to move out of their home, having lost his appeal to the Federal Court, Daryl says to his wife Sal:

I'm really starting to understand how the Aboriginals feel. This house is like their land, it holds their memories, the land is their story. It's everything. You just can't pick it up and plonk it down somewhere else. This country's gotta stop stealing other people's land.

Daryl's value of property is connected to a concept of place that is fundamentally different from the concept of a commodity. For the Kerrigan family, their property is also their place. The film goes to considerable effort to represent this place as ordinary, not spectacular or unique to the film's viewers. Indicators of the disadvantages of the place are also made clear to the audience: there is lead in the soil, it is walking distance from a major international airport from which there is constant and disruptive aircraft noise and associated atmospheric pollution. No one else might see what the Kerrigans see in their property, but the fact remains they are passionately attached to it and are entirely uninterested in leaving it and any related compensation for its acquisition. The point is that place is meaningful for the family and it is this alone that renders its alienability abhorrent to them.

The stunning achievement of *The Castle* is that it credibly represents the paradox of a mainstream family who hold a radical value of property.

The film did so (and to great commercial success) despite widespread opposition to the value of inalienable, placed-based property expressed by native title claimants and Indigenous land owners at the time of the film's distribution. The concept of place central to the idea that property is inalienable is made palatable to mainstream Australia precisely because the Kerrigan family is convincingly mainstream. The ultimate 'family-values' family, the Kerrigans are white, Anglo, heterosexual, *Channel 9* viewers[7] with a small business, a suburban home, a holiday house and a few pets. The characterisation of the family as regular 'little Aussie battlers' is careful and thorough, leaving no doubt that they and their values are collectively David against the Goliath of modern property law. Modern property law and its institutionalised commodity value of property are portrayed as a senseless machine destructive of a seemingly obvious connection of people to place. In the film, the law's miscognisance of its own value specificity troubles the Kerrigans. Struggling to be understood in his own terms, Daryl corrects his local council officer: 'No, no you've missed the point – I'm not interested in compensation.' The Kerrigan value of property is different from the law's value and cannot be enveloped by it. Furthermore, Daryl says to the High Court that the law's value of property-as-commodity excludes their value, leaving no place for an alternative meaning of property and leaving no place for place. Property law is thus characterised as perversely destructive:

> They're judging a place by what it looks like, if it doesn't have a pool, a classy front, or a big garden it's not worth saving. But it's not a house, it's a home. People who love each other. Memories. Family. But that doesn't mean as much as a big fucking driveway.

Daryl's placed sense of property undermines the abstractness of dephysicalised law. He makes the law seem artificial or fictitious. Thinking like a lawyer requires a suspension of belief in physical reality, a denial of experience. The law facilitates a culture of property articulated in terms of symbols, certificates of title, conflicting interests rather than places, homes and belongings. Living in a world of modern property relations involves an acceptance that the real is unreal, that places are spaces and that networks of complex relationships are commodifiable environmental products. To deny this sensibility, as the Kerrigan family does, is radical.

---

7 *Channel 9* is a national commercial television broadcaster in Australia, the programmes and news service of which were, then, consistently top rating according to daily media viewing habit polls published in the *Sydney Morning Herald*.

1.2 Location

This book is about the relationship between law and place. It is important to briefly locate the analytical approach of *Lawscape* to this topic in the context of the scholarship of law and other disciplines. Studies and theories of place in culture have, until recently, been predominantly limited to the behavioural sciences, geosciences and literary studies. These disciplines have focused on place as: constitutive of cultural and psychological identity; as natural environments; and as an aesthetic setting for art, literature and music respectively. In the behavioural sciences, there is a small but established study of place in terms of the social organisation of gender (McDowell 1999), race (Mohanram 1999) and ethnicity (Kristeva 1991; McCoy 1997) in the anthropological, sociological and political sciences. These disciplines focus on place as constitutive of social subjectivities such as the domestic, the fringe, the ghetto, the suburb, the electorate (Goot 1998), the diaspora (Grosz 1993), the global citizen (Massey and Jess 1995) and, more generally, of the character of modernity itself (Cushing 2002; Shields 1991). These studies have also been addressed in theories of architecture and urban planning (Rapoport 1972; Vidler 1992; Winikoff 1995). Significantly, place is abstract and dephysicalised in behavioural science studies of cultural identity. Anthropological, sociological and political studies emphasise the agency of place, only as a *social* environment, or social setting, in the formation of individual and social identities. Presenting place as a physical or natural environment is subversive to behavioural sciences because it suggests that social identities are determined not only by cultural materialities such as gender, race, ethnicity and class, for example, but also by natural or environmental materialities such as climate, meteorology, epidemic, topography, flora and fauna.

Physical geography (Holt-Jensen 1999) and environmental sciences including geology and biology (Dick 1996), have until recently, discussed place and the physical natural environment as distinct and separate from human culture and activity, with the significant exception of references to archaeology, which appropriates human activity into 'nature'.[8] Recently, geoscientific discourse has more directly related environmental contexts to human agency (Kohen 1995; Richter and Redford 1999). These disciplines increasingly employ such terms as 'crisis', 'responsibility', 'care' and 'necessity' when speaking of human interaction with the natural environment (Aplin et al. 1999). In other words, attention to the relationship between people and place, while emphasising its physical aspects, would present the relationship as one of unilateral agency of people over place in terms of environmental change or degradation.

Human geography presents analyses of people–place relations that are more subversive of the paradigm of modern law that separates people and

---

8 For a good critical discussion of this aspect of archaeology in geology, see McConnochie (2002).

place, nature and culture. American geographer David Harvey's *Justice, Nature and the Geography of Difference* (1996) while not an elaborate theory of property, critiques the dominant value of property by challenging the ongoing validity of the paradigm of nature/culture that ideologically sustains the production and economy of global capitalism. Harvey 'recognises that "the antithesis between nature and history is created" only when "the relation of man to nature is excluded from history" ' (Marx, cited in Harvey 1996: 184). Significantly, Harvey offers a critique of property that is not ecocentric. His model of the world does not privilege the natural environment because it does not separate humans from the world and excludes the hierarchical dynamic. Harvey offers a social theory that deconstructs the 'otherness' of nature that sustains both anthropocentric and ecocentric models of the world. In this way, his postmodern theory of property is intellectually reconcilable with notions of biodiversity in theories of physical sciences, notably, ecological studies. The environmental changes of modernity are neither natural nor anthropogenic in Harvey's geography and thus establish the possibility of incorporating theories of biodiversity within property theory.

Australian geographer Jessica Weir advances a theory of 'landscape connectivity' (Weir 2009) according to which the important parts of people–place relations are the connections, rather than the substances of those relationships (Weir 2009: 47). Drawing from French philosopher Bruno Latour and Australian philosopher Val Plumwood, Weir critiques the 'hyperincommensurability' and 'hyperseparation' of people and place, nature and culture in modern cultural thought and practice. The problem, she argues, is that the modern paradigm of people–place relations is twofold: it '[I]ncreases human power to transform nature, and limits human capacity to respond to ecological devastation' (Weir 2009: 48). Weir's critical geographical analysis of people–place relations in the Murray River country of southeastern Australia identifies the universalism of the paradigm of modern people–place relations as presenting one of the most substantial obstacles to connectivity. 'Central to this power to transform nature is the assumption in modern thinking that modern knowledge is universal and thus can be applied anywhere' (Weir 2009: 48). Her own place-based analysis demonstrates the benefits of her critique. Following Donna Haraway's theory of 'situated knowledges' (1988 cited in Weir 2009: 49) Weir presents the relationships of indigenous traditional owners to Murray River country that subvert conventional categories of economy, ecology, knowledge and law. Weir's analysis highlights the vulnerability of 'the moderns' in their blindness to and denial of their dependency on place (Weir 2009: 16–18).

There is a significant body of research in literary studies and art theory about the iconography of place as landscape or, in other words, as metaphor and setting (Daniels and Cosgrove 1988). These studies concentrate on the visual (Daniels 1993) and sensual elements of place in human perception. They predominantly relate place to human creativity and metaphysics through

detailed analyses of art (Beilharz 1997; Bonyhady 2000; Casey 2002), literature (George 1996; Nightingale 1986; Pollack and MacNabb 2000; Williams
1973) such as (especially) poetry (Barrell 1972; Fitter 1995; Turner 1979),
tragedy and romance in dramatic art (Burt and Archer 1994), romanticism in
music and painting (Barrell 1986) and the 'pastoral' and 'new world' genres.
The 'trans' discipline of cultural studies has recently developed theories of
place that primarily focus on place as a form of spatiality manifest in aesthetic and political areas. There is a significant body of work in the cultural
studies of aesthetics that addresses place and space in art, film, architecture
and urban planning. The focus of these studies is the degree and or significance of place as landscape, setting, metaphor, home and identity in individual and social imagination (Haynes 1998).

Histories and theories of culture and its discourses describe the role of
place in the formation of cultural identities (Arthur 2003; Drew 1994; Hodge
1999; Muecke 1992; O'Carroll 1999; Ryan 1996; Shaffer 1987). An interesting
and valuable variation of this approach to place is the work of Peter Read
(2000). Read is not explicitly interested in the abstract construction of cultural identity, rather he is interested in the lived experience of cultural subjectivity. In particular, he argues that subjectivities are informed either by a sense
of place, or placelessness. Paul Carter's *The Lie of the Land* (1996) also
theorises the relationship between place and subjectivity via a discussion of
property and in terms of cultural identity. Carter focuses on the dichotomy
of movement and stasis in the cultural discourse of place. He theorises property as a struggle to control or to repress the openness and changeability of
nature. Carter claims that the modern cultural 'preoccupation' with property
is symptomatic of a desire to be grounded or placed. His connection of place
to cultural identity is not unconventional, but it is different because it
acknowledges that the dominant sense of place in modern cultural discourse
is private, alienable property:

> Our homes are tumuli erected over the slaughtered body of the giant
> ground; only our nervous decoration, our attention to monumental detail,
> our preoccupation with property, give us away. We build in order to stabil-
> ise the ground, to provide ourselves with a secure place where we can stand
> and watch. But this suggestion that the ground is treacherous, unstable,
> inclined to give way, is the consequence of our cultural disposition to fly
> over the earth rather than to walk with it. Is it not odd that ours, the most
> nomadic and migratory of cultures, should found its polity, its psych-
> ology, its ethics and even its poetics on the antithesis of movement: on the
> rhetoric of foundations, continuity, genealogy, stasis? Is it not odd that a
> culture intent on global colonisation should persistently associate move-
> ment with the unstable, the unreliable, the wanton and the primitive? But
> perhaps it is inevitable; for a culture that is ungrounded, movement,
> however integral to its survival, must always constitute a threat.
>
> (Carter 1996: 2)

I would add to Carter's theory that private property is an ideal vehicle for the schizoid tension between the desire to be grounded and the cultural imperative of nomadism. It seems that only when property is alienable and exchangeable, a meaningless commodity, that security is purchased.

Theories of law and justice in modern western philosophy and law despite enormous and diverse variation are predominantly anthropocentric. Legal theory and theories about law are concerned with relations between individuals, between communities, between states and between these elementary groupings themselves. Rarely do modern western philosophies of law explicitly theorise relations between people and place, although the separation and hierarchical ordering of the human and non-human worlds constitutes the primary assumption from which most western legal theory begins. Peter Fitzpatrick, however, does not make this assumption in *The Mythology of Modern Law*. Fitzpatrick's analysis of law as myth presents the force and purposiveness of the paradigm of modern law. And while he does not theorise place, the tension he describes between property as colonised lands and property as positive, universal law, proves fruitful for an understanding of the necessary absence of place to modern property law.

Legal positivism, like other scientific discourses, describes law and legal relations according to the conventions of the genre of objectivity. The generic conventions of legal positivism identify and define aspects of law according to abstract categories, called doctrines, which are considered authoritative rules applicable to each question and dispute requiring legal adjudication. Legal positivism claims that law is a science, devised methodically and practised clinically. This philosophy of law considers the influence of the social sphere remote, inappropriate and unnecessary to the operation of law and the influence of the non-human world even more so. Accounts of place, land and the natural world are irrelevant to legal positivism except as the concealed ground from which law asserts its authority and force. The anthropocentrism of legal positivism is expressed by its refusal to admit material aspects of dispute, both cultural and natural or environmental, except passively, as evidence. By imagining and juxtaposing objective and subjective thought, abstract rules and particular contexts and then by privileging objectivity and abstraction, legal positivism epitomises anthropocentric logic.

Critical legal studies (CLS) takes the contrary view that law is intimately connected to the social realm and that, indeed, law and legal practice are socially significant, socially informed and socially produced. As such, CLS admits materialist analyses to legal philosophy. However, the materialism of CLS is qualified as being an exclusively cultural materialism. Questions of natural, environmental or non-human materialism are usually beyond the human-centred, sociopolitical framework of CLS. Recently however, CLS has theorised environmental justice (see, for example, Deimann and Dyssli 1995; Hayward and O'Neill 1997). These accounts are presented in conjunction with critiques of race and class within global geopolitics. Thus while increasingly considering the role of law in terms of the regulation of the natural world and its resources, CLS approaches it from the perspective of social justice and therefore remains an anthropocentric philosophy of law that excludes place, except as a resource for providing social justice.

The closest legal theory has come to non-anthropocentric philosophies of law is the newest comer to the 'law-and-' fold, law-and-geography. The law-and-economics and law-and-literature movements have unsurprisingly contributed little to a theory of the relationship between place and law. The notion that it is fruitful to approach law from its outside is important in the material analysis of this book. Legal scholar Desmond Manderson's theory that law is a discourse begins where the 'law-and-' movements stop: that law can be approached and understood textually, as part of cultural discourse. This philosophy of law (law-as-discourse, not law-and-discourse) is evident in the work of a number of 'legal geographers' (see, for example, Blomley 1994, 1998; Bonyhady and Griffiths 2002; Godden 1998). Law-and-geography analyses the role of place, space and nature in law. The *Legal Geographies Reader* (Blomley, Delaney and Ford 2001) presents critiques of a range of doctrinal laws including property, heritage, environmental and planning from the perspective of the lived experience of cultural and geographic materiality. These critiques mostly conduct sociological analyses of law rather than advocate a reconceptualisation of the relation between society and the natural world itself.

The analysis of modern property law in *Lawscape* is from neither the doctrinal or positivist perspective nor the sociopolitical perspective of critical legal studies. The analysis of property law here is materialist in the sense that it asks in what, or rather where, modern property law can be said to be grounded. *Lawscape* does not draw a relationship between land and law in the way that law-and-geography might, in terms of the function of space in matters of social justice. Rather, the mutual economy of land and law is considered to place law so that property law is not 'the' or 'a' universal and global abstraction – but local laws of particular places. *Lawscape* contends that despite the claimed irrelevance of place to property law modern property law is defined precisely by its placelessness. The absence of place in property law renders indigenous land claims subversive and implicates property law in ongoing environmental change. This is a materialist analysis of law that does not repeat and then reverse the paradigmatic opposition of law, as culture, to nature – rather it asks how place, particular places, can be understood and related to in different ways. *Lawscape* does not advance an essentialism about land neither is it advocating a kind of geographical determinism. *Lawscape* advocates a change in the paradigm of modern property law that would replace the absence of place with its centrality to law. *Lawscape* asks what a particular paradigm of law leads to and what lessons can be learned in the shaping of a property law that reveals and regulates the connections between people and place.

Property scholarship most often conveys the idea that law can exist independently of place largely by excluding place from its discourse. But this approach 'disables our responses' (Weir 2009: 3) to current intellectual and material crises in the functionality of modern property law. Theories of property predominantly focus on people in terms of politics, economics, ethics, law and morality. Judgments about property, about who should get what in the distribution of the goods of life (Kerruish 1999), are value judgments that describe a vision of human nature, meaning, the past and the future (Bowrey 1993). Theories of property usually present descriptions of what 'should be' in terms of what possibilities are to be allowed. But what is allowable in the world cannot be determined against an imagined uniformity and stability of natural environments. Narratives of property law offered by most property textbooks present a unified community in possession of accepted truths, rights and lawful relations. These textbooks also present an absent or at the very least, an assumed homogeneity of natural environments across its jurisdictions. The inadequacy of this narrative is especially evident in native title claims and environmental critiques of property law.

Historical sources of the dominant value of dephysicalised property in English common law such as John Locke's *Two Treatises of Government* (1689) and William Blackstone's *The Commentaries on the Laws of England, Books 1 & 2* (1765–1766) are the foundational narratives of imperial sovereignty and colonial property law. Their theories of property explicitly speak to the placelessness and transportability of the paradigm of modern law. Twentieth-century theorists repeat and clarify the dephysicalised value of property. The work of Wesley Hohfeld (1913, 1917) and Kevin Gray (1991) have become authoritative sources of values and definitions of property in law in contemporary legal practice. Their only account of the relation between property and the material, physical world is that material 'things' do not exist in modern law.

English property theorist Alain Pottage's essay 'Instituting property' (1998b) argues that property has become sufficiently abstract that, as Kuhn described in his theory of paradigm shift, it has ceased to be meaningful and functional:

> The problem for property theory is not simply that nature has been socialised . . . rather, it is that the process of social evolution has so decisively overtaken the conditions in which property categories were formed, that the category of property has little or no explanatory value. In law, the vocabulary of property is animated by operations which cannot be described in terms of that vocabulary.
>
> (Pottage 1998b: 344)

Pottage links the representation of property to its material operation, yet Pottage's preliminary claim that nature has been socialised locates nature outside culture, positioning law as the active centre. *Lawcape* argues that it is the paradigm itself, and not the abstract envelopment of nature, that renders the vocabulary of contemporary property law inadequate. The crisis of the paradigm is apparent by its increasing dysfunction but it is in part caused by physical or 'natural' limits that it claimed to have transcended. A more profound critique of the paradigm of modern property law is offered by his attention to its cultural specificity (Pottage 2001). This study both historically situates and geographically locates property law in European thought and place.

Environmentalist critiques of property may initially seem the exception to the anthropocentric tradition of property theory. The importance of these critiques is that they interrogate the cultural specificity of the dominant instrumentalist value of nature and thus point to the way in which it is a discursive construction rather than a truth across time and place. Environmental lawyer Christopher Stone's renowned environmentalist critique of property law (1972) is based in the idea that property rights should be attributed to things in the extra-human world, such as trees. Legal scholar Donald Large (1973) critiques property in terms of the dispossession of Indigenous North Americans, but by referring only to compensation as a human and cultural right, does not directly challenge the dominant or colonial cultural value of property itself. More recently, the work of American legal scholars Eric Freyfogle (2003) and Joseph Sax (2008) provide in-depth environmentalist critiques of the idea and institution of private property in terms of its historical development and logical incompatibility with environmental law and policy.

Interest in the ownership and use of land and natural resources, particularly the cause and response to environmental change, shared by both environmental science and environmental philosophy has contributed significantly to the debate about modern western concepts of place. The philosophy of a movement now called deep ecology insists that nature is intrinsically valuable and provides consistent critiques of anthropocentrism (Sessions 1995). The value of deep ecology to a theory of place is limited, however, because it generally replaces anthropocentrism with either environmentally qualified articulations of anthropocentrism or ecocentric models of life. Ecocentrism offers nothing more than an inversion of the hierarchical value or position of the paradigmatic categories nature/culture and thus does not so much depart from anthropocentrism as mirror it through opposition. Ecocentrism disallows the notions of possession and ownership at the basis of most theories of property if it attends to the question at all. The concepts of network and interconnection open a space for the notion of inalienable relationships between people and place. The idea that relationships are interdependent and multilinear works against the idea that relationships are oppositional within the dichotomous nature/culture paradigm of anthropocentrism.

The popular and controversial book *The Future Eaters* (1994) by Australian biologist Tim Flannery highlights the tension between two important points about the relationship between science and law. Regardless of the controversy over the objective merits (or otherwise) of *The Future Eaters*, the ideas themselves are deeply subversive of the dominant paradigm of nature/culture and the discourse of anthropocentrism. In this light, it is unsurprising that the book met with hostility from lawyers and scientists alike. Flannery's conclusion is that anthropogenic environmental change in Australia has not been exclusively conducted by European colonists and that Indigenous Australians caused the extinction of some flora and fauna, notably megafauna. This suggestion disrupts the notion that Indigenous Australians are intuitively well adapted to, or simply an extension of, Australian 'nature'. It refuses the idea that some cultures are more 'natural' than others. It debunks the imagined scale of cultural progress from primitivism to civilisation. Flannery's suggestion also disrupts the notion that Australia was a *terra nullius* because it indicates the shared transcultural history of human agency in (as exploitation of) nature. Published amid the debate about land and property stimulated by the recognition of native title in Australian law 2 years earlier, Flannery's work offended both supporters and opponents of native title.

What is lost or excluded by reading anthropogenic environmental change in terms of race is the idea of adaptation. The interpretation of anthropogenic environmental change in terms of adaptation deconstructs the paradigm of nature/culture because unlike the notion of human agency, it is both and neither natural and cultural. Flannery's work leaves the category of culture and the ideal and measure of 'progress' behind in his thesis that humans are a species, which like any other, must adapt to live. The notion that humans are a species is not new or radical – what is valuable about Flannery's work is that it situates the human species neither at the top or the bottom of an ontological hierarchy but within a 'network' of 'interconnected' physical activity. Shifting the ground from a discussion of race or cultural agency in environmental change to human agency or adaptation is fruitful to a critique of the nature/culture paradigm. In terms of property law, Flannery's work shows that although adaptation may be anthropocentrically conceived as a 'cultural' response to a 'natural' situation, it implies a connection with material environmental conditions that modern property law disavows. The question is not whether property relations are 'natural' or 'cultural' or if alternative property relations are more 'natural'. The point is that property relations are lived through traditions or paradigms that are at once natural and cultural and that are particular to the times and places in which they take root. In this way, thinking of property law in terms of adaptation links it to land use and creates a different relationship between people and place.

1.3 Map

The question *Lawscape* asks is how the materiality of property came to be so challenging to its operation. The origins and traditions of private property law and land use are recognisably European. The ontological paradigm of European property relations conceived the world as dual but oppositional categories – nature/culture. This paradigm is apparent in the parallel framework of persons/things in property law. The enclosure or privatisation of the English commons and the appropriation and colonisation of foreign countries practised and made real the ideological relations between people and place expressed in the paradigm of nature/culture. The different histories of England's colonies meant that the development of colonial property laws diverged substantially from English land law in important, mostly doctrinal, ways. Nonetheless, colonial property laws evidenced an alien, European ontological paradigm manifest in theories and practices of land use that property law enabled and encouraged. The evaluation of colonial property law is best considered against the materiality of its operation, by which I mean both its application and consequences. This analysis demonstrates not only that the dominant values and practices of property law were alien, but that they were maladapted.

Modern legal discourse is both closed to questions of place in disputes over property and disrupted by claims that place matters, in native title claims, for example. The inadequacy of property law is increasingly evidenced not only by its insistent retreat from native title but also by problems encountered by farmers in meeting social and economic expectations of agricultural production despite increased environmental regulation and degradation of their properties. Conservative factions call on property law to protect the private rights of farmers against the irreconcilable demands of economy and ecology. Other farmers condemn property law for creating those demands and for degrading the land.

Chapter 2 argues that the paradigm of modern property law is not fixed or universal, rather it emerged within particular material conditions. The function of the chapter is to provide an understanding of the intellectual basis and heritage of contemporary property law. It begins with an analysis of the dichotomous meta-concept nature/culture that describes the world divided into human and non-human realms. The separation and opposition of nature/culture is structured hierarchically, positioning people as the 'masters and possessors of nature'.

Chapter 3 connects the domination and possession of nature and the elevation of humanity to the rise of private property. Historically, private property transformed common property into enclosed privately owned land, which itself became increasingly valued as an alienable commodity in the context of a market economy. The ideological justification of enclosure, based on the idea of improvement and cultivation, was as important to the ubiquity of private property as the creation of physical boundaries themselves. It changed land use and the economy of natural resources. Resistance to the dispossession and alienation of people from place in the process of enclosure demonstrates, however, the existence and strength of prior experiences and values of property relations. The peasant and poet John Clare articulated a different value of place in his concept of property, a concept arguably shared by the illiterate, peasant and later working class to which he belonged. Clare's work consistently laments the marginalisation of a mutual relation or connectivity between people and place. His critique of a unilateral relation of dominance over nature is a rare and detailed record of a land ethic in Anglo culture that preceded and was irreconcilable with the principles and practice of private property.

Chapter 4 links the transportation of the European paradigm of nature/culture to England's colonies with particular land laws and land use practices. The ideas of improvement and progress in Enlightenment philosophy that justified enclosure also justified the colonisation of northern America and Australia and the imposition of private property law in those countries. Like the commoners in England, Indigenous peoples were dispossessed by the enactment of ideas of cultural progress and improvement that were contingent on a paradigm that separated people and place. The principle that property and land are alienable and tradeable was not derived locally but imported from England. The viability of that alien and alienating law has increasingly diminished because it has excluded any consideration of its practicability within the limits of the land itself. In this way, property law can be regarded as maladapted.

Chapter 5 explores the development of modern property theory and its exclusion of place, particularly in regard to the concept of 'dephysicalisation'. The opposition of nature to law is articulated in property theory in terms of transcendence, abstraction, alienation, commodification and fetish. The function of the chapter is to present dephysicalisation as an elaborate and established theory of property that has become the basis on which the separation of people and place is regulated by contemporary legal practice.

Chapter 6 argues that the theory of dephysicalisation is practised, making real the separation of people and place in contemporary property relations. Having established the theory of dephysicalisation in the previous chapter, Chapter 6 examines how theory creates and is created by practice. Specifically, how the theory of dephysicalisation is practised judicially, how it is taught in law schools and how that feeds and is fed by broader cultural discourses and cultural practices of property relationships. The function of the chapter is to show how paradigms are practices as much as theories and how the current paradigm of placelessness affects and abstracts relations between people and place. In legal practice, property is a discourse of rights. Rights discourse is so dominant in understandings of people–place relations that environmental regulation of private property is regarded as inappropriate interference with rights. The chapter links legal expressions of property to cultural discourses of property and land use, particularly farming and custodianship.

The point that Daryl Kerrigan made in his claim that place is 'everything', that it can't be alienated, exchanged or compensated, is that places are particular not general, local not universal. The paradigm of modern property law that 'things' are irrelevant, that they can be readily 'picked up and plonked down somewhere else' – this is a paradigm of displacement. *Lawscape* traces the historical, geographical and philosophical development of the paradigm and questions whether it can sustain people–place relations into the future.

Chapter 2

Conceptual origins

> Does a field make progress because it is a science, or is it a science because it makes progress?
>
> (Kuhn 1996: 162)

2.1 Introduction: separation of people and place

The separation of nature from culture in the foundational history of contemporary social, legal, geographical and geopolitical order breathes logic into the uncanny practices of current laws and crises about land. This chapter explores the origins and power of this theoretical framework and its importance in the development of contemporary law and, specifically, how it came to dominate a particular understanding of property. In this continuing history, law constructs itself as a metaphysical discourse that simultaneously constitutes and is constituted by the absence of the physical. In property law, this 'dephysicalisation' of the world began by dividing the people–place relationship into the active agents of the property relation, 'people', and the passive objects of the property relation, 'things'. However, the passive function of 'things' within this property equation means that those 'things' in the biosphere are not, in fact, irrelevant to property law – they are *vital* to it. This is because the ongoing practice of property law depends entirely on a very particular, instrumentalist value of the biosphere. This view or philosophy of the natural world or 'nature' legitimises current modes of the production, distribution and consumption of those 'things'.

The chapter begins with a brief exploration of the language and discourse of property. Legal scholar James Boyd White, in his essay on language and law, suggests a view of people as creators of their world rather than mere players in it. Language is not merely a mode of communication in that world, it is a technology: it makes things:

Language can not be seen as transparent or neutral but as a real force of its own. Language does much to shape both who we are – our very selves – and the ways in which we observe and construe the world.

(Boyd White 1990: xi)

This chapter examines precisely how language shapes 'our very selves', our psychic world and extends this idea to examine how language shapes the physical world and environment, not only our 'selves', but also our 'others', the 'things' we claim to own. 'Property is a way of looking at the world, as well as a means of sharing it out' (Langford 1991: 4–5). Despite the contentiousness of remarking that humans bear an enduring, or at least serious, impact on the natural environment, 'there is increasing public acceptance of the idea that much of what we call "natural", at least as far as the surface ecology of the globe and its atmosphere is concerned, has been significantly modified by human action' (Harvey 2000: 119). To accept the connection of people and place proposed by critiques of environmental (mis)management is to recall an integrated relationship between people and place that confounds the schismatic logic of nature/culture. It is a relationship revealed in the etymology of property.

The etymology of the word 'property' reveals a strange inversion of the people–place relationship that it originally described. Originally, what was 'proper to' a person were the physical qualities or things so closely associated with the person that he or she could be identified by them. In contemporary usage, this definition of property is the secondary meaning of the word and remains only the primary meaning of the word in the physical sciences, e.g. 'what are the properties of hydrogen?' The primary meaning of the word 'property' today pertains to abstract relations between people, rather than with or over physical things. The mitosis of what was once the singular meaning of 'property', identity, into two modern unrelated meanings of the word reveals a separation of the world into physical and cultural realms. The two definitions of property, however, are not different or progressive points on an evolutionary line of cultural development, rather they are antithetical. Today, the defining principle of the dominant meaning of 'property' is alienability – the inverse of the original defining principle, identity. In relation to land, the use of the word 'property' originally indicated the identification of or defining connection between people and place. The legal priority of the category 'real property' articulated a human relationship to the physical or real that mattered more than lesser forms of property. The legal remedies that attached to land reflected this priority. In contemporary usage, however, the use of the word 'property' in relation to land indicates the alienability and disconnectedness of people from place. Today, jurists and legal scholars debate the extent to which the category 'real property' remains relevant. The historical and etymological development of the word 'property' indicates that this legal category is neither inevitable nor enduring. It reminds us that any given property regime or set of people–place relations is limited by a specific set of geophysical and cultural conditions.

The central aim of this chapter is to extend the discussion of language and property to consider its parameters and the players of the people–place relation: nature and culture, in more depth. Nature and culture emerge as discursive constructions that signify not different and independent concepts, but rather the positive and negative values of the same meta-concept (which I will refer to as nature/culture). The chapter contends that this paradigm of nature/culture functions as the condition, as well as a parallel to, the coupling of people/things in legal thought. The epistemology and taxonomies of nature/culture and people/things are the primary means by which the law of real property orders the world. The notion of order is important here because it connotes both classification and force, suggesting that property law is a particular practice of structuring people and place as separable and separate.

2.2 Ancient origins and etymology of property

Many inquiries and studies in real property law begin by asking 'what is property?' The attempt to identify and define property in its normative sense, as a social institution, is ambitious and difficult and is usually acknowledged as such by theorist and lecturer alike (see Chapter 5 and 6). The most common remark made in pedagogical and theoretical definitions of real property is that 'the term "real" is oxymoronic' (Carney 2001b). So misleading is the word 'real' in the law of property today that students and 'laypeople' are warned from 'assuming' its 'simplistic' and 'everyday' sense – reality, the tangible and physical. The modern English word 'real' derives from the Latin *res* meaning 'thing' and the classical meaning of real property specified the real, tangible and physical nature of property interests in land. However, the 'real' in contemporary real property law, the 'thing' is unreal – it is an abstract 'right' to a thing and not the thing itself (see Chapter 5). The 'right' to property exists only in law which makes defining real property difficult and self-referential. Defining property in its contemporary semiotic sense is no less difficult. Tracing the historical development of the word 'property' sheds light on the contemporary meaning as well as on the extraordinary shift itself in people–place relations in modern Anglocentric thought and culture.

The history of the English word 'property' indicates the way in which modern Anglo-European relationships between people and place have changed over time. The English word 'property' comes via the Old French *propreté*, which comes from the Latin word *proprietas* meaning 'proper to, one's own, or special character' (Chambers Dictionary of Etymology 2000).[1]

---

1 All etymological references are to this dictionary.

The French word *propre* meaning clean and suitable, originally indicated the sense of something 'close or near' and 'in place'. The Old French and Latin meanings of these words derive from the Greek word *idiotes*. *Idiotes* refers to the peculiar nature or specific character of something. The *idiotes* of something is the quality that makes it distinctive and distinguishable from other things – and it was the means by which ownership could be claimed – the proximity of the thing to the person was considered sufficiently close as to be associated with that person. Thus, to say that 'this is my own' would suggest that it is connected to my identity, that it forms part of who I am. The immediate connection here between 'people' and 'things' in the western origin of the concept suggests that 'property' and 'identity' were mutually formative. Indeed, the idea of authenticity itself derives from this meaning of property where 'there is a distinct and particular link between the object and its owner' (Davies 2007: 25).

The relationship between property and identity continued and remained an important one in medieval England and in the early common law view of land. Legal historian David Seipp wrote: '[L]and had significance greater than the sum of its economic production and use value. Land was also an important component of identity' (1994: 46). For this reason, disputes over land were addressed by reference to location and use rather than to abstract legal categories – in other words, land was treated differently, because it was recognised and valued materially (Seipp 1994: 49). In his archival research, Seipp found that the word 'property' in Anglo-Norman texts from the 1180s to Middle English texts from the 1380s meant an 'attribute' or 'characteristic' of a person or thing. However, there was a secondary and less common usage of the word 'property' in medieval England and this was a person's *interest* in having a thing. Usually the context of this meaning was religious 'and the connotation is overwhelmingly negative' (Seipp 1994: 69):

> Dozens of surviving manuscripts from the fourteenth and fifteenth centuries praised monastic establishments for holding all goods in common and shunning 'property', or condemned them for doing the opposite. To have 'property' of goods (or goods 'in proper') was a sin, and monks guilty of this vice were denounced as 'proprietaries' or 'owners'.
>
> (Seipp 1994: 69)

The original and primary definition of property is, today, the secondary definition of the word. In its modern usage, the primary meaning of the word 'property' divorces property from identity. Indeed, it denotes the alienability, rather than the mutual identification, of the owner and the owned. 'Property', in today's usage, refers to an object or thing whose only relationship to the owner is that it is owned. The transition from the mutually defining relationship of 'ownership' and 'identity' to a unilateral relation indicates a shift in the ideology and practice of people–place relations. Human subjectivity is defined not via identification or association with a place, but via alienation from it. According to the original sense of 'property', the thing possesses me, I belong to it and am identified by it. But according to the modern sense of 'property', I possess the thing, it belongs to me. Where place once characterised and identified a person, now place and person are disconnected. The particular and physical qualities of place have been erased from property relations in legal discourse and replaced with entirely social relationships using a vocabulary of rights.

The legal discourse of property rights has come to dominate the cultural discourse of property generally. Even so, numerous legal scholars and educators have noted that older, even ancient definitions or concepts of property as something real and particular, such as land, have persisted in cultural discourse. There are even, still today, individuals and communities who rationalise their property interest in terms of their identification with the land over generations. And so, as Australian legal scholar, Margaret Davies argues: '[T]here is a tension in the legal idea of property between seeing it as a disaggregated bundle of rights and seeing it as something more solid, specific, and identified with a particular person' (2007: 27). Canadian legal scholar David Lametti also observes that 'the intuitive appeal of making things the mediator of the relationship is evidenced by the pervasiveness of "thingness" in the lay person's understanding of property' (2003: 354). But despite residual and persistent views of property as something real and specific, the dominant view of property, in both legal and cultural discourses, is one of abstract entitlements as between persons which are alienable from, rather than proper to, a person. Indeed, the contemporary usage of the word 'property' refers almost always to something fungible, rather than something distinctive and that is detachable from, rather than attached to or even integrated with, the identity of an individual or community.

2.3 Nature/culture

> When we say nature, do we mean to include ourselves?
>
> (Williams 2005: 67)

The paradigm of nature/culture operates via the dichotomous logic of anthropocentrism. Anthropocentrism divides the world into two categories: human beings and 'the rest', then places humans at an imaginary centre of that world:

> Man, if we look to final causes, may be regarded as the centre of the world; in so much that if man were taken away from the world, the rest would seem to be all astray, without aim or purpose . . . and leading to nothing. For the whole world works together in the service of man; and

there is nothing from which he does not derive use and fruit . . . insomuch that all things seem to be going about man's business and not their own.
(Bacon, cited in Marshall 1994: 184)

According to this model, people are not human in the sense of being a physically determined species – rather they are human in the sense of being a culturally determined and distinguished species from all other uncultured species. Cultural practice exists on a linear scale of development that is regarded as evolutionary. The evolutionary line stretches from nature at one end to culture at the other end. Nature and culture are thought to be as different as it is possible to be. They are opposite. They are not, therefore, two distinct concepts, but two poles of the same meta-concept, nature/culture. This meta-concept or paradigm of people–place relations holds together what Foucault (1973) called the 'order of things' in modern discourse. This modern discourse classifies things according to their location on a grid of arbitrarily determined qualities and properties that they either lack or possess in relation to other things. This grid is imposed onto a view of the world that perceives and characterises things not according to their own particular qual- ities but according to the logic of the grid's structure. 'By virtue of structure, the great proliferation of beings occupying the surface of the globe is able to enter both into the sequence of a descriptive language and into the field of a *mathesis* that would also be a general science of order' (Foucault 1973: 136–137). Natural things are classified as natural 'not in their organic unity' but because they conform to a pattern or list of properties. 'They are paws and hoofs, flowers and fruits, before being respiratory systems or internal liquids' (Foucault 1973: 137). Nature and culture are not just different con- cepts or realms; they are mutually exclusive and mutually defining categories of being. Natural things could be classified as much by the cultural qualities they lacked as much as by the natural qualities they possessed. Similarly, culture could be known as the absence of nature and the loss of natural qualities. Together, through their mutual opposition, nature and culture make sense of the system of knowledge that classified them. The dynamic of opposition is central to the process of classification:

An animal or a plant is not what is indicated – or betrayed – by the stigma that is to be found upon it; it is what the others are not; it exists in itself only in so far as it is bounded by what is distinguishable from it.
(Foucault 1973: 144–145)

In the scientific revolution of the sixteenth and seventeenth centuries, the idea of civilisation became the basis of human self-perspective. Human dis- tinctiveness was expressed not in terms of perceptible differentiation from the world but in terms of the uniqueness and status of human development as culture. Humans were thought to be a species without equal and, through their imagined superiority, became the standard or measure by which all other things could be understood and evaluated.[2] Understanding things in the world was not based on what those things actually were in their own right, but on how they compared to 'Man, the measure of all things'.[3] 'Everything else' was everything not human, which, according to the conceptual model of humanity as the centre of the world, became simply 'the environment' – meaning 'the aggregate of surrounding things' (Macquarie Dictionary 1992). The model 'assumes that humans are at the very centre of a system of nature' (Serres 1995: 33). The centre of the model is differentiated from its periphery by mutually exclusive qualities. The relationship between humans and 'their' environment is expressed as an opposition between culture and nature. It is a structure fundamental to the discourse of the human sciences and it is 'congenital to philosophy' (Derrida 1978: 282–283).

2.3.1 Masters and possessors of nature

The key word in seventeenth-century epistemology was 'method'. Method constituted the modern genres of science, philosophy and law. These modern 'disciplines' deployed the discourse of method in their development of a bifurcated body of knowledge: reason/emotion, proof/faith. The conceptual division of the world into the categories of nature and culture is vital to the discourse of method. Francis Bacon's epistemology posits 'a violent shift in perspective' (Berman, cited in Hay 2002: 123): rejecting knowledge 'received' through faith in favour of 'active' scientific inquiry. He argues in *The New Atlantis* (1626) that the purpose of philosophy and more broadly of human society is the acquisition of 'the Knowledge of Causes, and Secrett Motions of Things; and the Enlarging of the bounds of the Humane Empire, to the Effecting of all Things possible' (Bacon 1990: 34–35). Significantly, the idea of knowledge-as-science advanced by Bacon is based on the specific concept of nature-as-object. Humans are thought to be separate from, outside and above the category of nature. The idea of knowledge-as-science nominates humans as subjects: the conductors of inquiry. The objects of scientific investigation are the 'things' of nature. It is not possible to be both the subject and the object in the ontology of science: something is either of culture or it is of nature; human or not human; the inquirer or the object of inquiry. The scientific study of people (as groups and as individuals) thus immediately renders them objects (e.g. cadavers, women, Indigenous peoples). In so doing, this inquiry situates these people in the category of nature, at the periphery of

2 It is important to note that although humans were considered a species without equal, this same paradigm also constructed discourses of gender, race, disability, sexuality and age (for example) that constantly transgressed the notion of a homogenous human species. Indeed, the measure was almost always qualified as white, male, able bodied, heterosexual and adult.
3 Attributed to Protagoras.

the anthropocentric model of the world as a biological species. The process imagines that it is possible to isolate the aspect of the object's being that is subject to the inquiry from the whole of the object's life (and/or death) as a person such as their intellect, culture, spirituality, family, community and psychology. The force of modern reason finds its power and authority to fragment, sever, alienate and possess the world through the discourse of method. As advanced by Bacon and Descartes, this imagined order of things:

> delimits in the totality of experience a field of knowledge, defines the mode of being of the objects that appear in that field, provides man's everyday perception with theoretical powers, and defines conditions in which he can sustain a discourse about things that is recognised to be true.
>
> (Foucault 1973: 158)

Carolyn Merchant's history of science *The Death of Nature* (1980) states that Bacon's model of *subject* and *object* in his theory of scientific method works through the deployment of metaphor, itself a mechanism of objectification. Merchant argues that the discursive category of nature is personified as woman:[4]

> Nature must be 'bound into service' and 'made a slave', put 'in constraint' and 'molded' by the mechanical arts. The 'searchers and spies of nature' are to discover her plots and secrets. This method, so readily applicable when nature is denoted by the female gender, degraded and made possible the exploitation of the natural environment. As woman's womb had symbolically yielded to the forceps, so nature's womb harboured secrets that through technology could be wrested from her grasp.
>
> (Merchant 1980: 169)

The use of the metaphor of woman to define nature renders the project of science more accessible, less radical, because it taps into a 'pre-existing logical order' (Ricoeur 1977: 17). As philosopher Helene Cixous argued in her seminal essay 'Sorties', pre-existing or prior logical order of man/woman 'transports us . . . through centuries of representation' (Cixous 1986: 63). The success of the metaphor is thus available only 'within a community whose members had previously assimilated their literal use' (Kuhn, cited in Harvey 2000: 164). Bacon's concept of nature thus rapidly crystallises through the use of this metaphor. Yet, while metaphor renders Bacon's specific concept of

---

4 The word woman refers not to women or to a particular woman but to a concept of people knowable as a category: whose behaviour and qualities are consistent and finite. I use the word woman to indicate the distinction between the stereotype or discursive category of women and actual women.

nature more readily understandable, it simultaneously undermines its viability as a scientific category. The epistemological authority of science and law is contingent upon the purity of knowledge: absolute truths 'found' by objective method. The understanding of the concept of nature through metaphor contaminates the scientific category of nature by conflating it with a cultural value. David Harvey concludes: '[W]e find that the values supposedly inherent in nature are properties of the metaphors, of the human imaginary internalising and working on the multiple effects of other moments in the social processes, most conspicuously those of material social practices' (2000: 164).

The material production and operation of science via metaphor indicates that we cannot 'speak about nature without, at the same time, speaking about ourselves' (Capra, cited in Harvey 2000: 164). Bacon's concept of nature binds itself to his concept of culture and in the process advances ontological as well as epistemological claims. The imagined separation of the world into the categories, nature and culture, was not therefore exclusively a matter of discourse and knowledge. It was a way of being and the basis of doing. Descartes' *Sixth Discourse on Method* (1637) speaks of method not only philosophically but also in terms of experience and experimentation. The imagined mind/body separation associated with Cartesian philosophy is enacted through the examination of animals (for example) as objects. Descartes argues that 'coercing, torturing, operating upon the body of Nature ... is not torture' because 'Nature's body is an unfeeling, soulless mechanism' (Descartes, cited in Hay 2002: 125). Descartes advanced a relationship of power through a specific ontological behaviour or, in Foucauldian terms, a practice of knowledge, separating or *othering* nature from culture.

This violent coupling of the emerging nature/culture paradigm indicates that the discourse of method was based not simply on a binary structure but, more significantly, on an hierarchical order. The conceptual and actual separation of nature and culture was not important in and of itself; it mattered only to the extent that it produced a measure of esteem. Human subjectivity was defined not merely in opposition to its physical 'environment', but by its superiority to it, by being the 'masters and possessors of nature' (Descartes 1978: 78).

The function of method in philosophy and science is more than the development or acquisition of knowledge in and for itself; it is principally to use nature for the elevation and meaningfulness of humanity. Harvey argues that the reification of nature as a thing – a purely external other – entirely separate from the world of thought deprives nature of having meaning in itself (Harvey 2000: 134). The thingness of nature indicates the absence of any defining quality. A thing is a thing because it is meaningless: 'Deprived of any autonomous life force, nature was open to be manipulated without restraint according to the human will. Nature became, as Heidegger later complained, "one vast gasoline station" for human exploitation' (Harvey 2000: 134). More than an epistemological revolution, the age of science carried with it a new ontological order and a new people–place relation. Science continues to make it possible 'to describe natural processes in their own terms; to examine them without any prior assumption of purpose or design, but simply as processes, or to use the historically earlier term, as machines' (Williams 2005: 76).

2.3.2 The eyes of the manufacturing period

The conditions under which the paradigm of nature/culture operated and proliferated were the growing capitalist market economy, the agricultural and the industrial revolutions. The ideas of the Enlightenment had made possible these revolutions and the accompanying political economy by using the conception of nature as a 'mechanism': 'The Cartesian division allowed scientists to treat matter as dead and completely separate from themselves, and to see the material world as a multitude of different objects assembled into a huge machine' (Capra, cited in Harvey 2000: 27). Karl Marx argued that when Bacon and Descartes developed their instrumentalist view of nature as unfeeling objects of human inquiry, they essentially 'saw with the eyes of the manufacturing period' (cited in Harvey 2000: 121). Descartes' notion that animal behaviour was determinate in the same way as a clock, for example, not only separated human culture from animal nature, it advanced the idea that nature was meaningless and therefore inferior to culture. His *machina anima* was the precursor to the consideration of nature not simply as something that might be exploited as an economic resource, but as an economic resource and nothing more. Harvey argues however that the nature/culture paradigm and its subsequent domination of nature:

> never deliberately embraced the destruction and despoliation of the natural world ... If destruction and depletion could be found, then it was a sign of such immense abundance that it did not matter. When it mattered, the price system would adjust to indicate a condition of scarcity that required attention.
>
> (Harvey 2000: 125)

2.3.3 Cultivation: nexus and nascence of nature/culture

Culture is a positive concept of activity. Raymond Williams notes that the word 'culture' 'in all its early uses was a noun of process: the tending *of* something, basically crops or animals' (1976: 77). Culture was not a state of being, but a state of doing. It was not originally separate from the idea of nature, but related to it. Indeed, nature was the physical and logical condition of this idea of culture. Importantly, in the early sixteenth century:

[T]he tending of natural growth was extended to a process of human development, and this alongside the original meaning in husbandry, was the main sense until the late eighteenth century and early nineteenth century.

(Williams 1976: 77)

Williams demonstrates how the extended usage of the word 'culture' distinguishes biology from social development. Bacon's phrase 'the culture and manurance of minds' (Bacon, cited in Williams 1976: 77) clearly refers not to the agricultural tending of human brains but is a metaphor for the increased social worth and value of human development in the realm of abstraction. The idea of social status could thus be conceived not only in terms of birth and blood, but also in terms of knowledge.

The extension of the word 'culture', from describing a physical activity pertaining to land and soil, to its use as a metaphor for describing cultural status foreshadowed the subsequent shift in the dominant signification of the word from meaning physical improvement to meaning metaphysical improvement. In his study of English husbandry manuals and the representation of agriculture, Andrew McRae finds that in the sixteenth and seventeenth centuries, the term 'improvement' was undergoing similar transformation. From agrarian improvement 'propelled by a sense of moral duty to exploit more efficiently the riches of the natural world' to 'a more explicitly pecuniary sense' (McRae 1992: 36–37) improvement, like culture, was becoming a dephysicalised and denatured concept: 'Improvement was a favourite word of the 1760s and 1770s, carrying with it a great mass of material aspirations and moral assumptions. In nothing is this seen more clearly than in immense resources devoted to the exploitation of the most basic of national assets, the land' (Langford 1989: 432).

The seventeenth-century discourses of improvement and progress, abundant in husbandry, enclosure and colonisation literature indicate the development of a metaphysical sense of the word 'culture' that was profoundly abstracted from its physical sense. The improvement of nature was increasingly thought to mark the improvement of human society. Paradoxically, the improvement of human society was also esteemed by its departure and distance from nature. Improvement discourse, although based on the very real and physical relationship between people and place in agriculture, was also principally used to establish the metaphysical subjectivity of modern man as transcending nature – as being cultured.

Improvement discourse put into everyday language and land use practices the ideological separation of nature and culture. Its focus on the purpose of activity also redirected the existing ontology of feudal theology. In her study of the socioeconomic discourse of this period, Laura Brace found that improvement was 'a contested concept', hinging on the objectification of nature:

which regarded land as having the potential for investment, sustainable productivity and a re-establishment of people's *original* dominion over nature. To exploit this potential and to be improved, land required labour and careful husbandry.

(2001: 5)

Debate about improvement therefore revealed a dispute about both the concept of nature and the concept of culture. Resistance to the extension of the notion of culture-as-cultivation of nature to culture-as-transcendence of nature undermined the epistemological and ontological claims of the nascent nature/culture paradigm.

2.3.4 A deformed chaos

The heavy reliance of improvement discourse on religious concepts (especially the Creation) and language worked strategically. The appeal to the pre-existing epistemology and ontology of Christian theology was a means to articulate and validate values of nature that continued, rather than departed, from those norms. In the *Book of Genesis*, culture precedes nature. It is the 'Word' of God that creates and orders the world. Improvement discourse similarly defined culture metaphysically by locating it prior to nature, thus relating it to an act of creation. The claim that husbandry and colonisation were part of God's will made the physicality of these activities less significant than the inevitability and metaphysicality of divine providence.

The Christian story of the Creation is repeatedly cited in justifications for husbandry, enclosure and colonisation. These cultivating processes were considered 'fundamental to God's intentions for the Earth and for mankind' (Brace 1998: 68). Man improves and orders nature either as a repentant act of repair or as a dutiful act of (re)creation depending on particular readings of the Fall of Man. Francis Bacon argues that man's Fall damaged both himself and nature, yet is reversible:

> For man by the Fall fell at the same time from his state of innocency and from his dominion over creation. Both of these losses however can even in this life be in some part repaired; the former by religion and faith, the latter by arts and sciences.
>
> (Bacon, cited in Brace 1998: 69)

According to this idea of man, culture is the active realm: transforming a dormant nature from something useless and menacing into something fruitful and known. Cultivating the land meant 'converting the desolate wastes into fruitful fields, and the wilderness into comfortable habitations' (Brace 1998: 68). Bacon's commentary suggests that without human intervention, nature alone is 'regarded "like a deformed Chaos" which brought discredit to the Commonwealth' (anon, cited in Brace 2001: 6). The characterisation of nature as a 'deformed chaos', however, cannot convey an idea of nature without an idea of culture that has been abstracted from it. Nature here signifies abnormality, imperfection, disorder and anarchy only because it functions as referent to its opposite, positive term culture. The concepts of nature and culture in this emergent sense are meaningful only through their opposition to each other. The idea of culture as a general process relating to abstract human development, rather than as a particular and physical land use practice, in this example indicates also that 'culture' is intimately bound to the ideas of civilisation and order, as transcendence: 'To speak of man "intervening" in natural processes is to suppose that he might find it possible not do to so, or to decide not to do so. Nature has to be thought of, that is to say, as separate from man, before any question of intervention or command, and the method and ethics of either, can arise' (Williams 2005: 75).

The anthropocentric concept of nature complements ontological principles in Christian theology such as man's place in the divine universe. But as Brace notes in husbandry literature, for example, the idea of man as the 'Vice-Regent and Deputy of Almighty God' (Hale, cited in Marshall 1994: 180) suggests that the Creation was incomplete. Improvement discourse thus does not simply follow Christian theology – it reworks it. God appears as the:

> great or mystical husbandman who created the pattern for all subsequent improvement of chaos. He made all creatures, plants, fruits, trees and herbs serviceable to mankind who was expressly created to 'husbandize the fruits of the earth.' All other callings were supplementary. Husbandry had a special status because it was ordained by God.
>
> (Blith, cited in Brace 2001: 6)

Accordingly, nature depends on man to deliver it from meaninglessness to meaningfulness hence fulfilling God's plans and restoring the world from chaos to paradise. Land use binds culture to nature both conceptually and physically.

The theme of the worthlessness of nature prior to man's intervention via culture and cultivation of land also recurs in theories and criticisms of enclosure. Common fields were considered spoiled and wasted by the defenders of enclosure:

> This to them constituted the sin of wasting God's workmanship. Nature provided a valuable treasury, but people would not be able to reverse the Fall unless they were prepared to labour and improve. Paradise was made paradise through dressing and keeping, and gardens were only perfect so long as they were cultivated.
>
> (Brace 1998: 77–78)

The project of colonisation further demonstrates the prevalence of theology, especially narratives of Creation, in the coupling of nature and culture as a meta-concept of the world. Colonisation was contingent on the physical and metaphysical splitting of the world into the categories of nature and culture. Peter Fitzpatrick (1992) argues that the dispossession of Indigenous peoples from their land is consistent with the idea of savagery that 'constantly receded in proportion to the inexorable advance of progress' (Pottage 1993: 615). Colonisation, dispossession and 'settlement' are 'equivalent to an act of Creation' (Fitzpatrick 1992: 82). These 'creative' acts were then put into practice thought to evidence what was hitherto only abstract knowledge of the world: that culture was separate and superior to nature.

2.3.5 A common origin, abstract and sacred

Fitzpatrick argues that the nature/culture paradigm constitutes and sustains what he calls the *mythology of modernity*. Method, the ideological and practical basis of science and law, Fitzpatrick argues, is actually part of this mythology. The selective interpretation and strategic deployment of theological narratives and values in the literature of husbandry, enclosure and colonisation evidence such mythology. The development of the law in the seventeenth and eighteenth centuries made extensive use of such mythology and, indeed, wrote itself into the Enlightenment version of the Creation story. So successful was the use of metaphor and religious narrative that Fitzpatrick contends that the dominant myth in the discourses of science and law in this period was not simply the belief that they were post-mythic epistemologies, but in their claim to have exceeded the specificity of epistemology altogether. Law and science became regarded as truths. Michel Serres also observes something mythical about the idea of culture in *The Natural Contract* (1995): 'Law precedes science and perhaps engenders it; or rather, a common origin, abstract and sacred, joins them' (1995: 53). The idea of origin is central to both theorists' critiques of nature/culture, because it brings into focus the transcendental claims of the paradigm. Fitzpatrick and Serres argue that the contradiction of the discourse of reason is located in its foundation on metaphor and religious narrative.

Yet Fitzpatrick and Serres do not challenge the paradigm nature/culture itself, rather, they critique its administration and effect. Fitzpatrick is concerned especially with the conflation of Indigenous peoples and nature through the idea of savagery (Fitzpatrick 1992). His critique of the notion of savagery points out that the negative qualities of nature define, through juxtaposition, the positive qualities of culture. But it is the separation and not simply the hierarchical opposition of nature/culture that underwrites modern law. Similarly, Serres leaves as true the separation of the world into the oppositional categories of nature and culture. His work is concerned with the relationship between nature and culture and what he sees to be the modern degeneration of that enduring relationship. He is particularly concerned with the disrespect shown to the natural world by human society and questions the moral and physical sustainability of this dynamic. His contention that environmental degradation may be arrested through the development of a contractual relationship between nature and culture certainly attributes agency to both 'realms', but it nonetheless simultaneously upholds the categories as real and right, which ultimately maintains the notion that humans exist separate from and outside nature.

Marx observed that the human economy exists only as a mixture of the person/thing categories via production and consumption: '[A]s long as men exist, the history of nature and the history of men are mutually conditioned' (Marx, cited in Harvey 2000: 26). The mixture may be so fluid that while it may be possible to think of nature and culture as separate categories, it is impossible to live as such. Raymond Williams says that 'the idea of nature contains, though often unnoticed, an extraordinary amount of human history' (Williams 2005: 67). The inextricability of the categories of 'nature' and 'culture' is not only symptomatic of their complex relationship, but also indicates that the two categories are referents to the same concept. They are simply the positive and negative values of the same thing rather than things of difference. Derrida refers to this incidence as the law of genre:

> Genres should not intermix. And if it should happen that they do intermix, by accident or through transgression, by mistake or through lapse, then this should confirm, since after all, we are speaking of 'mixing', the essential purity of their identity.
>
> (1992b: 225)

The following section explores the role of law in regulating the nature/culture paradigm of people–place relations through the conception and elaboration of a model or theory of property as a relation between persons and things.

2.4 Persons/things

> The distinction between persons and things may be a keystone of the semantic architecture of Western law.
>
> (Pottage and Mundy 2004: 3)

The practice of reason through science established the human 'subject' as the agent of knowledge of the studied 'object'. Similarly, the law of property established the human 'person' as the agent of dominion over the possessed 'thing': 'The distinction between persons and things is a foundational theme in Western society, and that legal institutions have played an essential role in constituting and maintaining that distinction' (Pottage and

Mundy 2004: 4). Law, like science, is both idea and practice. Where the dynamic of the subject/object relationship in science is mediated through knowledge, the dynamic of the person/thing relationship in law is mediated through possession.

The anthropocentric division of the world into nature and culture formed the basis of the modern idea of property in law. Indeed, property law fortified and actualised the paradigm of nature/culture. Evaluations of non-English human societies were articulated in terms of their laws and economies, particularly with regard to the use of land as a resource or 'thing': 'The "cultural development" of any given society was measured by its "sufficient removal" from the common state Nature placed it in' (Locke, cited in Fitzpatrick 1992: 82). People–place relations were translated into systems of property and measured against the standard of English property law as though those people–place relations or property systems were culturally and geographically non-specific. People–place relations were not compared in terms of differentials but in terms of degree of attainment of a universal (English) standard. The conceptual separation of the world into the categories nature and culture was regarded as universally correct, legitimate and desirable, as was the actual separation in the world of people from place. People–place relations, articulated as systems of property, formed the basis of law: 'In the state of nature, Austin confirmed: "men ... have no legal rights" ' (Fitzpatrick 1992: 82). In the state of nature, people are possessed by place rather than in possession of 'things'.

The power of culture over nature articulated by Bacon's and Descartes' instrumentalist value of nature is expressed in modern property law as the power of people over things: to alienate and enjoy things without restraint. The modern legal right that guarantees property (and sovereignty) identifies possession as the primary basis of ownership. The owner of the property right possesses the right to, and over, a thing. The idea of ownership as possession indicates not simply an economic relationship between humans and their environment, but also a political relationship.[5] For example, to speak of the dispossession of Indigenous peoples' land 'rights' suggests that what has been taken is the 'right' as well as the land, so that power has been taken through the vehicle of land. The idea of property articulated in terms of rights reinforces an anthropocentric understanding of the world and so it is to politics and power that our discussion of property now moves.

---

5 The word 'possess' derives from the Latin *potis* meaning 'able, having power' and combines with the English verb *sidere* meaning 'sit down' to form the verb *possidere*, meaning literally 'sit down as the person in control', hence by extension 'take possession of' and ultimately 'have, own' (Ayto 1991: 406).

2.4.1 Land as power

> Land gives so much more than the rent. It gives position and influence
> and political power, to say nothing of the game.
>
> (Trollope's Archdeacon Grantly, cited in Sugarman and Warrington
> 1995: 121)

The Norman property regime, with its hierarchical super-structure, characterised feudal property interests as political interests. So important was land
to power that even the most basic of property rights, possession, was legally
subject and subordinate to the ultimate sovereign power over the land. The
feudal system of tenure meant that even the tenant's power or political and
ownership rights in respect of the land 'stopped at possession' (Baker 1979:
199). The social value of property in feudal England, the symbolism of
power and status that attached to land tenure, was more important, at least
theoretically, than its economic value. Property was about social order and
political structure, or as Carol Rose (1994) argues, property was propriety.
The gentry's land tenure 'provided them with their main title to power and
prestige' (Briggs 2000: 9).

The idea of land as power remained stronger than the idea of land as
capital in English law through to the seventeenth-century. The power to enjoy
land and its direct connection to political participation even at this time were
generally more important at that time than pecuniary gain and advantage:
'When discussion took place of the relationship between property and power,
most people had in mind one particular form of property – land' (Langford
1991: 58). The developments of the property law creations of primogeniture
and the equity of redemption for example indicate that, despite the increasing
importance of land as wealth according to the growing economy of capital,
the dominant value of land was socio-political. In feudal England, property
was the possession of rights to revenue 'rather than a right to any specific
material thing' (Macpherson 1975: 110). But revenue conveyed not simply
economic gain. Revenue conveyed, more importantly, political gain. The distinction of revenue from mere access to the goods of life can be grasped by
an explanation of the precise forms of power consisting in property rights.
Macpherson qualifies this:

> In the first place, the great bulk of property was then property in land,
> and a man's property in a piece of land was generally limited to certain
> uses of it and was not freely disposable ... A substantial segment of
> property consisted of those rights to a revenue, which were provided by
> such things as corporate charters, monopolies granted by the state, tax
> farming rights, and the incumbency of various political and ecclesiastical
> offices.
>
> (Macpherson 1975: 110)

Land, as the 'object' or 'thing' of property, was to the 'subject' or 'person' of that relation, what nature was to culture – an instrumental prop. More than a parallel, however, the instrumental value of nature within the nature/culture paradigm is the condition of the possibility of this particular property relation. Until land was devisable and then alienable, land exceeded economic value. Possessing land meant holding power and social status in a society that was principally ordered and governed politically. And even as land became devisable and alienable toward the end of the feudal period, as the land market developed and became important, the strength of the relationship between land and power persisted.

David Sugarman and Ronnie Warrington argue that in England the alienability of land did not diminish its role and value as power. The emerging capital-based economy did not bring with it an immediate and corresponding shift in the role and value of property in land:

> In the strange, half-timeless world of the traditional English landed estate, feudal concepts blissfully lingered long after their semi-feudal relations had been eradicated. Land was not just the most valuable form of property; both to its owners and to non-owners it was a socio-political nexus, a way of life.
>
> (1995: 111)

The 'lingering' attachment of power to land is well evidenced by the creation and development of the equity of redemption in the seventeenth and eighteenth centuries. This rule 'minimised the possibility that landowners would lose their land when they mortgaged it in order to raise cash, or use it for security for the debts they incurred' (Sugarman and Warrington 1995: 111). The important result of this reform preserved, if not increased, the power of the landholder against all others, including the mortgagee. At common law, the date of repayment agreed to at the time of the mortgage would see one of two outcomes: either repayment in full and reconveyance of the property back to the mortgagor or delay in payment and forfeiture of the property to the mortgagee. The courts of equity challenged this common law rule by contending that the true object of the loan agreement or transaction was the security symbolised by the land and not the land itself. The terms of the loan agreement, such as its duration and the mechanism of foreclosure were deemed irrelevant by the Court of Chancery: 'The rights of the landed were thus entrenched as against the lenders, even though this might involve rewriting the transactions between the parties' (Sugarman and Warrington 1995: 111). This rewriting of mortgage agreements effectively meant that the parties to it were no longer equal in power for no other reason than the one who originally granted the mortgage was regarded as 'properly' owning the land whereas the other, the lender, held only the interest in the money and because money was inferior to land, the interest holder, the mortgagee was inferior also. Lord Nottingham states in *Thornborough v Baker* (1675) that 'in natural justice and equity the principal right to the land is only as a security for the money' (Sugarman and Warrington 1995: 117). The law actively restrains the alienation of land through this rule and thereby distinguishes land from capital: 'The property, that is, the land, really belonged to the borrower; the lender was only entitled to the money' (Sugarman and Warrington 1995: 117). Although the feudal period was ending, the link between land and power remained and, it has been argued, this reform of the common law 'helped the aristocracy to retain its landed estates and at that time political power' (Kerruish 1999).

The significance of the equity of redemption was that it had become synonymous with an estate in real property and demonstrated the degree to which property was valued as power. The possession of land in law, like the mastery of nature in science, claimed to produce human subjectivity esteemed not by physical or material reality (biology or force) but by metaphysical transcendence. Yet, as the critiques of seventeenth-century scientific discourse contend, the creation of the paradigm left indelible, material traces. The English courts' rationale in applying the equity of redemption was that land should be returned 'to its rightful (often meaning historical or traditional) owner'. Despite accusations of the unfairness of the rule, for example, the equitable creation was defended abstractly: '[I]t was as if it was inconceivable that an English gentleman would give up his land' (Sugarman and Warrington 1995: 120). In their critique of the rule and the historical reporting of its rationale, Sugarman and Warrington find significant the deployment of terms such as 'fair', 'rational', 'noble' and 'ideal'. The principle is significantly compared to the transcendental wisdom of mathematics, inciting the critics to remark wryly 'here was a doctrine that could indeed perform miracles' (Sugarman and Warrington 1995: 120). But there is nothing miraculous about property law and its equation of land with power when it is noted that:

> [F]rom 1621 to 1844 the kingdom's supreme judges were not professional lawyers of King's Bench or Chancery but England's nobility assembled in Parliament. Although the law remained the law of the Crown, the largest owners of property became the highest judges of the law of property.
>
> (Sugarman and Warrington 1995: 122)

Having land meant having power. It was not power delivered by justice, but power delivered by judges. As St Germain had argued during the Reformation: '[P]roperty was not a divine institution and thus property rights were firmly vested in the temporal sphere of jurisdiction, where they were subject to regulation by the law of man' (Guy 1985):

It was a common claim that Parliament, including that portion of its charged with representing the community at large, the House of Commons, was pre-eminently a legislature of landowners, whose vested interests as a class it was frequently tempted and sometimes induced to advance. In fact this was not so much an admitted vice as a boasted virtue of the 'landed gentlemen', as Hume put it, 'in whose hands our legislature is chiefly lodged'.

(Langford 1991: 288)

The relationship between person and place here is governed by the dynamic of possessive ownership according to which, land is an unmediated referent to political status and thus to the transcendence of human subjectivity. The seemingly apparent paradox of this idea of property is that the inalienability of land suggests an identity between person and place while the land itself rarely rates a mention. In fact, there is no such paradox: the law upholds not the inalienability of land, but rather, the inalienability of power.

2.4.2 Land as capital

In an economical point of view, the best system of landed property is that in which land is most completely an object of commerce; passing readily from hand to hand, when a buyer can be found to whom it is worthwhile to offer a greater sum of money for the land, than the value of the income drawn from it by its existing possessor.

(Mill 1978: 255–256)

During the transition from feudalism to capitalism, the idea of property changed from power to thing and the justification of the law grew more elaborate and abstract, the anthropocentric model of people and place became increasingly explicit. Land was no longer considered to provide power but to be vulnerable to it, as object. The scientific revolution was matched by the legal revolution of the sixteenth and seventeenth centuries following the secularisation of land in the reformation[6] and the growth of the capitalist market economy. The idea of nature was fundamental to the discourse of science. Similarly, the idea of real property in land was fundamental to the discourse of law (Buck 1990: 200). But did the changed ideas of property and law indicate a changed idea of land itself? Certainly, land gradually became thought of as capital rather than as power, but it maintained its function as metaphor, a vehicle of representation rather than a materiality. Due to the dominance of capital, land was eventually and explicitly understood

---

6 Between 1536 and 1603 one-quarter of the land in England changed hands as a consequence of the programme of dissolution (Elton 1982: 378–394).

to be primarily and principally, a resource. Combined with the prevalence of the discourse of improvement and the justification of private property in labour, land became not only the implicit condition of the human economy, but as the hidden condition of law itself.

The shifting function of land in law, from being the foundation of socio-political power to being the resource or 'thing' of wealth presented questions about the authority of law. The very idea of a resource connoted inter-dependence between people and place, not just economically, but legally. The authority of law was supposed to transcend the physical realm, to be independent and, more importantly, original – beyond question. The authority of law could not merely be constituted by the accumulation and control of resources and 'things' (what kind of social order would that be?) Yet with the transition from feudalism to capitalism, it was no longer possible to regard the law's authority as transcendental and metaphysical because power and authority were also increasingly and transparently pro-vided by the ownership of actual, physical land and its resources as capital assets: 'For political and parliamentary purposes land was losing both its special identity and its unique status' (Langford 1991: 288). The more specif-ically valuable land became as a marketable physical resource, the more important it was for the law's authority to be distanced from the realities of the market economy. Accordingly, the ownership of lands and resources was translated into an increasingly elaborate and complicated concept of prop-erty in legal theory and practice. It was at this time that the view of people–place relations was converted from the diverse and various relations they were between different communities and different places into a national and imperial discourse of property as a legal relation between a 'person' and a 'thing'.

The divisibility and alienability of land meant that property could be thought to be the land itself whereas in pre-capitalist England property was an intricate network of social and political relations and obligations: 'As rights in land became more absolute, and parcels of land became more freely marketable commodities, it became natural to think of the land itself as property' (Macpherson 1975: 111). Furthermore, the legal protection of the property right 'could be so much taken for granted that one did not have to look behind the thing to the right. The thing itself became, in common parlance, the property' (Macpherson 1975: 111). The problem with this observation of the reality and socioeconomic effect of the land market and property transactions was that it meant that the authority of law was still tied up with the ownership of land and resources. Grounding law's authority in the physical foundation of land and resource ownership was antithetical to the hitherto apparently metaphysical and transcendental nature of law and divine or natural order of the universe. It would also prove an obstacle to affording the same protection of property in land to property other than land: 'The ways in which commercial development complicated definitions of property and the political priorities which were supposed to flow from respect for property' (Langford 1991: vii). Law and property needed to transcend the physical realm and, to achieve this, legal theory and specifically property theory developed and elaborated various models of land and resource owner-ship that effectively removed even the mention of them from the discourse. The use of the words 'thing' and 'object' were important and necessary to this end. As Bentham noted in 1789:

> It is to be observed, that in common speech, in the phrase *the object of a man's property*, the words *the object of* are left out; and by an ellipsis, which, violent as it is, is now become more familiar than the phrase at length, they have made that part of it which consists of the words *a man's property* perform the office of the whole.
>
> (Macpherson 1975: 111)

What exactly was the 'thing' of property? It didn't matter. Bentham's point was that property was not the land, it was the right. He defends this by replacing land with 'object' or 'thing' to indicate the irrelevance of the quali-tative nature of the 'thing'. 'Things' matter to property law only in so far as 'people' own them. The quality of thingness is that it has no quality. Defi-nitions of the word *thing* number 29 in the Macquarie Dictionary, which in itself alone, if not in combination with the first two definitions, well illustrates this point: '1. A material object without life or consciousness; an inanimate object. 2. Some entity object, or creature which is not or cannot be specifically designated or precisely defined' (Macquarie Dictionary 1992). The signifi-cance of the partner term to 'thing' in the private property relationship, 'person', denotes the singular of people. The idea of the 'person' in property corresponds with the primacy of individual proprietorship in the theoretical model of private property. Possessive individualism was increasingly preva-lent in the growing economy of capital (Macpherson 1962). Its unilateral dynamics paralleled the diminishing relevance of communities and their multilateral dynamics. Individualism and separation from place are mani-festly situations of alienation. Writing 4 years before Bentham's remarks were made, the gentleman agriculturist Thomas Coke (1752–1842) while resonat-ing the feudal connection of property to sovereignty, articulates modern property as alienation from community. He foreshadows the late modern usage of the word 'alienation' (by Hegel, Marx and Freud) as the effect or character of the estrangement of humanity from nature through civilisation (Williams 1976: 31–32):

> It is a melancholy thing to stand alone in one's own country. I look round; not a house to be seen but mine. I am the giant of the giant-castle, and have eaten up all my neighbours.
>
> (Coke, cited in McLeod 1999: 164)

Coke's remark indicates that alienation is not simply a cultural condition, a feeling of estrangement from other people. Coke, as an individual and private proprietor living on enclosed land is estranged from the land itself. His home is not 'his' country, but his 'giant-castle'. For Coke, property is not the land, but the ownership of it. Coke lives neither with nor of the land, but on his property. His lament does not regard the land at all. His only relation to the land around him is his alienable possession of it. The property relation articulated here is of power, objectifying, abstracting and then absenting land. Alienation is an effect both of estrangement from land or nature and from other people. Indeed, it would not be a great exaggeration to say that this sense of alienation is contemporaneous with the paradigmatic splitting of the world into nature/culture: 'If we alienate the living processes of which we are a part, we end, though unequally, by alienating ourselves' (Williams 2005: 84).

2.4.3 Land as other

Only after land is conceived as capital, a non-qualitative object of property, when property is commerce, can it be alienated 'readily from hand to hand' (see Mill 1978). The theoretical and material structure of people–place relations as persons and things affected alienation at three levels: of land as property with the fluidity of capital; of people from place with enclosure, colonisation and emigration; of people from people with urbanisation and individualism. Alienation denotes neither agency nor passivity; rather it describes a relationship. Derived from the Latin *alius* meaning 'other' and *alienus* meaning 'of or belonging to another person or place', 'alienation' is used in English to describe the state of estrangement or the act of estranging (Williams 1976: 29). Williams notes the changed uses of the word from the fourteenth century, when it referred to the severance of relations between an individual and God or between an individual or group and the state, to the fifteenth century when it referred to the transfer of rights, estates or money. The transfer, however, was not regarded as being voluntary or intentional and therefore positive. Rather, *alienation* was used during this time to describe transfer in the negative sense of loss, force or impropriety (Williams 1976: 29). Alienation was imbued with positive meaning (and was positivised) in the seventeenth and eighteenth centuries with the increased prevalence of absolute private property. While alienation is well understood as a founding principle of modern property law, it is barely acknowledged that alienation is a relationship or dynamic referring not to one thing but to two: the person and the thing are alienated from each other. Modern property discourse erases the bilateral aspect of alienation, because it constructs alienation as agency and will: the person is the active, alienating subject, and the land is the passive, alienated object or thing of the land market. In this sense, the modern discourse of property constructs land as culture's *other*. The notion of unilateral alienation renders the modern paradigm of property, placeless.

Private property instantiated the greatest physical alienation of people from place in the history of English land law and yet, theoretically, it coupled people and place via the justification of private property as labour. Locke's justification of property in labour was the legal parallel to Bacon and Descartes' justification of science as cultural improvement and elevation. It carries the same logical holes and manoeuvres. It also carries the same influence in contemporary people–place relations. Although the rules of absolute private property were modified by an emphatic relative rights-based discourse, Locke's justification of private property, published anonymously in the seventeenth century, carries immense influence in contemporary legal and political order. His work has long been considered a defence of enclosure law and since the 1990s it has also been regarded as a justification and defence of British colonialism (Arneil 1994). Yet his argument not only justifies private property and colonialism as socio-political institutions (and the condition of inequality of landholding). Locke's lingering but understated contribution to modernity is his uncanny rationalisation of the physical severance of people and place in terms of their metaphysical union. Locke understood land not as something intrinsically vital, active or as an agent of power, but as something passive and vulnerable to power. To Locke, land was literally, powerless. The anthropocentric model of person/thing at the centre of his theory of property relations was that the person is or has the power while the thing, the land, is powerless.

Locke's justification of private property rests on three premises. First, that 'every Man has a *Property* in his own *Person* . . . [and] . . . the *Labour* of his Body . . . are properly his' (1988: 287–288). Second, that mixing or joining one's labour with the earth, annexes that person's labour to that land, creating exclusive title to the land and its produce. Third, that 'men had agreed, that a little piece of yellow Metal, which would keep without wasting or decay' (1988: 294) enables uneven distribution and unlimited accumulation of property 'without injury to anyone' (1988: 302). Locke defines persons and things in his labour theory of property as part of a process of improvement and production. He relates people and place to each other only via the mediation of wealth. The premise of his theory presents people as persons, constructing an individualism at odds with the existent shared economy of open field or common agriculture. He presents nature as things valued solely through human labour, use and ownership, constructing an idea of nature in itself (lacking cultivation) as waste (Locke 1988: 299–302).

Yet, while metaphysically coupling persons and things through the process of labour, the actual and physical foundation of Locke's logic is their alienation. For if it were not possible to remove commoners from the commons, Indigenous communities from their nations and alienate land through 'conquest or commerce' (Locke, cited in Arneil 1994: 605), Locke's economy of property could not succeed. Although he makes labour the centre of his justification of private property, he fails to acknowledge the contentiousness of the particular form of labour he advocates. Locke has a specific idea of labour as it relates to land that is different to the labour of the commoners on the commons pre-enclosure. He begins with gathering acorns and apples from 'the Trees in the Wood' and shifts this as his description on enclosures develops (Kerruish 1999):

> Locke speaks almost exclusively, in the Second Treatise, of labour in terms of crop growing, agrarian activity rather than mining, grazing, manufacturing, or other forms of industry which could theoretically provide an equal claim to proprietorship through labour.
>
> (Arneil 1994: 603)

Locke's justification of property is based not only on the agency or alienability of land, but on the agency and alienability of a particular form of labour. This shift in agency decisively alienates people from place, prioritising culture and cultivation over nature in the modern paradigm of property. Locke did not suppose that landowners would labour their land alone. The degree of industriousness advanced by Locke necessitates wage labour and/or slavery:

> Locke produced a defence of private property based on the natural right of man to that with which he has mixed his own labour, and many thousands of people believed and repeated this, in periods when it must have been obvious to everybody that those who most often and most fully mixed their labour with the earth were those who had no property, and when the very marks and stains of the mixing were in effect a definition of being propertyless.
>
> (Williams 2005: 76)

As Macpherson points out, the justification of private property through labour 'was only needed when and because a moral case had to be made for putting every individual on his own in a market society' (1962: 204). In Locke's theory, the landholding customs of people closest to the land, had the least claim to title to it:

> Enclosure and cultivation (as distinct from herding, extracting, communal production) became the kind of labour that justified title to land because cultivation increased the value of land more than any other use.
>
> (Kerruish 1999)

For Locke, the primary relationship between people and place is the labour of the land. His theory of property as alienation thus plays out in a 'state of nature' (1988: 290). Absolute private property rights, he argues, are natural rights.

2.4.4 Nature as law and the antilogy of natural rights

By the late seventeenth century, when Locke was writing his justification of enclosure and colonisation, the medieval concept of property that was merged with status and obligation and that was appointed by God, was challenged by the modern ideas of commonwealth, contract and capital. Epistemological faith in theological doctrine was being supplanted by faith in scientific method, the order and certainty of which provided protection from chaos. But the question of the legitimacy of law, still vested in its origin, proved problematic for Locke's theory of property. Though he stressed the rectitude of the 'law of Reason', the question of law's origin proved difficult:

> In the sixteenth and seventeenth centuries landowners had asserted their titles in land against the prerogative of the king, and copyholders had asserted their titles and customs against their lords. They therefore discarded theories of the origin to title in divine right. Yet if they fell back upon Hobbesian violence or on the right of conquest, how could they reply to the telling counter-argument of the Norman Yoke? When Locke sat down to offer an answer, all this was stewing around in his mind.
> (Thompson 1991: 159–160)

Locke's justification of private property asserted natural rights and the wisdom of the market against divine rights and the wisdom of kings. His appeal to nature worked as an escape route via which he could maintain the idea of origin as the guarantor of law's legitimacy while displacing the conventional connection of origin to force. In its place, Locke constructs an idea of nature as order, balance and design. Nature is the provider of both subsistence and reason (1988: 286–287). Locke anticipated a concept of nature as abundance, gradation and eternity that seemed counter to Bacon and Descartes' concept of nature. It was epitomised in the early eighteenth century poetry of Alexander Pope (1688–1744):

> First follow Nature, and your judgment frame
> By her just standard, which is still the same:
> Unerring NATURE, still divinely bright,
> One clear, unchang'd, and Universal Light,
> Life, Force, and Beauty, must to all impart,
> At once the source, and End, and Test of Art.
> (Grant 1950: 16)

This poem was published within 22 years of Locke's *Two Treatises on Government*. The imagined complementarity of nature and culture here seems different from the nature/culture paradigm supporting Locke's theory, but, in fact, simply inverts the hierarchy of the terms. Where science had subordinated nature as the object of knowledge, Pope now elevates nature as the provider of knowledge. But people, now abstracted as culture, are still the centre of the universe and the division of the world and its simultaneous severance and coupling of nature and culture remain. The relationship Pope ascribes to nature and culture repeats the relationship of God and man that science had replaced. Nature is eternal and omniscient in the same way that God had been. Science had discovered the workings and eternal laws of nature. Similarly, Locke's justification of property constructed an idea of law that married reason and eternity. The laws of nature were synonymous with the laws of reason, which as with science and philosophy, provided law with authority vested neither in God nor in force. The idea of natural law or law in nature was not the subordination of culture to nature. Rather nature is cultured and elevated to replace God. The role of nature here remains utterly the legitimisation of culture and thus does not disrupt the nature/culture paradigm. The paradigm continues to deploy nature ideologically, but with a new rhetorical purpose – to legitimise culture and conceal its agency. The process of naturalisation removes the question of agency so that what protects or authorises the new world order is not force, but something transcendental, beyond question. The paradigm seems 'natural' in that it is represented as true, inevitable and universal.

The idea that the legitimacy of law and culture is vested in nature contradicts the idea that nature is subordinate to culture advanced by the improvement discourse that Locke deployed to advance his specific idea of labour. One sense of nature refers to the passive, meaningless object of law and science, connoting everything that man is not, and another sense of nature refers to the prior condition of that paradigmatic structure, connoting the authority of an origin. The contradiction or double meaning is an incidence of antilogy that Jacques Derrida calls the scandal of play in the discourse of the human sciences (1978: 283). For Derrida, unlike Foucault, nature and culture are not separated by the force of modern reason. The opposition between nature and culture:

> is congenital to philosophy. It is even older than Plato ... it has been relayed to us by means of a whole historical chain which opposes nature to law, to education, to art, to technics – but also to liberty, to the arbitrary, to history, to society, to the mind, and so on.
>
> (Derrida 1978: 282–283)

Derrida explains that because nature and culture do not exist outside the logical frame of the paradigm that constructs them, incidences or things that arise which cannot easily or convincingly be categorised as either natural or cultural, disrupt the ability of the paradigm to make sense. He draws his example from Levi-Strauss who noted that the incest prohibition does not fit neatly or obviously within the nature/culture opposition. It is something that '*simultaneously* seems to require the predicates of nature and of culture' (1978: 283, emphasis in original). The incest prohibition 'is universal; in this sense one could call it natural. But it is also a prohibition, a system of norms and interdicts; in this sense one could call it cultural' (1978: 283). The scandal of the incest prohibition is that it makes the categories of nature and culture meaningless, thus threatening the validity of the paradigm itself. However, the scandal of meaninglessness occurs not only because nature and culture are discursive constructs, but also because meaning is possible only through mutual exclusion and opposition. In other words, it is precisely because law and nature are defined in opposition to each other that the play or disruption occurs. The incest prohibition, like anything else must be either natural or cultural, but not both or neither. Precisely because it is not exclusively natural or cultural, questions of its origins arise. Similarly, the idea of natural rights, the right of culture from nature, asks questions of origins. Questions of origins undermine the atopic and ahistoric claims of the nature/culture paradigm.

The tension in Locke's theory of property that nature is the source of a law that insists culture improve and appropriate the meaninglessness and chaos of nature, presents a scandal or lacuna in anthropocentric discourse. The origin of law, its authority or right, is both and neither natural and cultural. An origin, a place and a time, 'escapes these concepts and certainly precedes them – probably as the condition of their possibility' (Derrida 1978: 283). Locke's idea of property is both natural and cultural. His defence of enclosure and colonisation do not reveal inevitable or enduring principles of property or necessary relationships between people and place. Rather Locke's theory of property relates the modern paradigm of nature/culture to the legal paradigm of people/things. The new world order of enclosure and colonisation advanced by Locke was not brought to being by method and reason, but by violence and force. The material dimensions and carriage of Locke's idea of property from theory to law further disrupt its claim that nature/culture is true and transcendental because it is based in the contested and the physical. The following chapter will elaborate this point with reference to the discourse and process of enclosing the commons in England and the resistance that it met.

Chapter 3

Material origins

Nation

3.1 Introduction: building a placeless nation

How did the conceptual origins of modern property law, the theoretical model of people and things, apply in the real world? The answer to this question lies principally in the enclosure of the English commons. The customs or laws of the commons were locally specific and responsive to geographic capacities and limits defined by forests, fens, marshes, wetlands and heaths. These specificities were regarded as irrelevant to the development of an abstract law of private property. The material origins of the modern laws of property were thus the physical processes of transforming very particular local geographic and ecological relations into uniformly productive fields and pastures across the nation through enclosure.

Enclosure is the name given to the process of enclosing and appropriating land – hitherto worked and enjoyed by a peasant community in common – usually with a hedge, fence or other physical boundary. Enclosed land is privately owned land; it excludes the interests and access of all but the owner, usually an individual. The land and its fruits are legally alienable, that is transferable and tradeable by the owner at their discretion. Privately owned land carries no obligation or responsibility to anyone for anything unless noted on the title. Enclosure is also the name given to a protracted but revolutionary period in English history in which a substantial portion of English lands were transferred from common, inalienable interests to private, alienable property. Enclosure occurred where an individual appropriated land held in common by the community, and/or where open fields held in common or in severalty for either cooperative or separate husbandry were parcelled out permanently (Langford 1989: 435). Although lands were being enclosed intermittently well before the eighteenth century, from 1750–1820, almost 21% of English lands were enclosed by acts of parliament. Enclosure was contested and resisted, locally as well as more broadly in ideological terms, because enclosure dispossessed entire communities or parishes, whose populations often became hire labour on the now privately owned land or else migrated to urban centres: 'The stranglehold of enclosure, by which means the open fields and commons where smallholders grazed their animals were legally stolen in the interest of the large landowners' (Reeves, cited in Barrell 1972: 190). As that quote indicates, enclosure can be critiqued in political terms which may or may not include 'an idealisation of feudal and immediately post-feudal values: of an order based on settled and reciprocal social and economic relations of an avowedly total kind' (Williams 1973: 35). Williams warns against such idealisation, noting that the social order of feudalism was 'as brutal as anything later experienced' and arguing, more significantly, that enclosure was part of a 'concentration of landholding' that developed over a longer period of time. His account of enclosure is one that describes this 'revolution' rather as an episode in a continuous history of 'conquest and seizure' of English lands, which, while an important, defining and 'decisive' episode, is nonetheless too easy to sentimentalise or approach uncritically and nostalgically.

In part, this tendency to look back at enclosure sentimentally is because enclosure was fundamentally a transition to a more complicated and detached relation between people and place. Many important and enduring questions about the relationship between humans and their environment date back to the process of enclosure. Margaret Davies asks of enclosure, for example: '[W]ere the enclosures an *inevitable* part of agricultural modernisation and rationalism? Did the rural population necessarily become proletarianised, that is less able to support themselves from the land and more reliant on employment in an increasingly capitalised economy?' (2007: 68). English law, land use practice and culture changed irrevocably through the enclosure of the commons. So powerful was the enclosure of the commons in terms of nationhood that it was conflated with the construction of both nation and empire: 'Nationalist propaganda in favour of enclosure equated the domestic privatisation and "improvement" of land with war and colonial conquest' (Davies 2007: 69).

This pivotal event in the foundational history of contemporary property law consistently deployed the ideas of improvement and progress. The paradox of improvement discourse is that its logic marries people to place while its counteractive practice physically separates and severs this relationship. The rationale of enclosure (and colonisation) is that cultural progress can be measured only by the improvement of nature. The condition of any given society is apparently, therefore, known via its relationship to and precisely by its distance from nature. In improvement theory, there is necessarily an immediate proximity of nature and culture. Conversely, in practice, both enclosure and colonisation physically removed people from their indigenous places through eviction, transportation and dispossession. These events deplace and displace people. The irreconcilable logic and practice of improvement however, does not belong only to the annals of a supposedly defunct British Empire. It is found on the shelves of lawyers and economists, thus demonstrating the continuing relevance of the paradigm of nature/ culture and its manifestation in law: people/things.

3.2 Ordering place: enclosure

The story of enclosure is an ecological story. Enclosure changed the relationship between people and place. Yet it has most often been regarded and recorded not in terms of that relationship but according to the nature/culture paradigm as either (traditionally) a social history or (more recently) a natural history. This chapter weaves together these separated histories to reveal the fact of their separation as characteristic to the paradigmatic splitting of people and place in English modernity.

The land laws of the peasant economy, its 'customs', were locally developed and thus were relevant and responsive to various local geographic conditions. These laws were necessarily strictly enforced. This is because as well as providing rights of access, use and enjoyment of land, waterways and local resources, they also provided highly specific limits or conditions to those rights. In other words, the land laws of the peasant economy were clear and rational rules of resource management. The social and ecological viability of these land laws was indicated by their continued observation over centuries. Communities established near forests and woodlands, for example, enjoyed the right of estover, which permitted the gathering fallen timber for fuel, and the right of hay bote, which permitted the use of dry forest wood lying on the ground and 'any dry wood they could knock down with hooks' for repairing fences and ploughs (Hoskins and Stamp 1963: 47). The local law or custom of the land was therefore a system providing both entitlement to and management of the land's resources. These laws can be traced back to at least the thirteenth century where local manorial court records indicate that these rights were well known and understood. Given these laws were developed in a cold and wet climate in which fuel and building resources were vital for life, it is not surprising that breaches of these laws were regarded as serious offences. Manorial court records dating back to the early seventeenth century in Gartmel (Lancashire) indicate the community's dependence on and protection of the local resource of bracken, which was used for thatch, bedding and fuel (Hoskins and Stamp 1963: 47). Being a highly valued resource, the right to use it was accompanied by the rule to cut it in a certain way and at a certain time. Commoners were forbidden from cutting bracken before a certain date (which varied from year to year depending on seasonal conditions) and even then the taking of the resource was limited to a 3-day period. The first of these 3 days was marked by the creation of a special day on the local rural calendar, Bracken Day (Hoskins and Stamp 1963: 47). This custom or law that strictly governed the use of the resource indicated both the notion of a right or entitlement to the resource and the notion of dependence on the resource giving rise to a responsibility for sustainable usage.

Given the geographic diversity of England, it is unsurprising that the land laws that supported peasant economies were various rather than uniform. The examples given by historians indicate a substantial range of laws and customs governing land and resource use depending on the physical context of those laws. Even grazing rights, the most important rights held by commoners, were highly specific to local geographic conditions. Certain species of animal were permitted to graze on common pastures while others were not, or permitted to graze only until a certain age (Hoskins and Stamp 1963; Karsten 2002). The key point here is that there was no universal right of grazing that applied across the nation, rather there were locally developed and responsive rights and rules governing the grazing of particular numbers of particular animals of particular ages at particular times in particular places. The geographic specificity of the law evidenced the connection between communities and the ecological conditions of their existence. The law reflected a connection between people and place. This intimate people–place relation gave rise to viable community cultures and economies over very long periods of time. That laws were determined and defined by the place of their origin and operation demonstrated that the commoners were cognisant of the dependence of their economy on maintaining the conditions of local resources.

The cultural significance of the laws or customs of the commoners relating to land use and management is that they protected an economy which 'made use of all the resources of the neighbourhood and was very largely self-sufficient. For the majority of English and Welsh people, money played only a marginal part in their economy until the early years of the nineteenth century' (Hoskins and Stamp 1963: 44). The ecological significance of the laws or customs of the commoners relating to land use and management is that they protected an economy which was not only locally specific but which fundamentally ensured its viability over time. Many of these laws operated in the same places for several hundreds of years, which reveal both the success of the economies they served and the intelligence of the resource management they provided.

The death of the laws and customs of the commoners and the peasant economy was not brought about by any intrinsic failure or inevitable collapse. Contrary to the claims of the improvers (those who stood to benefit from enclosure), the laws and customs of the commoners were neither unproductive nor non-viable. Rather, their laws were extinguished either by the legal seizure of the lands to which the communities and their laws belonged or by declaring illegal the various land use practices involved. The extinguishment of these laws or customs was the principal objective and the consequence of enclosure and private property in land:

> In the great attack on the commons which reached its climax in the late eighteenth century and the early nineteenth, it was frequently alleged that the commons were mismanaged and neglected and gave rise to every kind of evil from sheep-rot to dissolute vagrancy; but these criticisms, even if they were well founded at the time, do not provide a true picture of the

way in which the commons were managed in earlier centuries when the manorial organization and machinery were still effective.

(Hoskins and Stamp 1963: 48)

Enclosure demonstrates the agency of law in transforming the paradigm of nature/culture from theory to practice through the introduction of private property relations. Locke's concept of property in labour, consistent with his contemporary improvement theorists, argued that cultivation and husbandry would deliver man from sacrilegious idleness and restore him to the rightful and active domination of nature. But Locke's ideas of property extended far beyond theoretical contemplation and debate. He linked improvement theory to the practices of enclosure and colonisation and, in so doing, endeavoured to legitimise the appropriation of common property and the exclusion of long-established communal rights:

Enclosure, labour and the subjection of the earth were all part of the same process. This provided the basis for his justification of property in the earth itself. To reiterate: 'As much Land as a Man tills, plants, improves, cultivates and can use the Product of so much is his Property. He by his labour does, as it were, inclose it from the common'.

(Locke, cited in Brace 1998: 161–162)

By presenting private property as reasonable and natural under the arch-discourse of rationality and its appeal to the paradigm of nature/culture, Locke provided a new story of law. Lawyers, judges and scholars reiterated his justification of private property for years to come because it reformed myriad diverse and complex people–place relationships of feudalism into rational, simple and finite relationships in law. While legal categories were fixed and knowable, law's authority, though historically abstract and sacred, could be vested in the inevitable rectitude of the Lockean method. This discourse was used to justify both the enclosure of the common property in England and the colonisation of property of foreign countries. The actual displacement and dispossession involved in this process effectively materialised the mythic division of the world into people and things. E.P. Thompson argued that the role of law was pivotal to the construction of that mythic world which not only reordered itself, but also its *other*: 'It was law (or "superstructure") which became the instrument of reorganising (or disorganising) alien agrarian modes of production and, on occasion, for revolutionising the material base' (1991: 164).

The gradual and widespread splitting of open fields, woodland and marshes into enclosed, mapped and discrete parcels of cultivated and horticultured land profoundly changed the economy of English society and ecology. Enclosure changed a practice that was at once cultural and natural: land use. It transformed the land use practice of agricultural cultivation into one fitting firmly within the ontological category of culture.

3.2.1 Making culture

The change from open field agriculture to enclosure indicated radically changed farming practice, from subsistence to enterprise via science. Human relationships to place were increasingly articulated as unilateral consumer and producer relationships within the developing economy of capital. The contribution of the scientific revolution to that economy and to the enclosure movement cannot be understated. Jethro Tull (1674–1741) and Charles Townshend (1674–1738) for example are regarded as having reconceived farming as a science. Their aim, however, was not to change farming as a form of knowledge about 'things', but as an economic mechanism. Their work advocated the idea of 'improvement' in terms of the increased production of the quantity of the goods yielded by farming rather than as increased quality or diversity of those goods – ultimately profit.[1] The word 'improvement', derived from the Old French word for 'profit', connected a particular form of land use to monetary gain (Williams 1976: 160–161). Tull 'invented' the mechanical, horse-drawn seed drill and Townshend 'discovered' the four-course rotation system of planting without fallowing. But neither 'invention' nor 'discovery' was valued as knowledge in itself, rather they were valued as utilities of economic development: 'Tull serves to underline the important fact that the ongoing agricultural revolution was the necessary precursor and partner of the better known Industrial Revolution' (Davies 2000: 636). Townshend's discovery was more probably a refinement and popularisation of an agrarian practice that had gradually developed in England over several years (Tudge 2003: 68). Fallow lands, which were important in the existing two-course or three-course rotation systems, were replaced with pastures of grasses or fodder legumes or roots such as turnips (Mazoyer and Roudart 2006: 313). This meant that the land was productive every season 'with almost no break' so that the land reached the maximum possible productivity at the time. The result was the production of 'at the very least twice as much as the older systems' (Mazoyer and Roudart 2006: 314). The increased produce was surplus available for trade on relevant food markets and was possible only by making illegal the long-established usufructuary rights and practices of commoners, which supplemented their income and supported rural society. Charles Townshend was known as 'Turnip' Townshend because he introduced the turnip as cheap winter food for livestock: 'The more livestock that can be maintained through the winter, the more there are to make use of next year's pasture' (Tudge 2003: 68). Townshend's advocacy of the idea of improvement was very much related to economic gain. Indeed, it was the market economy that encouraged the beginnings of industrial scale agriculture.

---

1 The English word 'improvement' was derived from the Old French word for 'profit'. In the English usage, improvement connected a particular form of land use with monetary gain (Williams 1976: 160–161).

Progress was conceived almost entirely in terms of a market economy:

> Farmers began to concentrate on particular agricultural products rather
> than producing a wide range of commodities to satisfy the needs of
> the local community. They chose the crop or animal to which their
> land was most suited, taking account of climate, the soil, and location,
> and they produced that crop or animal for sale on the national market.
> Thus regions developed which were devoted to a single type of agriculture.
>
> (Bellamy and Williamson 1987: 96)

Science and the new economy worked hand in glove. The economic function
of science in changing agricultural practice is indicated by the class of
farmers responsible for producing the burgeoning improvement and husbandry literature. Their literacy and independent wealth distinguished them
as gentlemen and professionals: Charles 'Turnip' Townshend was also known
as Lord Townshend.[2] The Board of Agriculture formed in 1793 consisted of
31 founding members, 14 of whom were titled (Barrell 1972: 65). As John
Barrell notes, the great proprietors were concerned mainly:

> with the revenue they derived from their estates: with ways to increase
> rents and to save costs in more efficient management; and precisely how
> these aims were achieved were of secondary importance.
>
> (1972: 66)

The members of the board who did not represent the peerage were agricultural experimentalists because they were 'bigger tenant-farmers and the more
substantial owner-occupiers' (Barrell 1972: 66). The growing landholding of
the rural professional class was related directly to the wealth of that middle
class. The new bourgeoisie of the countryside 'were responsible for virtually
all the agricultural literature produced between about 1750 and 1820' (Barrell
1972: 66). Land ownership became tied to land use: changes to one practice
were changes to both:

> Farming gradually became a capitalist industry based on a sophisticated
> market economy, but this development was only possible because of the
> evolution of the concept of absolute ownership, and the emergence of a
> few wealthy landowners and large farmers in place of the multiplicity of
> peasant proprietors.
>
> (Bellamy and Williamson 1987: 95)

---

2 For an interesting discussion of class, farming, literature and agrarian capitalism see Thirsk,
'Making a fresh start: sixteenth century agriculture and the classical inspiration' in Leslie and
Raylor (1992).

The agricultural revolution and its connection to the advancement of private property demonstrate that cultivation was the nexus of the modern discourses of individualism and economic efficiency: 'If we ask, who the genius of the place may be, we find that he is its owner, its proprietor, its improver' (Williams 1973: 123). The value and utility of nature as things, that were separate from culture, was then and remains the basis of both science and law. The institutionalisation of private property is the practical coincidence of these discourses. The alienation of humans from 'everything else' imagined in science and law was enacted by enclosure.

Culture was made by changing property law. Enclosing open fields that had been held in common for hundreds of years meant changing the laws of possession and ownership, especially the rights regarding fallow lands. Agricultural historians have called the common rights of grazing 'the largest and most widespread' of obstacles to the agricultural revolution (Mazoyer and Roudart 2006: 333):

> Open field farming, while not such a rigid or inefficient system as has sometimes been suggested, was incompatible in most places with the long-term tendency to increase the size of farms or with the desire of individuals to specialise in the immediately profitable use of land.
>
> (Briggs 2000: 35)

The cultivation of lands periodically left fallow meant prohibiting commoners' rights to graze. As these rights had been exercised over open fields, the process of enclosing them required either the total acquiescence of the commoners or strategies to counter their resistance. The economic objectives of private property were simply incompatible with common property. Open field agriculture was an obstacle to agricultural productivity and profitability, they could not coexist. A legal solution was necessary.

The connection of custom and tradition to law in feudal society was similarly incommensurate with private property because the alienability of land, that the latter required, relied on the a-historicism of the science of farming and 'improvement' theory. The values and uses of land within the peasant and capital economies were very different and this difference fundamentally challenged the functionality of land law. Whereas property had been about obligation and reciprocity in feudal law, modern property law conceived of property in terms of rights and unilateral relations. The new, private form of property severed the connection of law to tradition and custom, because capital was created not by historically and geographically defined obligations and responsibilities but by the alienability and exclusivity of land and its resources. Private property law required the alienability of property in terms of relationships that were universal and dichotomous, rather than particular and pluralistic. It was necessary to abolish the collective obligations of the peasant economy protected by the laws of the commons to enable the freedom to exclude, cultivate and alienate land and its produce (Mazoyer and Roudart 2006: 333). Contemporary customs expressed specific people–place relations that revealed a diversity of long-established cultures. Modern English property law, however, prescribed generalised people–place relations in producing a universal culture – the English nation.

As with the 'pioneers' of new farming practice, the agents of property law reform represented and protected the interests of one class, the same class that claimed absolute and exclusive (private) property rights. This class personified culture. It was the class of landowners and the new order of professional farmers or 'improvers'. Entrepreneurial 'gentleman' farmers, members of the parliament and judiciary belonged to the same class: the ruling class. This fact is overlooked in a recent account of enclosure by a landscape historian who presents legal and agricultural change as separable:

> Considerable changes in the rural landscape of Britain were brought about either by changes in the legal framework of man's relationship with the soil, or else with by changes in his agricultural practices, and quite frequently by changes in both.
>
> (Reed 1990: 205)

Changing the landscape can only be read as 'either' or 'both' agricultural and legal when the framework of class that supports their activity is omitted. Parliamentarians, judges, lawyers and enclosure commissioners, who were often the 'gentleman' farmers and landowners, ensured the successful carriage of enclosure: 'The enclosures did not stop at the boundaries of the estate. Many peasants were deprived of their lands in all sorts of ways: non-renewal of limited leases, seizing lands upon deaths and transfers, and abusive evictions' (Mazoyer and Roudart 2006: 340). The attention of the law-making and landowning class to gleaning, for example, was an attempt to guarantee the exclusivity of property by reducing or 'translating' customary rights over common property into permitted usage of private property (Thompson 1991: 163). Gleaning by women and children of straw and grain from wheat and cornfields after harvest was common practice and was regarded as a legitimate custom until 1788 when the common law ruled that it was not a property right (*Steel v Houghton* (1788) 1 H.Bl 34). Customs in common were diminished and simplified into rights in common. Customs were newly categorised, for example as the right to pasture (common of pasture), right to cut peat or turf for fuel (common of turbary) and right to collect firewood and repair wood (common of estovers) (*Halsbury's Laws of England IV* 1932, cited in Neeson 1993: 313: 'In reality, on the ground, the range of common produce was magnificently broad, the uses to which it was put were minutely varied, and the defence of local practice was determined and often successful' (*Halsbury's Laws of England IV* 1932, cited in Neeson 1993: 313). But formally, at common law, common right was the right to share the produce of land, not the ownership of the soil. Peasants became trespassers on land they did not own but to which they felt they belonged. Alienation redefined law and property; it also redefined legitimate relationships to place.

The elimination of obligation and responsibility from law was an important aspect of the reconceptualisation of people–place relations in the capitalist economy. But as E.P. Thompson argues, enclosure was not only an important element in the transition from feudalism to capitalism in England; it was an essential element in the transition from community to nation and from nation to empire. Enclosure demonstrated changed values and uses of land, the accelerated pace of which corresponded with the universalising movement of the legal discourse of alienable and exclusive property. In the fifteenth and sixteenth centuries enclosure evidenced gradual and localised incidents of economic change, but by the eighteenth century enclosure was so wide-spread that it evidenced the basis of a national and imperial economic programme:

> The concept of exclusive property in land, as a norm to which other practices must be adjusted, was now extending across the whole globe, like a coinage reducing all things to a common measure.
>
> (Thompson 1991: 164)

The metaphoric description of property as a coin points to the way in which the rise of capital made law a function of its quantitative economy. Law no longer protected the diverse rights and obligations of various and specific interests in particular localised resources; instead, it protected the standardised rights and wealth of the private realm independent of location. Private property law homogenised the plurality of local cultures and various relations to place into a national market of land and labour. But as private property recast human subjectivity, it changed the scenery too. The law inscribed itself into land. If it can be said that enclosure made culture something transcending the physical, it might also be said that enclosure made nature. This means enclosure changed the non-human world of 'everything else' from diverse, particular networks of things and local ecologies, into the contained and framed setting of culture – the landscape. The following section explores the ways in which enclosure and the privatisation of property trans-formed English lands into the English landscape – how property law shaped and continues to shape the land.

3.2.2 Making nature

> Scrutiny of historical change is the condition for comprehension of human landscape perception.
>
> (Fitter 1995: 8)

The eighteenth-century vision of 'Man'[3] as *homo faber* extended beyond the realm of culture to nature, through the immense alteration of land use practices and fabrication of landscape. The seventeenth-century meaning of 'landscape' had been the visual perception and representation of country in painting. However, by the eighteenth century, this term had become a broader referent to the appearance of country. Importantly, the knowledge and appreciation of country became a mark of cultural distinction:

> Between 1776 and 1800, it became increasingly fashionable for landed proprietors with no trading interests at all to display interest in agriculture as well as in hunting or painting: indeed, there grew up an 'agricultural school' of painting, and great landowners and statement, including Thomas Coke of Norfolk, first Earl of Leicester, the Duke of Bedford, and Lord Althorp, were happy to be portrayed in the centre of farmyard scenes.
>
> (Briggs 2000: 33)

Culture was measured in the language of nature: 'During the eighteenth century the contemplation of landscape – in nature, or as represented in literature and the visual arts – became an important interest of the cultivated' (Barrell 1972: 3). Wealthy landholders brought home landscape paintings from their 'grand tours' of Europe, which they would then realise on their English properties through the hired skills of eminent landscape architects (Williams 1973: 122). Landscape was fashionable in two senses: it indicated a modal aesthetic of land and, in addition to the land market itself, became a commodity: 'Landscape very quickly became the most popular genre of painting, and in the private collections of the very rich it was the newly acquired Claudes and Salvators that were most admired' (Barrell 1972: 4). Indeed, the demand for landscape art 'exceeded the sources of legitimate supply, and the trade in imitations, copies, and forgeries was considerable' (Barrell 1972: 4). The representation of country as landscape was executed according to particular aesthetic values that consisted of distinctive:

> principles of composition that had to be learned, and were indeed learned so thoroughly that in the later eighteenth century it became impossible for anyone with an aesthetic interest in landscape to look at the countryside without applying them.
>
> (Barrell 1972: 6)

---

3 The male pronoun is used and capitalised here to underline the gendered paradigm of nature/ culture.

The application of this aesthetic value constructed a landscape. Art, as a cultural form, constructed nature as external to it and in so doing expressed an aesthetic of alienation. Aesthetic preferences are not divorced from the paradigm of people–place relationships of any society. While not necessarily prescriptive, the aesthetics of landscape are imbued with values of nature and correspond to values of land use: 'To the English improvers this art, with its close associations with bourgeois improvement and with scientific inquiry into nature and into modes of perception, was a close analogue' (Williams 1973: 122). The connection between the aesthetic of landscape painting and values of land use is well demonstrated by the later usage of the word 'landscape' as a verb: referring to the professional and large-scale activity of gardening, landscaping. The experience of 'seeing the world as a landscape' (Turner 1979: 8) therefore did not preclude *making* the world as landscape. Nature was cultured and culture was naturalised. The division of the world into natural and cultural realms that defined modern Anglo-Saxon subjectivity was made real. Landscape no longer referred only to a specialised genre of visual art – it referred to the actuality of topography and farming and gardening practice:

> It was that kind of confidence, to make Nature move to an arranged design, that was the real invention of the landlords. And we cannot separate their decorative from their productive arts; this new self-conscious observer was very specifically the self-conscious owner. The clearing of parks as 'Arcadian' prospects depended on the completed system of exploitation of the agricultural and genuinely pastoral lands beyond the park boundaries. There, too, an order was being imposed: social and economic but also physical.
>
> (Williams 1973: 124)

W.G. Hoskins was an economic historian whose famous study *The Making of the English Landscape* (1955) became a popular television series *Landscapes of England*. He is credited with having inaugurated a new branch of history with his investigation of the relationship between human social change and changing topography (Taylor, in Hoskins 1988: 7–9). In his study, which spans the western farmsteads of the pre-Roman landscape to the power stations of Oxfordshire in the 1970s, the largest chapter is *Parliamentary Enclosure and the Landscape*. Hoskins observed that the practice of transforming land from common and open fields (including moorland and mountain) to enclosure:

> had been going on intermittently and at a varying pace in every century. But from the 1750s onwards, enclosure by private act of parliament . . . was the great instrument of change. From then onwards, the transformation of the English landscape went on at a revolutionary pace.
>
> (Hoskins 1988: 144–145)

Hoskins continues to provide figures and dates of the extent of enclosure acts, the most notable of which is the contrasting pace of enclosing open arable fields prior and subsequent to the 60-year rule of George III. Under the rules of George I (1714–1727) and George II (1727–1760) there were 18 and 229 Acts respectively enclosing an area not exceeding 400,000 acres. Yet between 1761 and 1801 under George III 1479 Acts were passed enclosing over 2.5 *million* acres. Between 1760 and 1801, 750,000 acres of 'wasteland' were also enclosed (Hoskins 1988: 151). In total, between 1755 and 1815 over 4000 Acts enclosed over 5 million acres of English land (Davies 2000: 637). In the reign of one king almost 13% of England was enclosed, contrasting to 1% in the reigns of the two preceding kings. Jeanette Neeson figures that between 1750 and 1820, 6.8 million acres (or 21%) of England was enclosed by Act of Parliament (Neeson 1993: 329). Enclosure is mostly recorded as a process with cultural effects and socio-political change: evicting, relocating and destroying peasant communities. Enclosure is less often recorded as a process with natural effects and ecological change: burning and felling forests and woodland, draining fens, marshes and wetlands, dividing and fencing villages and open fields. Enclosure was an early form of what is now called 'planning'. It was, in every sense, the fabrication, the making of landscape. The change to land wrought by enclosure was rapid and radical.

Social historians generally agree about the contribution of class interests to the emergence of private property and enclosed lands (see, for example, Brace 1998; Davies 2000; Langford 1991; Neeson 1993; Thompson 1991; Turner 1979). The significance of class in the process of enclosure is not explained by the size of the class, but by the size of their landholding. The 'revolutionary pace' of enclosure from 1750 rapidly consolidated large areas of land into the ownership of a few. The powerbase of owners of enclosed land was different from the powerbase of feudal landowners. Enclosed land was owned exclusively, without obligation or responsibility in the way it had been in feudal England. The labour and produce of enclosed land were alienable, marketable surplus not supplies. As such, they were sold at a price greater than the cost of their production rather than on a basis of exchange or mutual obligation. Private and exclusive land ownership transformed land into a market resource. But in the same way that corporate responsibility is today considered an important parallel if not a vital contributor to remedial social and ecological work, the same landowning class whose power grew through enclosure attracted criticism for failing to recognise their responsibilities in addressing some of the environmental damage wrought by the agricultural and industrial revolutions.

The depletion of forest and woodland was a serious concern in the seventeenth and eighteenth centuries. While most preferred to attribute this to extensive shipbuilding and the use of charcoal in the iron and glass industries, John Evelyn implicated enclosers in the diminution of the nation's trees through their 'grubbing out of woodlands to create arable land' for profit

(Hayman 2003: 82). In 1664, Evelyn wrote: '[T]here is nothing which seems so fatally to threaten dissolution of the strength of this famous and flourishing nation, than the sensible and notorious decay of her wooden-walls' (cited in Hayman 2003: 82). Trees and nationhood were famously linked by the symbolism of the oak tree. The depletion of forest and woodland therefore could be linked to a threat to the nation itself, both symbolically and politically. The tension between improvement theory and its advocacy of enclosing land for profitable productivity and concerns about the state of English forests became the focus of gentlemanly attention at the time. Concern was so substantial that an essay on improvement in 1728 entitled 'Sure Method of Improving Estates by Plantations of Oak', Batty Langley urged cautious felling and the replanting of trees in order to avoid the complete loss of timber, as a resource, in England:

> Indeed at this juncture we have very little building timber in our woods and forests to boast of and are already much obliged to foreigners for great quantities of our civil uses. But should we ever happen (which God forbid) to be obliged to purchase some of their timber for our Shipping (by want thereof at home) 'tis to be feared that this glorious nation that governs the Seas, must submit to every invasion that's made, for want of its wooden walls of defence.
>
> (Langley, cited in Schama 1995: 165)

Cultivating private oak plantations was not the same thing as conserving forests and woodlands, but by linking the logic of improvement with the language of national security, Batty reconciled profitability with a form of land use that did not necessitate land clearing.

Concern had become so serious by the 1760s that regrowth and mass planting programmes were established as competitions for proprietors and aristocrats to sow the most acorns, chestnuts, elms and firs: 'Acres of ducal property were immediately studded with acorns, and fir saplings by the hundreds of thousands began to sprout across the country ... William Mellish (won a prize) for 101,600 spruce and 475,000 larch on his estates at Blyth, Nottinghamshire' (Schama 1995: 168). Yet the programme was related to the welfare of the nation in terms of defence and particularly shipbuilding for the navy. The efforts to restore the natural realm via tree growing were not natural heritage or conservation efforts, rather they were conceived in terms of the economics of patriotism. Schama later compares English efforts to their French counterparts on the eve of the French Revolution observing that both were fighting a 'triangular (and unequal) contest for precious timber' (1995: 179). The timber triangle he suggests consisted of merchants, contractors, stewards and tenant farmers at one corner who 'looked at the trees as standing capital, to be realised or reinvested as the market dictated'. The landless poor were at the second corner 'whose survival depended on the defence, violent if necessary, of traditional rights to gleaning, gathering, and cropping'. At the apex were, of course, the state officials and large landowners 'increasingly desperate about the shortage of ship timber and suffering from nightmares of the last pine and the last oak snatched by the Other Side' (Schama 1995: 179–180).

The values of nature and land use indicated by mass tree growing competitions were identical to the values of nature and land use that rationalised the larger projects they supported: enclosure and global colonisation. Private enclosed land was the condition of the property regime required for ducal tree plantation of such magnitude. It was also the condition of the dispossession and appropriation of alien property regimes. The histories of enclosure and colonisation are ecological histories. Both their conceptual programme and their materiality corresponded with dominant social and aesthetic values of nature and land use in England in the seventeenth and eighteenth centuries. Just as the poet Alexander Pope had equated beauty and utility[4] similarly when agriculturists contrast open and enclosed country, they 'are most willing to identify a beautiful landscape with one which is well-farmed' (Barrell 1972: 75). The pleasure derived from cultivated landscape was complemented by the fear and hostility that characterised the agriculturists' relationship to wild or natural places such as marshes and woodlands. The negative perception of uncultivated nature could be elaborated in terms of fear and hostility generally. In particular, the attachment of negative sentiment to nature was continuous with negativity concerning foreigners and foreignness. Sir John Sinclair, President of the Board of Agriculture, so loathed nature that he likened it to foreign enemies with whom the cultivated Englishman was at war:

We have begun another campaign against the foreign enemies of the country ... Why should we not attempt a campaign also against our great domestic foe, I mean the hitherto unconquered sterility of so large a proportion of the surface of the kingdom? ... let us not be satisfied with the liberation of Egypt, or the subjugation of Malta, but let us subdue Finchley Common; let us conquer Hounslow Heath; let us compel Epping Forest to submit to the yoke of improvement.

(Sinclair, cited in Neeson 1993: 31)

Here, the idea of nature as *other* is highly pronounced. Improvement was synonymous with enclosure, landscape gardening and colonisation. Improvement was the condition of each of these programmes as was the objectification of place as *other* to English nationhood. Improvers, enclosers,

---

4 'Epistle IV to Richard Boyle, Earl of Burlington, Of the Use of Riches' [1735], in Alexander Pope *Poems* (D. Grant (ed.)) (1950), Harmondsworth: Penguin, 163–170.

gardeners, legislators and colonisers preferred the preordained cartographic structure of abstract space, to the physicality and particularity of place. The idea of space cultured place by bringing it within the realm of human knowledge and control. Standardised, universal and measurable space could be grafted over place so that the physicality and particularity of places became irrelevant. The irrelevance and absence of place underwrote the legitimacy of enclosure and colonialism because:

> If it were admitted that different cultures produce different spaces, then negotiating these would be difficult, if not impossible. Constructing a monolithic space, on the other hand, allows imperialism to hierarchise the use of space to its own advantage. In imperial ideology the Aborigines do not have a different space to that of the explorers; rather, they underutilise the space imperialism understands as absolute.
>
> (Ryan 1996: 4)

As Ryan notes, spatialising place made the appropriation of lands seem a rational and constructive process of discovery and exploration rather than a political and destructive process of dispossession and spoilage. This discursive movement was important to the epistemological and ecological revolution of enclosure:

> The process of enclosure replaced the chaos of the open fields and common lands with a neat patchwork of hedged fields and securely held as private property by virtuous, improving individuals.
>
> (Brace 2001: 9)

The notion of space removed place as nature from culture. The concept of space and spatial technologies, such as cartography, were instrumental to enclosure and the ordering of place both conceptually and actually: 'One might ask whether the role of maps in organising and exploiting land and labour did not in fact begin to impose a "linear" or "rational" perspective upon the landscape' (Pottage 1994: 361, 370). Changes to law and property relations indicating changed perceptions of land were physically expressed through the regulation of enclosure by changes to the land itself:

> To enclose an open field parish means in the first place to think of the details of its topography as quite erased from the map. The hostile and mysterious road system was tamed and made unmysterious by being destroyed; the minute and intricate divisions between lands, strips, furlongs and fields simply ceased to exist: the quantity of each proprietor's holding was recorded, but not among what furlongs it had distributed.
>
> (Barrell 1972: 94)

3.2.3 Property and landscape

The mutually defining relationship between culture and nature that animated the development of property law during the period of enclosure conveys a fact of immense significance. The idea and representation of land as place in human culture is intimately bound to the materiality of land. Law determines, in part, how land is regarded aesthetically and how landscape is made materially. As the law of private property and enclosure objectified or *othered* land into landscape, the law erased the specificities of those lands as places from its discourse. Recent historical accounts of enclosure maintain this erasure. Norman Davies, writing a brief history of the British Isles in 2000 records the history of enclosure in predominantly cultural or social terms:

> The enclosure of communally held open land had long been the occasion both for agricultural progress and social distress. Farmers gained control of large closed fields suitable for the production of cash crops and surpluses, while local peasants and humble tenants lost their means of subsistence.
>
> (Davies 2000: 637)

The political control of land, Davies notes, served an economic purpose with social effects. The sense of 'land' to which he refers is the anthropocentric sense of land as resource, the control of which is really the control of its products and access to them. What such anthropocentric history does not note is that the *isles* of which Davies writes (and their creatures) were themselves controlled and effected as nature. Davies separates and privileges the social history of enclosure from the natural history, or more precisely, from the history of the effects of enclosure on nature. Landscape historian W.G. Hoskins, by way of contrast, records enclosure and the rise of private property as affecting major change to the topography and landscape of England. Hoskins' history highlights rather than assumes the way in which law makes or physically determines the landscape via enclosure. He notes that, in 1764, Lancelot 'Capability' Brown dammed the River Glyme to make a lake at Blenheim Palace. In 1775 Brown made a lake at Burghley, 'nearly a mile long and moved trees of the most enormous bulk from place to place, to suit the prospect of the landscape' (Hoskins 1988: 137–138). Hoskins links these landscaping events to the notion of cultural control of nature. Furthermore, this control is noted in terms other than socioeconomic. Contemporaneous praise of Brown's 'control of land' did not contemplate the land in terms of its economic value or even entirely as a source of aesthetic pleasure. Rather, Brown was hailed as being a creative genius, recalling Locke's concept of colonial settlement as the 'equivalent to an act of creation' (Fitzpatrick 1992: 82). The control of land in this sense of (re)creation contemplates land as the means by which culture is transcendental:

It was the genius of Lancelot Brown, which brooding over the shapeless mass, educed out of a seeming wilderness, all the order and delicious harmony which now prevail. Like the great Captain of the Israelites, he led forth his troop of sturdy plants into a seeming barren land; where he displayed strange magic, and surprised them with miracle after miracle.

(*Guide to Burghley House* [1797], cited in Hoskins 1988: 138)

Landscape historians Bellamy and Williamson record the social impact of enclosure and private property indirectly or as consequences of primarily geological and biological change. For them, the physical and biological 'control of land' is central to the programme of enclosure. The idea of nature as instrument is significant to their history only insofar as it is enacted and performed physically. Their account of enclosure draws attention to major and permanent alterations to nature as physical rather than as ideological changes. Private property and agricultural experimentation altered the direction and flow of rivers and thus affected the physical qualities of the soil, most deliberately, its fertility. The vigorous drainage of fens in the seventeenth and eighteenth centuries (Langford 1989: 432) resulted in the loss of wetlands and their ecologies (Tudge 2003: 67). Channels and sluices were constructed from rivers to flood meadows, enriching grasses and soil for the concentrated production of a single lucrative crop that could maximise returns on capital (Bellamy and Williamson 1987: 96). New crops such as root vegetables, carrot, parsnip and turnip for example, were grown to feed livestock now kept in stables and stalls rather than grazing on fields, and this increased the quantity of livestock. 'This highly efficient system of arable farming facilitated tremendous improvements in animal husbandry' (Bellamy and Williamson 1987: 100). The techniques of rotation farming and cross-seasonal growing required intensive use of land throughout the year. The increased availability of feed for livestock changed the quantity *and quality* of animals: 'Not only were more animals kept, but individual beasts were healthier and much larger. From the seventeenth century, great improvements in stock had been made by selective breeding. Agricultural shows and awards acted as a further stimulus in the eighteenth century' (Bellamy and Williamson 1987: 100). Bellamy and Williamson argue that 'these innovations directly encouraged the enclosure of the landscape, but they also served as an indirect stimulus, since they accelerated the decline of the small owner-occupier' (1987: 100). The point that can be drawn from the history of the biophysical effects of enclosure is that both the natural and the cultural worlds were the conditions and effects of change brought through enclosure. They are not neat and distinctive worlds so much as the same world exhibiting the effects of major changes in land use and land law.

Nature is the condition of agricultural change in the same way that culture is the condition of the enclosed landscape. Things of nature were cultivated and thereby attributed with having inherently cultural significance, e.g. oak trees. Similarly, things of culture were naturalised and attributed with having inherently natural origins, e.g. entitlement to private property through labour: 'Landed wealth is transformed into the "natural" wealth of land-scape. The behaviour of those who possess it is correspondingly naturalised, and all sense of arrogance and violence is removed' (Turner 1979: 141). Praise for the work of 'Capability' Brown at Burghley House, for example, presents the cultured garden as being so natural that it is impossible to distinguish between nature and culture:

> Though the beauties with which we are here struck, are more pecu-liarly the rural beauties of Mr Brown, than those of Dame Nature, she seems to wear them with so simple and unaffected grace, that it is not even the man of taste who can, at a superficial glance, discover the difference.
>
> (*Guide to Burghley House* [1797], cited in Hoskins 1988: 138)

The slippage of the terms nature and culture between their apparently distinctive and mutually exclusive realms seemed to further legitimate rather than challenge the paradigm of nature/culture. But not everyone was con-vinced and neither, argues Raymond Williams, should they be:

> Reading some of these histories you might almost believe – you are often enough told – that the eighteenth-century landlord, through the agency of his hired landscapers, and with poets and painters in support, invented natural beauty. And in a way, why not? In the same ideology he invented charity, land-improvement and politeness, just as when he and his kind went to other men's countries, such countries were 'discovered'.
>
> (Williams 1973: 120)

3.3 Traces of place

3.3.1 Anti-enclosure discourse

Pro-enclosure literature was largely advocated by those who stood to gain from it. But because enclosure was a form of 'legalised seizure enacted by representatives of the beneficiary class' (Williams 1973: 98), unsurprisingly and invariably, the seizure of lands, rights and village communities met with opposition. Yet while opposition to enclosure was widespread and long standing, it was defeated by property law. Nonetheless, it is important to consider and to value that resistance as a means to understand the roots of ongoing resistance to contemporary property law. An understanding of various forms of resistance to the dominant values embedded in property relations is vital to recognising their placed specificity without which univer-salising claims flourish. As Edward Said wrote against the universalising claims of imperialism in *Culture and Imperialism* (1994): '[T]here was *always* some form of active resistance' (Said, cited in Brace 2001: 17).[5]

Against the universalising claims of improvement theory and enclosure law, anti-enclosure discourse suggests that culture, law and landscape are as impermanent and variable as 'nature' itself. Resistance to enclosure situates modern property law within specific historic and geographic conditions. By refusing the universalising claims of improvement theory and the nature/culture paradigm, anti-enclosure protest and discourse locates property law, making it particular and placed. Foucault wrote that resistance emerges within the discourses it opposes: 'Where there is power, there is resistance, and yet, or rather consequently, this resistance is never in a position of exteriority in relation to power' (1990: 95). Similarly, Raymond Williams observes that the anti-enclosure riots marked the end of the local resistance to local instances of enclosure and led to the broader class-based organisation of resistance in trade unionism: 'The maturity of capitalism as a system was forcing systematic organisation against it' (1973: 112). Resistance to enclosure did not 'succeed in halting it' (Siemon 1994: 22) and the paradigm of nature/culture and the discourse of private property flourished. However, the fact that there was resistance to enclosure and that this resistance is still debated today, works, in Derrida's words, as indelible traces or *Erinnerungsspur* (Derrida 1978: 216) of difference within what is otherwise an homogenising discourse of universal relations to place. Anti-enclosure discourse critiques enclosure from various perspectives, mostly economic, political and moral. All these critiques evidence anthropocentric values of nature in so far as they are concerned with the distribution of, and access to land in terms of its economic resourcefulness and the social meanings and consequences of that distribution. One particular critique, found in the writing of peasant and poet John Clare, resists enclosure in a different way. Clare's writing evidences a non-anthropocentric relation and connection to place and his passionate struggle against enclosure is unambiguously a struggle against the new people–place relation prescribed by the nature/culture, person/thing paradigms developing at the time.

Resistance to enclosure was strongest until and including the seventeenth century: 'Even after it was imposed, decreed, or consented to, this exclusion from grazing long remained poorly accepted, so much so that it was necessary to enclose the lands with quickset hedges, rock walls, or ditches in order to enforce respect for the exclusion' (Mazoyer and Roudart 2006: 340). After this time, enclosure became increasingly publicly defensible (Kerruish 1999). When Locke published his justification of private property anonymously at the end of the seventeenth century, significant enclosing had already taken place through 'private agreement': 'Private in the sense that they were

---

5 Emphasis in original.

promoted and paid for by private parties, but all too public in the sense that they involved changes in the organisation of property and in the social structure of rural areas' (Langford 1989: 435). Prior to 1730, when the period of parliamentary enclosure began:

> Commentary on enclosure, whether derived from the testimony of the people in court or through petition, or from the official proceedings and polemic of those making assertions in their behalf, is overwhelmingly negative – and remarkably consistent.
>
> (Siemon 1994: 21)

After this time, anti-enclosure discourse did not diminish, rather it was countered by pro-enclosure discourse. Siemon relates the rise of pro-enclosure discourse to the 'emergent values of nascent capitalism' (1994: 22) and the emergent class of capitalists who held them. John Barrell argues that the increased size and influence of the rural professional class was directly related to the growth of the pro-enclosure movement. He points out that the success of parliamentary enclosure required:

> [T]he services of lawyers to draw up the enclosure-bill; of paid enclosure-commissioners, to supervise the whole business of putting the act into execution and redistributing the land; of solicitors to draw up the claims of those whose land was to be enclosed, and who could afford the services of a solicitor; of quantity-surveyors, to mark out the course of new roads, and to measure out new allotments of land; and to auditors, to check through the commissioners' accounts of the expenses of the enclosure.
>
> (Barrell 1972: 70–71)

The establishment of the professional class or bourgeoisie was linked to and supported by parliament. This small group of decision makers, who created law, consisted predominantly of landowners who were significantly 'the only gainers of the agricultural revolution: real rents increased sevenfold from the middle of the fifteenth century to the middle of the nineteenth' (Allen 1992: 285). The juncture of land ownership and parliamentary power indicates a second reason for the rise of pro-enclosure discourse after 1730: when an enclosure bill became enacted, it also made opposition to it illegal: 'Parliamentary enclosure could be employed by way of coercion when voluntary efforts had failed' (Langford 1989: 436). Resistance to enclosure thus became resistance to law. Disagreement about concepts and values of property became conflicts before the law. In this way, anti-enclosure discourse was translated into criminality.

Legal forms of opposition were available, but expensive, and usually unsuccessful (Neeson 1993). Indeed, it was to shortcircuit expensive and protracted litigation that landlords increasingly turned to parliament to enclose (and engross) their properties:

> Simple convenience and the desire for a watertight legal title ensured that a statutory device, once created, would regularly be employed in preference to other methods. Expensive though it was, in terms of both parliamentary fees and the cost of fencing, reorganising, and new instrument, it compared very well with the unlimited potential expense of litigation in case of disputes in the future.
>
> (Langford 1989: 436)

Parliament 'turned a deaf ear to legal protest' (Neeson 1993: 260) and so opponents to enclosure resisted through physical actions. Newly created and enforced laws designed to protect private property discouraged such resistance by imposing 7-year transportation penalties: 'Under 9 Geo. III c.29 (1769) anyone convicted of wilfully and maliciously damaging or destroying any enclosure fence was guilty of felony' (Neeson 1993: 280). Those transported for resisting enclosure in England became the very agents of colonial enclosure in the colonies. The introduction of the penalty of transportation turned resistance into colonisation.

Despite the protection of law, 'enclosers' farms were plainly vulnerable' (Neeson 1993: 280). Resistance varied from parish to parish and in some villages there were traditions of protest 'that looked back to earlier resistance to enclosure, one that owed much to the habits of communal agriculture' (Neeson 1993: 263). Brace cites instances of 'local opposition' expressed by 'stubborn non-compliance, foot-dragging and mischief' such as:

1. burning of trees, fences, hedges, gates and summerhouses;
2. anonymous threats in letters and the forms of poems;
3. theft of newly completed enclosure books and plans;
4. blockading fence construction fences until forcibly removed at the enclosers' cost;
5. rumours, newspaper advertisements and letters regarding enclosers' motivations;
6. digging up sand and soil onto the road;
7. felling young trees planted immediately after enclosure.

(Neeson 1993: 259–293)

Affecting over 3000 parishes (Hoskins 1988: 145), enclosure met with widespread and ongoing (though localised) resistance, over a 200-year period. Bellamy and Williamson cite similar examples:

> In 1639 the men of Corby in Northamptonshire marched to Thackley Green and spent three days pulling down the hedges of the enclosing

landlord Sir Christopher Hatton ... As late as 1870 the stakes and railings dividing the common at Fakenham in Norfolk were pulled up and burnt.

(1987: 115)

The authors attribute this resistance to the economic effects of dispossession on the lives of commoners, small farmers and cottagers: 'In many places and in many sections of society there were those who deeply and bitterly resented the enclosure of the landscape . . . (because) it meant the ends of a subsistence that was a valuable safeguard against unemployment and economic hardship' (Bellamy and Williamson 1987: 114). It is important here to relate some anti-enclosure activities such as the felling of trees, hedgewood stealing and fence breaking to resistance not only in its symbolic and political sense, but also in the literal or physical sense of resisting hardship. When the commons were enclosed, commoners lost vitally important waste and pasture, including especially the necessities of wood (see Clare 2000: xxxvi; Neeson 1993: 280). The value of waste was lost to the enclosers (and to colonists (Tully, cited in Brace 2001: 16)), who consistently contrasted waste to improvement and cultivation.

Economic changes contributed substantially to the anti-enclosure movement. Economic historians record the increased hardship of consumers, labourers and farmers with the dramatic fall of real wages (Allen 1992: 285) and the long-term rise of real product prices (Allen 1992: 284). In 1862 John Aubrey, nostalgic for the days of feudalism, remarks that England was enclosed 'for the private, not the public good' and now was 'swarming with poore people' (Aubrey, cited in Siemon 1994: 21). The appearance of increased poverty relates in part to the decreasing number of landowners: 'When the manor of Feckenham was surveyed in 1591, sixty-three different owners held some 2900 acres. By 1900 there were only six owners, who held all this and another 3000 acres besides' (Hoskins 1988: 166). It also relates to the fact that enclosure concentrated poverty into fixed locations and increased its visibility. Commoners were dispossessed of property in an abstract sense of rights, but they were also dispossessed physically of homes and subsistence leading them to urban centres if they had not already been forcibly 'relocated'. Hoskins notes that private property heralded 'the age of territorial aristocracy' in which village cornlands vanished inside park walls: '[W]hole villages were destroyed and built elsewhere when they were found to stand in the way of a "prospect" or some grand scheme of landscape design' (Hoskins 1988: 134). The first Earl of Dorchester for example bought the entire site of the town Milton Abbas:

which had stood for many centuries at the gates of the Benedictine monastery at Milton. He decided to build a great family mansion where the ruins of the abbey stood. The little town stood in the way and was demolished. In 1786–7 a model village was built on a new site a mile away.

(Hoskins 1988: 134)

But other, non-economic factors also account for the bitterness and strength of the anti-enclosure movement. Historian Robert Allen relates resistance to enclosure to what he calls the accompanying 'narrowing of the mental life of the rural population' (1992: 289). The cooperative management of open field or common agriculture meant that farmers were jointly responsible for decision making and participated in public life (Allen 1992: 290):

> They deliberated the rules within the framework of the manorial court and provided necessary public officials to manage the system. Leveller demands for national democracy were an extension of village democracy rather than a whole new departure. As the open fields were enclosed, this political forum vanished. Furthermore, as the yeoman lost their copyholds and beneficial leases, they ceased to be ratepayers and so lost the public responsibilities that followed from that obligation.
>
> (Allen 1992: 289)

Enclosure altered local socio-political relations as landlords were no longer necessarily connected to the local community in terms of their cultural identity. Landlords were no longer necessarily connected to the land either in terms of having 'an affinity for a particular setting or place' that had 'played such a major role in the social and cultural dynamics of England until the early modern period' (Estabrook 1998: 20):

> The government of the countryside belonged in the supposedly safe hands of landed proprietors. But there were growing fears in the eighteenth century that this class was opting out of its responsibilities at the very time when commercial farming and the social changes which accompanied its most called for attendance to duty.
>
> (Langford 1991: 367)

Anti-enclosure discourse is usually discussed in terms of resistance to the development of private property and the modern social organisation it supports. Historians such as Neeson and Hoskins are also interested in anti-enclosure discourse because it reveals ontic and epistemic dimensions of life pre-enclosure, particularly relationships between people and place. They are interested in enclosure not only as a social or environmental event evidenced by riots and petitions and transformed landscape and topography – but also as an event that fundamentally changed ecological subjectivity. The pre-enclosure relationship between people and place, articulated especially by commoners, Neeson calls 'possession without ownership' (Neeson 1993: 3). This form of property held by commoners pre-enclosure was not alienable and not exclusive, the significance of which is not entirely economic. Neeson's definition of 'possession without ownership' suggests a property relationship closer to the ancient or original sense of the word 'property' referring to identification with and from place, rather than ownership over it. This relationship creates subjectivity from place. In this sense, it is neither atopic nor ahistoric:

> Commoners were not labourers. They were peasants. The value of the name is that it emphasises a continuity with the past, a continuity based on the occupancy of land and the rights in the common-field system . . . they are descendants of other English peasantries, not a rootless eighteenth century phenomenon.
>
> (Neeson 1993: 297–298)

Commoners, Neeson contends, recognised their mutual dependence on the shared economy of open field agriculture (1993: 321) and their mutual relationship with the land (1993: 3–5). Their violent resistance of the commoners to the enclosures and the poetry of commoner John Clare (1793–1864) are renowned examples of the vitality of this mutual relationship. Clare's resistance to enclosure, through poetry, is substantially different from the forms of resistance outlined earlier. However, it is also different from the literary tradition of his contemporaries. Other poets wrote about enclosure, but Clare's poetry cannot be understood completely as anti-enclosure discourse neither can it be understood completely as part of the environmental idealism of Romanticism and pastoral genre.

3.3.2 Romanticism

Romanticism was reactionary: '[I]t is easier to articulate what romanticism was against than what it stood for' (Hay 2002: 5). The Romantics reacted against the ideas and aesthetic forms of the age of Enlightenment. They wrote against reason and replaced it with an epistemology of the imagination. Nonetheless, Romanticism was an intellectual project. Its focus was overcoming the intellectual legacy of Enlightenment:

> The Negation is the Spectre, the Reasoning Power in Man . . .
> To come in Self-annihilation & the grandeur of Inspiration,
> To cast off Rational Demonstration by faith in the Saviour,
> To cast off the rotten rags of memory by Inspiration,
> To cast off Bacon, Locke, & Newton from Albion's covering,
> To take off his filthy garments & clothes him with Imagination.
> (Blake 1972: 818)

Romanticism revered nature as the genesis of wisdom and locus of inspiration. Nature was not a metaphor for what civilisation ought to be, in the way that it was for Pope and the Augustans – it was its antithesis. The Romantics were critical of civilisation and modernity; they defined their project as an escape from the trappings of culture and a retreat to nature. Thus Romanticism did not subvert the nature/culture paradigm, it just polarised the terms differently. Romantics were ecocentric rather than anthropocentric. Although the Romantics juxtaposed nature and culture (as civilisation) their ideal of nature remains cultured, as a garden, rather than a wilderness. Clare, however, valued waste and wildness, nature was not to him a garden or paradise (Bate 1991: 34) but a loved one: 'Yer flat swampy vallies unholsome may be/Still refuse of nature wi out her adorings/Yere as dear as this heart in my bosom to me' (Clare [1812–1823] 1984: 46–47). The Romantics' relationship with nature was mediated through an elaboration of idealised culture that ultimately elevated the human spirit. The Romantics 'appropriated the natural as a delicate interior notation' (Fitter 1995: 277). Romantic representations of nature are highly specular and stylised. Ideals of nature were central to the Romantic critique of civilisation. The pastoral genre was therefore central to the Romantics' reaction against the institutions of culture because it articulates a value and ideal of nature most explicitly.

Jonathan Bate wrote that the work of the Romantics is part of a broader environmentalist tradition: 'What are the politics of our relationship with nature? For a poet, the pastoral is the traditional mode in which that relationship is explored' (Bate 1991: 19). Stephen Muecke describes the pastoral genre as one characterised by a relationship of alienation between viewer or artist and land:

> There is not landscape without a sense of otherness; landscape has to be seen or experienced, in the way a tourist does. So for the Indigenous person, there is really no such thing as the landscape. Perceptions of landscape depend on difference, therefore and on displacement.
>
> (Muecke 1992: 166)

Muecke argues that Australian Aboriginal narratives of place are noticeable for the absence of a specular perspective of the landscape. This degree of proximity with place changes the relationship from one which would use the word 'to' to one which would use the word 'from'. Clare's poetry comes *from* the land, because his relationship is not 'to' place, but 'from' it. The depth of feeling and knowledge that consists in such an indigenous relationship with place suggests that the commoners' resistance to enclosure is based on the dispossession of both their ecological relationships as well as of their material economy: 'It is not only the loss of what can be called – sometimes justly, sometimes affectedly – a piece of "unspoiled" country. It is also, for any particular man, the loss of a specifically human and historical landscape, in which the source of feeling is not really that it is "natural" but that it is "native" ' (Williams 1973: 138).

3.3.3 The poetry of John Clare

The conventions of the pastoral genre situated nature as a background to a story about a shepherd or alternatively as scenery appreciated visually. The aesthetic tradition of the pastoral genre and landscape painting required a level of detachment from the land that commoners, hitherto attached to the lands literally through their cultures and economies, did not experience: 'A working country is hardly ever a landscape. The very idea of landscape implies separation and observation' (Williams 1973: 120). The pastoral landscape was perceived from a position of exteriority, suspended above the nature it described comprehensively. Clare, however, perceived himself within, as part of the landscape. Natural elements in Clare's poetry are characters with whom we can engage rather than landscapes which we observe and admire. Clare's expression of nature has a subjective quality, contrary to the objectification of place as scenery within the pastoral tradition. Indeed the subject/object boundaries between people and place are altogether strange to Clare and he introduces and associates these boundaries with the process of enclosure. In *The Lament of Swordy Well* (1984: 147–152), for example, Clare writes of land in the first person, that is, the land itself is the narrative voice of the poem. The land narrating the poem is not land in general or lands arbitrarily chosen as example. Rather, the land is a particular land, a place that Clare refers to as Swordy Well. This song or poem expresses the geographical, biological and social changes of enclosure. The enclosed land has become barren and dull with the relocation of stones, felling of trees and bushes and the transformation of springs into an irrigation system. Soil properties have changed with these topographical changes and with multiple-season harvesting. The local fauna of the land have also been displaced by 'improvement', leaving it for more supportive feeding and nesting places. Human society is newly fractured into greedy and rapacious enclosers and the labouring poor related only through the 'strife to buy and sell'. Clare's poem combines these three different aspects of enclosure or, rather, he does not distinguish between them.

Swordy Well was known to Clare in his childhood and was greatly changed by agricultural improvement. The narrating land, Swordy Well, says:

> And me they turned inside out
> For sand and grit and stones
> And turned my old green hills about
> And pickt my very bones.

Swordy Well laments that agricultural changes have transformed it from land into a landscape. Swordy Well is no longer a particular place but a construction of a human ideal that seems indiscriminately designed: 'No now not een a stone can lie/Im just what eer they like.'

What drives the transformation of land to landscape, Swordy Well claims, is not an idea or understanding of the land itself, but an unknowing and unilateral relation to the land's resources. Swordy Well claims to have adequately participated, as a resource, in a different kind of people–place economy now past. According to Swordy Well's account of the pre-enclosure economy, neither person nor place was disempowered. By contrast, 'improvement' rendered both the land and the labourers, *slaves* of enclosure:

> There was a time my bit of ground
> Made freeman of the slave
> The ass no pindard dare to pound
> When I his supper gave
> The gipseys camp was not afraid
> I made his dwelling free
> Till vile enclosure came and made
> A parish slave of me.

The changed economy, Swordy Well says, requires more than the land already offers. Pecuniary gain objectifies land, denying its agency and particularity. Swordy Well appears not as itself, but as any or every enclosed land, in the dressing or 'dull suit' of limitless commercial resource:

> Yet worried with a greedy pack
> They rend and delve and tear
> The very grass from off my back
> Ive scarce a rag to wear
> Gain takes my freedom all away
> Since its dull suit I wore
> And yet scorn vows I never pay
> And hurts me more and more.

In addition to describing the motivation, process and appearance of enclosure, Swordy Well also connects the change from land to landscape to the departure of non-human species from it. The bees, rabbits and butterflies find themselves alienated from Swordy Well because of its transformation via the 'hasty plough'. Clare's critique of enclosure records noticeable changes to Swordy Well not as landscape, but as a place that is home and habitat to a network of things (including people):

> The bees flye round in feeble rings
> And find no blossom bye
> Then thrum their almost weary wings
> Upon the moss and die

Rabbits hat find my hills turned oer
Forsake my poor abode
They dread a workhouse like the poor
And nibble on the road

If with clover bottle now
Spring dares to lift her head
The next day brings the hasty plough
And makes me miserys bed
The butterflyes may wir and come
I cannot keep em now
Nor can they bear my parish home
That withers on my brow.

This aspect of Clare's writing clearly sets his resistance to enclosure apart from the socio-political protests described earlier and from the intellectual goals of Romanticism. Interestingly, Swordy Well refers to the people who have enclosed and improved it as '[t]hese things that claim my own as theirs.' For Clare, enclosure does indeed make persons and things of people and place. The undifferentiated partner or thing of the property couple is not land, but the human owners. Clare inverts the hierarchy of the paradigm and thus draws attention to its logic.

The final lines of the poem anticipate what Hoskins, Neeson, Robinson and Powell lament. That is, that history, written as maps and events, loses or erases almost everything of place following enclosure. What remains of Swordy Well is its name, its abstract, cultural form:

And save his Lordships woods that past
The day of danger dwell
Of all the fields I am the last
That own my face can tell
Yet what with stone pits delving holes
And strife to buy and sell
My name will quickly be the whole
Thats left of swordy well,

Clare's point was understood by scholar John Barrell in his study of the landscape of agricultural improvement, he argued that enclosure erased completely the physical particularity and diversity of places:

Everything about the place, in fact, which made it precisely this place, and not that one, was forgotten; the map was drawn blank, except for the village itself, the parish boundary, and perhaps woodland too extensive or too valuable to be cleared, and streams too large to be diverted.

The enclosure commissioner would then mark in the new roads he was to cause to have made to the neighbouring villages, running as straight as the contours of the land would allow. In this way the map was redrawn, and the new topography would begin to be realised on the actual landscape.

(Barrell 1972: 95)

Barrell's history of enclosure, like Clare's poetic record, links the transformation of place into space to the erasure and homogenisation of a network of natural things into the cultured and abstracted paradigmatic category, nature. Both Clare and Barrell emphasise the role of law in the imposition of the 'grid of property upon the land' (Guillory 1995: 392). That grid is an imagined line that invents and separates nature from culture, from which relationships to place become simply the possession of (improved) landscape. Michel de Certeau connects the abstraction of place directly back to Descartes' notion of man as 'masters and possessors of nature':

A Cartesian attitude . . . is a mastery of places through sight. The division of space makes possible a panoptic practice proceeding from place whence the eye can transform foreign forces into objects that can be observed and measured, and thus control and 'include' them within its scope of vision.

(De Certeau, cited in Ryan 1996: 6)

The panoptic vision of and over place is strikingly missing from Clare's anti-enclosure poetry. The universalising claims and practices of a Cartesian vision of place are antithetical to his insistent attention to the local and particular.

Unlike Romantic literature about place, Clare's writing is not simply reactionary. While he writes against enclosure and against the paradigm of nature/culture, his writing records an intimate relationship between people and place that is not an ideal but a lived experience of connection with place. Clare is nostalgic rather than intellectually reactive and his writing is an expression of feeling rather than a presentation of ideas regarding the Enlightenment. Clare's treatment of nature as subject, rather than object, enables him to express an emotional or spiritual relationship between people and place and indeed discards their separation. His writing is a rare instance and important articulation of relationship with nature that preceded the logic of enclosure and thus resists the erasure of place from the property discourse of people/things. His experience of property contains a concept of or relation with place that is radical to contemporary dephysicalised property law. Clare's writing is important because it locates and records the physical origins and conditions of private property.

Hoskins points out that although there are numerous condemnations of enclosures on economic and political grounds, condemnations otherwise are lacking. He laments that the nature of the commoners' relationship with the land was all but lost in history because this class of people was illiterate:

Perhaps it is not remarkable, after all, that no poet should have described this world to us before it expired, described it in language that would bring home to us what kind of world it actually was and how its inhabitants looked upon it, for it was above all a peasant world and the peasant was inarticulate.

(Hoskins 1988: 157)

John Clare was exceptional in his literacy and were he not, further evidence of this ecological subjectivity that his poetry provides might remain. The use of poetry and literature generally for historical and political study occasions debate in aesthetic philosophy, which cannot be addressed adequately here. Suffice to say that the writing of John Clare is valuable both aesthetically and politically. It is perhaps even more valuable than those of his contemporaries, because Clare was not a professional poet or intellectual – he was a commoner. This point is relevant for two reasons. First, commoners were the last of the English peasantry and their relationship to place is all but lost to their modern descendants. Second, while there are histories of peasantry from outside that community, there are very few records of peasantry from within it: 'Clare saw the change from where commoners stood: he looked with them not at them' (Neeson 1993: 12):

To deny that much of his poetry reflects upon the social conditions of his time or is valuable source-material for historical study is perversion. It must be recalled that his is one of the very few voices of the rural poor of his age still to be heard.

(Clare 1984: xxiii)

The geographical and social specificity of Clare's life as commoner is not transcended but is part of his very particular aesthetic form and style. Indeed, contemporary critics argue that Clare's work is uniquely valuable precisely because of its local and particular language, rhythm and content:

Clare's place in the tradition of English literature cannot be established by simple chronology or solely by reference to the leading writers of his age . . . in all his writing he achieves a voice that is unmistakably his own. A song by Clare published under an assumed name in a Victorian miscellany, cannot be confused with any other writer's work.

(Clare 1984: xv)

Clare describes identification rather than alienation as the basis of people–place relationships. Many of his poems present this through intense sentiments of affection for place and lament of its transformation. His writing does not express a purely aesthetic appreciation of place. Raymond Williams juxtaposed the aesthetic and material realities of landscape poetry by remarking that Sidney's *Arcadia* 'was written in a park which had been made by enclosing a whole village and evicting the tenants' (Williams 1973: 22). Contrary to such aesthetic abstraction, Clare's own subjectivity seems grounded in the specificity of place. It conveys not only the economic materiality of other anti-enclosure discourse but also the ecological reality of enclosure itself.

Clare strongly opposed the enclosure of his local area and the means by which it proceeded – but it was not his intellectual preoccupation, it was his personal life and experience (Barrell 1972: 196; Clare 1984: xxii). Clare's protest was neither abstract nor doctrinaire:

> Clare's experience of these events is essentially local. What mattered to him was not so much the general problem of enclosure but the local enclosure of the fens; not the Game laws so much as the fate of local men caught poaching.
>
> (Clare 2000: xxviii)

Clare does not write of place abstractly, rather he writes of specific places such as Helpston 'not as it is typical of other places, but as it is individual; and individual not because it is different, but because it was the only place he knew' (Barrell 1972: 120). Clare's knowledge of the natural world did not universalise and taxonomise things neither did it perceive a 'landscape'.

In the poem *Helpston Green*, Clare describes place with a familiarity that distinguishes it and perhaps disqualifies it from the conventions of the pastoral genre. It is emotional rather than rational, felt rather than reasoned. It is a personal, local account of the ancient common of his home. Clare's tone and use of metaphor when writing about enclosure sometimes express anger and disorientation. This poem, however, expresses sadness and loss in the language of grief and mourning: 'Long after enclosure created compact farms, and renting an allotment had become almost impossible, labourers still felt a longing for land' (Neeson 1993: 329). This description of land is not aesthetically descriptive, expressing an outsider's perspective. Instead, it is personally descriptive, written with or from place. *Helpston Green* does not present a landscape – it presents a particular and loved local environment with which the narrator is connected. The poem seems closer to love poetry than to nature poetry. Helpston Green is a sick and dying loved one.

Helpston Green, like Swordy Well, was a place changed dramatically by enclosure and agricultural 'improvement'. Clare describes the fields as 'injured' by the 'tyrant's hand' who wields the 'uplifted ax' that has, without 'mercy' or 'compassion' struck 'a fatal blow' to 'every tree' so that

'Whole Woods beneath them bow'd'. In addition to extensive tree felling, the improvers 'stopt the winding runlets course/And flowery pastures ploughed' so that the topography of the land has completely altered. Clare remembers it vividly nonetheless:

> Where ere I muse along the plain
> And mark where once they grew
> Remembrance wakes her busy train
> And brings past scenes to view
> The well known brook the favourite tree
> In fancys eye appear
> And next that pleasant green I see
> That green forever dear.

Enclosure for John Clare was not the end of ownership of place but the end of mutual possession and connectivity that brought personal loss as well as economic loss. His identification with place demonstrates a meaning of the word 'property' that resonates with the original Greek meaning connecting the possession and the possessor through a relationship not of ownership but of identification. Clare 'gained his identity through his bond with his native landscape and lost it in madness when he was displaced from that land' (Bate 1991: 54). The value of Clare's writing is that it evidences not only a history of land pre-enclosure, but also a history of a relationship to the land not as landscape. Clare describes land not as space but as place. His value of placed property remains radical to the paradigm emerging around him that dominates the contemporary discourse of property.

3.4 Conclusion

Displacement was the objective and the effect of enclosure. An understanding of the immense geosocial significance of enclosure in the history of modern English culture sheds light on the ongoing necessity and cost of the separation of people and place in dominant forms of contemporary property law. The erection of boundaries and fences through hedges, altered the landscape physically. The exclusion of commoners from land, from which they previously obtained their means to life, altered the landscape politically. Finding themselves and their children landless, their villages relocated or destroyed meant that rural and regional communities declined as urban populations increased. The direct dependence of human culture and income on land substantially diminished through the changes wrought by enclosure and by the nineteenth century less than half the English population derived income from land and farming. With more people living in urban centres and with rising poverty and crime, increasing numbers went or were sent to the 'new world' and took their values and land use ideas with them. The reorganisation and disorganisation of agrarian modes of production was part of the same idea of place that brought colonisation (Thompson 1991: 164).

Whence people and place were understood to be separable, rather than connected, in property relations, it was possible to 'allow, encourage and force' (Butlin 1993: 195) those dispossessed common populations, who lost their means of subsistence at home with enclosure to go to the colonies (Kerruish 1999). Because the relationship to place was already severed, the expression of 'will' through labour was an expression *over* place rather than *from* it. The concept of possession had transformed from a possession without ownership *in place* to possession with ownership *over place*. This transformation had an unmediated effect on the land. Enclosure and colonisation were more than social events, they were ecological events. The nature/culture paradigm constructed and exported not only new displaced legal and social subjectivities, but also new land use practices. The paradigm of modern property law was based on the alienability of quantified parcels of land rather than on the inalienable and specific qualities of land. Without place, this atopic model of property was readily exported by its own process of transporting British populations across the world, imposing the paradigm here described onto other nations and into other lands and ecologies:

> This practice of compulsorily transforming customary rights into Common-Law property would be repeated with results at least as tragic throughout all of the lands settled by the British Diaspora. But this time it would be the Aborigines who would lose their pike and ducks, their land, streams, and forests.
>
> (Karsten 2002: 29)

The following chapter examines the imposition of the modern paradigm of property law onto colonised lands and nations with regard to the histories and subjectivities that it inscribed.

Chapter 4

Material origins

Empire

Since land formed the most valuable natural resource of a colony, the way in which the government permitted the public estate to be acquired and exploited by individuals materially influenced every aspect of economic and social development.

(Burroughs 1967: 1)

Participants in the rush adapted to variations in environment and tried to alter what they found. Some complications and harmful consequences should warn against simplified prescriptions for economic ills which assume that the practices of acquisition and allocation refined during the great land rush offer an ideal model for development throughout the world today.

(Weaver 2003: 6)

4.1 Introduction: alienation and maladaptation

The conceptual origins of modern property law and its theoretical model of persons and things were made real by physically separating people and place through dispossession and diaspora. These material origins of modern property law, with the enclosure of the English commons, made it possible to replace localised and physically responsive land laws with universalised and abstract land laws. This chapter examines the material origins of modern property law beyond England's shores in what became her colonies. The model of persons and things that characterised modern property law in England was transported across the world through the project of colonisation. Thus, although the development of the property laws of England's colonies have locally particular histories and functions – these laws remain ultimately and demonstrably alien and maladapted.

In Britain, changes to the landscape, notably the creation of enclosures and hedgerows were associated with improved land use practices and private property laws. The increased landholding and economic power of fewer individuals made possible large-scale commercial agricultural development. The prerequisite and parallel of this change was the dispossession of more

than half the original landholders[1] and the destruction of the peasant economy (Siemon 1994: 17). In addition to the relocation or removal of entire
villages; the enclosure of open fields; the erection of physical boundaries;
and public warning notices against trespassing; the law also protected private property by instituting game laws and prohibitions against gleaning
and nutting. The social and ecological magnitude of these changes was
profound. Those who had depended on common property rights became
part of a different workforce – vital to the prosperity of the industrialised
market economy. The 'undeclared civil war between the British landed classes
and their underlings' (Hughes, cited in Flannery 1994: 346) increased convic-
tion rates for new crimes against newly created private properties. Penalties
for crimes against property, often transportation to distant penal colonies,
provided a vital supply of human labour for the 'improvement' of lands
beyond England.

Locke's idea of labour worked against actual labourers by devaluing their
former common landholding on the basis that common property was the
same thing as uncultivated waste:

> God gave the World to Men in Common; but since he gave it to them for
> their benefit, and the greatest Conveniences of Life they were capable to
> draw from it, it cannot be supposed he meant it should always remain
> common and uncultivated. He gave it to the use of the Industrious and
> Rational (and Labour was to be his title to it).
>
> (Locke 1988: 291)

Locke's treatise presented private property as a universal and transcendental good. The cultivation of land signified progress only to the extent that
practical improvement was linked to moral and intellectual improvement,
which was implicitly an indicator of greater social improvement. The connection Locke drew between civilisation and private property presented private
property as an achievement, a mark of a sophisticated society. Locke's ideology of labour suggested that private property benefited not only the private
proprietors but also and more importantly, the nation and the empire.

Hannah Arendt's critique of Locke (1958) argued that the rise of labour
was connected to a changing concept of nature. Nature was not an earthly
reality, but a subject of process. The Lockean ideas of private property and
labour were contingent on viewing nature not simply as the opposite of culture, but as something to be appropriated and transcended by culture. Other
critiques of Locke's property theory explored the extent to which Locke's
concepts of labour and law were instrumental justifications for colonisation

---

1 Between 1774 and 1874 more than 50% of original land holders lost all or part of their land
  through the process of enclosure (Neeson 1993: 242, 280).

and the unlimited accumulation of private wealth. Macpherson argued that Locke's property theory belonged to what he called the 'possessive individualism' of early capitalism (1962). Arneil argued that Locke's theorisation of private property 'has specific historical roots in England's colonisation of the new world' (1994: 609). Locke's property theory articulated and advocated both a new economy and the colonisation of foreign lands in the service of that economy. The application of Locke's theory of property influenced, indeed characterised the ideology and function of the property laws of England's colonies, variations between them notwithstanding.

The differences between the property laws of England and those of her colonies are clear in terms of doctrinal and socio-political variation. Colonial authorities, including courts, departed in significant ways from English doctrine in recognition of different local socio-political and geographic conditions. Thus, it is possible to view the property laws of British North America and Australia as distinctive, even unique in their historical development (Buck 1994, 1996; Edgeworth 1994; Girard 2005; Ziff 2005). But this view interprets local variations in land use practice and in the legal instruments regulating those variations, as definitive differences. The conclusion of leading comparative legal historians is that the differences between the property laws of England and her colonies, and indeed between the colonies themselves, were sometimes intellectual, other times socio-political but important differences all the same. It is true that one cannot overstate the differences between the socio-political conditions and intellectual debates of England and her colonies in many important ways, for example in regard to primogeniture (Buck 1996), dower (Girard 2005), conditional estates (Girard 2005) and mortgages (Buck 1994; Girard 2005): 'Legal historians with interests in the evolution of property law in the colonies have begun to recognize the value in locating property law and rights within the broader political, social, economic and intellectual contexts of the societies in which they operated' (McLaren, Buck and Wright 2005: 2). Yet, if we extend the analysis of the comparative historical development of property law in England's colonies beyond the socio-political and intellectual contexts of the colonies to include the material conditions of the colonies including climate, rainfall, soil and native fauna and flora, a different conclusion emerges.

The concepts of property and proprietary interests in operation in England's colonies were, despite colonial peculiarities, ultimately English: 'English law provided a large repertoire of devices for transferring, subdividing, qualifying and encumbering interests in land' (Girard 2005: 136) and these, for the most part, remain central to the property regimes of England's former colonies. The property laws of the colonies were 'really English transplants' (Alexander 1997: 43). The law of mortgages and succession may have developed differently in different colonies, but the categories themselves and the values of land and natural resources on which they are founded were English and maintained. The economy and discourse of property in the colonies turned on the same hinges that supported the economy and discourse of property in imperial England. The idea that the land and its resources should be used intensively, even exhaustively, and that entitlement follows such usage is common to the property laws and land use practices of both England and its colonies. Specifically, the idea that land use should take the form of agriculture and pastoralism (in that order) was also common to both England and its colonies (Weaver 2003). These particular forms of land use required and encoded particular instrumentalist values of land. It was true that colonial laws varied according to different material conditions, distinguishing them from their imperial origins to some extent. Yet the underlying philosophy, the nature/culture paradigm, on which these laws were based was the same. Accordingly, this chapter argues that the property laws of the English colonies of Australia and British North America were better described as alien than local.

From the earliest days of their colonisation, there was an incongruity between the English ideology of property and its practicability in different environmental contexts. The climates and geographies of other countries did not always support intensive agriculture and/or pastoralism without substantial and ongoing changes to the landscape and hydroscape to render English land use practices possible and productive. Property law in the colonies was not responsive to its local environment. Rather than adapt an appropriate economy to the 'new' or local ecology and then adapt their law to suit, colonial property law was imposed with the old or foreign economy regardless of its propriety. Colonial land law was inappropriate – literally out of place.

Even where local conditions rendered the imposition of an alien regime of property difficult or impossible, such as intensive agriculture in the arid regions of Australia and the USA and in the colder and heavily forested areas of Canada, colonial property law remained essentially alien. Certainly minor changes were effected to surmount these difficulties. For example, the size of land grants in Canada was adjusted downwards to accommodate the physical obstacles to grants of large tracts of land. In Australia, the unlawful use and occupation of large tracts of land by squatters were eventually permitted in recognition of the physical obstacles to agriculture and control over the limits of settlement. However, the changes were designed to allow the logic of the alien property law to prevail, rather than collapse, in the face of the physical obstacles presented by different conditions. Colonial property laws adjusted English property law only as necessary to ensure their perpetuation. The law was not adapted to the land, the land was expected to adapt to the law.

In biological terms, actual or successful adaptation is the 'alteration in the structure or function of organisms which enables them to survive and multiply in a changed environment' (Macquarie Dictionary 1992). Thinking within the logic of the nature/culture paradigm it would have seemed unnecessary, if not unthinkable, that the application of English property law to foreign lands required its adaptation to different physical environments because the law was considered cultural. Culture was thought to transcend nature and, therefore, property law would not have been thought to be subject to material conditions and physical constraints.

However, as Kuhn contended, a paradigm can work only on the basis that it remains functional and meaningful. The nature/culture paradigm of modern property law depended on its ability to provide and regulate a viable and meaningful people–place relation. Property law functions 'so long as the tools a paradigm supplies continue to prove capable of solving the problems it defines' (Kuhn 1996: 76). The ability of colonial property laws to solve the problems and disputes defined according to the principles of private property have been challenged by disputes of its own creation. In the English colonies, native title claims and environmental obstacles to the outright application of private property ideals indicate the difficulty encountered by the use of English property law in non-English places:

> At three disparate places – Upper Canada, New South Wales, and the Cape Colony – and in the satellite colonies of New South Wales, administrators addressed standard predicaments, ones like those encountered in the thirteen colonies and early republic; the presence of first peoples on frontiers; the operations of squatters and their disregard for government rules; the importance of occupation; the accumulation of land by speculators; the costs of mapping and organising the land; and the challenge of extracting revenues from settlers. The particular remedies were the unique outcomes of local politics and natural environments. At the same time, however, the shaping of property rights in roughly standard ways was a global phenomenon.
>
> (Weaver 2003: 116)

The remedies of which Weaver writes were mostly partial and always temporary. The dispossession of Indigenous peoples; the concentration of vast tracts of land in the hands of the few; and subsequent environmental problems attributable to these initial 'standard predicaments' remain long-standing concerns of (post)colonial governments. The inability of modern property law to resolve the disputes and problems that it in part created in foreign lands demonstrate its maladaptation to those lands as well as its insistence on adherence to the thoughts and ways of the distant homeland.

Agriculture and the attendant practices of land clearing, tree felling, ring barking and intensive irrigation evidenced the colonists' perception of the inadequacy of existing resources to accommodate their desires. Furthermore, these practices indicated the colonists' sense of entitlement to and incognisance of the actual availability of foreign resources for appropriation. Colonial literature about land juxtaposes the ideas of improvement and waste. Theories of improvement and waste were central to the proposal and carriage of important property-related legislation pertaining to sovereignty, land grants, land transfers and pastoral squatting. British sovereignty was asserted on the basis that Indigenous peoples had not improved the land and were therefore undeserving of proprietorship. Land was granted to non-indigenous individuals on the condition that it was improved.

The colonists did not perceive themselves as newcomers or strangers to foreign lands, rather they perceived the lands as new and strange. The process of aligning the known and the strange was therefore an inverted process of adaptation – a process of maladaptation. The failure of colonists to successfully adapt their economy and laws to the lands they colonised was evident in the numerous instances of starvation; the protracted importation of vital supplies from their homelands; extensive degradation of the lands and waterways; and the extinction of native flora and fauna.

4.2 Ordering place: colonisation

> The concept of exclusive property in land as a norm to which other practices must be adjusted, was now extending across the whole globe, like a coinage reducing all things to a common measure.
>
> (Thompson 1991: 164)

The long and complex historical development of property law in England was unique to England. It could neither be preserved against the institutionalisation of English capitalism nor applied completely by an imperial government to its colonies. Instead, the regulation of land use and proprietorship in Australia and British North America assumed a specifically and necessarily colonial character. But it is important to recall that the colonies were never intended to be foreign to England and her interests but rather expressed the 'interplay between the demands of imperial policies and the response of colonial conditions' (Burroughs 1967: 1). It is precisely the 'response' or adaptation of property law to 'colonial conditions' that legal scholars and practitioners have argued defines the property laws of Australia, Canada and the USA as local in character.

This chapter contends, however, that local responses are not the same as local origins and that the claim that the property law in the colonies was local can only be made by comparison to English property law. If we go beyond a comparative doctrinal and socio-political analysis of the identity of colonial property laws and extend the scope of our analysis to the material conditions in which they operated, then a different and more comprehensive conclusion emerges. Colonial property laws were not always, technically, the same as English property law. Yet despite the fact that the former have, from the earliest days of colonisation, differed from the latter in significant ways, the ideological foundations of colonial property laws and their material consequences were far from local either politically or materially:

Studies of legislation and case law show local variations in the evolution of property rights. For example, the property rights to water on western American lands – a well-studied area – comprise a complicated tale of local and regional experimentation. However, just as significant for our story as the reporting of particular events is the delineation of underlying cultural values (and) of common technologies.

(Weaver 2003: 94)

Property law was one of the key technologies of colonisation and its values and concepts were indeed common to a variety of English colonies. The concepts of the exclusive possession and alienability of land that form the basis of private property law were exported from England via the umbrella discourse of improvement. The discourse of improvement was *atopic* – it lacked any reference to locality and place. This absence made possible the blanket enclosure of various English and Welsh commons and the replacement of locally relevant land laws with abstract property laws. As in the country of its origin, the use of the discourse of improvement in the property laws of the British colonies also lacked reference to geographic specificity. This was the primary reason for its failure to sustain itself over time. The discourse of improvement could apply only within the very particular geographic conditions of England including, importantly, fertile soils, the availability of plants and animals suitable (and available) for domestication and a temperate climate. The use of improvement discourse as the basis for land law in different geographic conditions would prove its undoing. By examining the failure of this discourse to adequately prescribe land use and ownership in different geographic conditions, it is possible to recognise the importance of locally developed and responsive land laws not only in cultural (and political) terms but also in ecological terms. Rather than adapt to the particularities and diversities of place, the discourse of improvement articulated a universal and atopic people–place relation. The universalism of the concepts of exclusive possession and alienability that characterise modern property law locate colonial property laws within the twin ideologies of English Enlightenment and empire. It is in this way, in their ideological rather ecological foundation, that the property laws of Australia and British North America can be defined as alien and maladapted.

4.2.1 Sovereignty and exclusion

The separation of people from place is described, in property law terms, as exclusive possession. The idea of exclusion is central also to its public law parallel: sovereignty. It is something discussed at length by legal scholar Peter Fitzpatrick in *The Mythology of Modern Law* (1992). Fitzpatrick argues that modern law defines itself by what it is not, a process he calls *negative transcendence* (1992: 10). He observes that modern law cannot define itself positively in terms of what *it is*. Law he argues, defines itself as universal, unified and ordered by setting these qualities against or in opposition to the qualities of law's *other*: particular, diverse and disordered (Fitzpatrick 1992: 10). The law thus defines itself by the exclusion of the qualities of otherness. In addition to defining itself by what it *is* (or is *not*), modern law also defines itself by what it *has*. Exclusion is the consequence of possession and acquisition – it is not possible to exclude people from a place that one has not already acquired and of which one is, in legal terms, in possession.

French linguist, Emile Benveniste distinguished between two modes of subjectivity or verbs of being, *verbes d'état*: 'to have' and 'to be'. Benveniste uses these two modes, of being and of having, in his analysis of the relationships they describe between people. Extending this distinction to analyse relationships beyond those between people to those between people and place illuminates important differences between traditional and modern forms of property:

> *To be* is, the state of that who is being, the one who is something. *To have* is the state of the possessor, the one for whom something is. The difference appears thus. Between the two terms it joins *to be* establishes an intrinsic relation of identity: it is the consubstantial state of being. On the contrary, the two terms joined by *to have* remain distinct . . . it is the relation between the possessor and the possessed.
>
> (Benveniste, cited in Hage 1998: 139–140)

Recalling its etymology, the word 'property' originally described the intrinsic relationship between a particular place and the person or people living there such that the two were mutually identified. People and place were 'fused' (Hage 1998: 139–140) in a 'consubstantial state of being'. This sense of property or people–place relation described the mode of subjectivity that uses the verb *to be*. That is, people *are* (in) place. This mode of people–place subjectivity was evident in the poetry of John Clare in England (for example) and remains present in the scholarship, poetry, stories and songs of Indigenous Australians (see, for example, Neidjie 1989; Sveiby and Skuthorpe 2006; Watson 2002; Weir 2009) and Native Americans (see, for example, Blaisdell 2000; Swann 1996). This literature indicates a traditional form of property whereby people are connected to place to the extent that they are, in fact, identified by and with place: 'We are not merely on and in the land, we are of it, and we speak from this place of Creation of land, of law' (Watson 2002: 268). The modern usage of the word *property* is, however, atopic and lacks any reference to place. Here, people and place 'remain distinct' and separate. This sense of property or people–place relation describes the mode of subjectivity that uses the verb *to have*. That is, people *have* place. This mode of people–place subjectivity is evident in the theory and practice of modern property law. According to this form of property, people are regarded in the singular, person, or 'the subject who has' and place is regarded as a thing or 'the object that is had' (Hage 1998: 174).

The primary characteristic of the public law concept of sovereignty, like its private law counterpart property, is exclusive possession. As foreign lands were annexed, British sovereignty of those lands was constantly assumed and asserted. The land was regarded as always and everywhere Crown land. The assertion of sovereignty and jurisdiction by the British consistently under-wrote the development of modern property law (Dorsett 2002; Kerruish 2002). The imposition of modern property law in turn made possible the notions of unlawful occupation of land by squatters and unlawful purchase of land from first peoples. Only the Crown could grant proprietary interests and negotiate, where necessary, with any pre-existing interest holders (Springer 1986):

> Colonising governments punctiliously conceded property interests to first peoples on most frontiers, but then monopolised sovereignty. From that ascendant position, they insisted on their exclusive right to purchase from Indigenous peoples.
>
> (Weaver 2003: 140)

William Blackstone wrote in 1765 that the benefit of private property was the 'free use, enjoyment, and disposal of all his acquisitions, without any control or diminution' (Blackstone 1966: 134). The right to private property was the right to deprive others of the place and its resources. Thus, the similarity between the modern individual of liberalism and the (feudal and) modern sovereign is that they both claim *dominium*:

> The *dominium* of Roman law comprised both the legal title and the right of actual beneficial enjoyment. In other words, *dominium* treated as conceptually inseparable the owner's right to use, dispose of, and exclude others from, his property.
>
> (Gray 1993: 34)

The idea of dominium in private property meant that the private individual was as significant, if not more significant than the public: 'So great moreover is the regard of the law for private property, that it will not authorise the least violation of it; no, not even for the general good of the whole community' (Blackstone 1966: 135). The exclusion of others was the purpose of private property and also of imperial and national sovereignty.

The colonisation of Australia and the development of its property law indicated the importance of the concepts of sovereignty and exclusion. The Attorney-General of New South Wales successfully argued, in *Attorney-General v Brown* (1847) 1 Legge 313, that the Crown was entitled to mine and dispose of the coal on the land over which it was both sovereign and proprietor to the exclusion of all others. Against this argument, Windeyer, counsel representing the interests of Brown, the lessee of the land, argued that Brown was entitled to mine and dispose of the coal on the land he leased to the exclusion of all others. Both arguments were based on the idea of exclusive possession and an instrumental view of nature that was characteristic of the philosophies of classical political economy, notably those of Locke and Smith (see Harvey 2000: 121–131). Both arguments were claims to exclude all others from the land's resources. *Attorney-General v Brown* was essentially a dispute between private and public sovereigns. Both parties insisted that their right to the property could not be shared, limited or controlled. The idea of property as being, fundamentally, the right to exclude all others was not disputed by either party in this foundational case in modern Australian property law. The case is most often taught and understood in terms of the relevance of the feudal doctrines of tenures and estates (Buck 1994; Edgeworth 1994). What is often overlooked is that although sovereignty and property are distinct concepts at law and although this case collapses that distinction, both concepts hinge on the overarching idea of exclusion. What is often overlooked is that regardless of whether the case was resolved in terms of sovereignty or property the outcome depended on the exclusion and dispossession of particular people from a particular place. The pre-requisite of intra-colonial disputes over property was the dispossession of local Indigenous people from lands that defined both their economy and their cultural identity.

In a Canadian case not dissimilar to the *Attorney-General v Brown* case in New South Wales, an intra-colonial property dispute between the province of Ontario and the newly formed Canadian state also hinged on the concept of sovereignty in regard to natural resources. Unlike the Australian case, however, the Canadian case, *St Catherine's Milling and Lumber Company v R* (1888) 14 App Cas 46, was based on the status of 'Indian' tenure. Determined ultimately by the Privy Council, the case held that any interests held by the Indigenous peoples were not proprietary (property) but personal and usufructuary 'dependent on the goodwill of the Sovereign' (Young 2008: 126). As in Australia, one of the earliest cases in Canadian property law was decided by overt recourse to the ideas of sovereignty and exclusion. In both cases, the dispossession of Indigenous peoples was the condition of putting those ideas into practice yet, also in both cases, the articulation of the process by which that dispossession took place was absent.

The colonisation of North American lands similarly depended on the dispossession of first peoples. Unlike Australia and Canada, the imposition of British Crown sovereignty in America did not last long. The American Revolution 'disposed of the crown and installed allodial tenure' (Weaver 2003: 66). Yet the ideas of sovereignty and exclusion remained central to the establishment of modern property law in this jurisdiction too. Historian John Weaver writes that the distinction was abstract and concealed the similarity between the land laws and land use practices of Britain's colonies, the revolution notwithstanding:

These were symbolic changes affecting few Americans, while practical ideas about land – the doctrine of improvement, squatters' possession, the marketability of interests, and the quest for a complete but cheap bundle of rights – pervaded frontiers in both the United States and the British empire for a long, long time.

(Weaver 2003: 66)

In the years immediately prior to revolution, individuals and syndicates negotiated land purchases from the Indians against British instructions that prohibited the practice. These transactions, if disputed, were usually declared invalid on the basis that the Crown was the only source of proprietary interests in the colony. This rule was the source of one of the earliest leading cases of modern American property law, which, like Australian and Canadian case law, was an intra-colonial dispute over land. In *Johnson v McIntosh* (1823) 21 US 543 the court declared that the plaintiff's purchase of land from the Piankeshaw 'Indians' was invalid and that the defendant's interest, derived from state grant, would prevail. The reasoning of the case was based on the idea that property rights could only derive from sovereign grant or a transfer thereof and were 'not to be unravelled by speculators' (Weaver 2003: 139). The link between property and sovereignty was exclusion and in particular, the exclusion of traditional forms of property which maintained a connection between people and place. Sovereignty was principally an instrument of dispossession and disconnection of people from place.

4.2.2 Dispossession and progress

The assertion of British sovereignty in Australia and British North America dispossessed and disconnected people from place. Contrary to popular myth, British colonists never believed that the lands to which they travelled were unpopulated, only uncultured. The British asserted sovereignty by whatever means possible and realised, indeed hoped, that this would dispossess Indigenous peoples of their lands or at least of their use and control over the lands. The legitimisation of this process was important to the colonists but difficult – ideology proved vital. The Enlightenment idea of progress became the rationale of colonisation and the measure of civilisation. Progress was measurable in terms of land use and, as in England, land use of Australia and British North America was progressive only where it was intensively productive. 'Improved' and productive land use practice was the logical basis of private entitlement to property. The idea of *terra nullius* was, therefore, never one expressing the absence of Indigenous people from their lands. *Terra nullius* was ultimately a code for the absence of agricultural use of those lands, particularly intensive agriculture. Without this form of land use, the British saw no basis for property rights to that land: 'Since resource exploitation figured centrally in all colonial empires, rudimentary recognition of native personal and property rights was universally eroded' (Weaver 2003: 134).

To the British, the signal of the availability of foreign lands, as wastelands in need of improvement and legitimising the assertion of British sovereignty, was economic. How were the lands used? *Terra nullius* was part of the narrative of the spread of a benign empire of improved people–place relations. The narrative mythologised conquest and imperialism as improvement and progress: 'The cause of improvement and that of empire were closely intertwined' (Gascoigne 2002: 74). In Australia, the assumption of *terra nullius* formed 'part of the mental furniture of the founders of New South Wales' (Gascoigne 2002: 8). The phrase signified unimproved land that could rightfully belong to no one until, as Locke had said, someone 'removes it out of the State that Nature hath provided . . . [and] mixed his Labour with, and joyned to it something that is his own, and thereby makes it his Property' (Locke, cited in Gascoigne 2002: 8).

The following editorial in the *Sydney Herald* of 1838 well articulates the ideological coupling of cultural progress and agricultural improvement in England's colonies. It also highlights the link between British sovereignty and private property in Australian law and culture:

> This vast land was to them a common – they bestowed no labour upon the land – their ownership, their right, was nothing more than that of the Emu or Kangaroo. They bestowed no labour upon the land and that – and that only – it is which gives a right of property to it. Where, we ask, is the man endowed with even a modicum of reasoning powers, who will assert that this great continent was ever intended by the Creator to remain an unproductive wilderness? . . . The British people . . . took possession . . .; and they had a perfect right to do so, under the Divine authority, by which man was commanded to go forth and people, and till the land. Herein, we find the right to the dominion, which the British Crown, or, more properly speaking the British people, exercise over the continent of New Holland.
>
> (cited in Rowley 1972: 37)

The 'belief in the possibilities of improvement' was so pervasive that 'in many ways it informed the terms on which Aboriginal–European relations were conducted' (Gascoigne 2002: 167). Indeed, faith in the idea of improvement supplanted any rational approach to a comparison between the British economy and Aboriginal economies. The British appreciated neither the dependence of their own economy on specific geophysical conditions nor the fact that their economy was younger and untested by comparison to the one it had replaced when the commons were enclosed. Because of this incognisance, the British believed their economy could be transplanted to countries with entirely different geographical conditions and with it, the legal regime that facilitated and protected that economy – private property law. Property law and its person/thing model blinded the colonists to other regulatory models of people–place relations. There was no scope within the model for a thing to be a specific place or for a person to be a specific community whose identity and economy were defined by a specific place:

> The ethic of improvement – which had been so closely linked with agricultural growth through enclosure and the substitution of individual ownership in place of the common fields – heightened that sense of individualism which stood in such conspicuous contrast to the communal identity of Aboriginal culture.
>
> (Gascoigne 2002: 12)

Indigenous Australian economies and the land laws that facilitated and protected them were very long established and very successful. These laws had, over a long period of time, gradually become adapted to a variety of local geophysical conditions. The aridity of the continent and the variability of rainfall meant that Australian economies could not have endured for as long as they did had they failed to do otherwise. Indigenous Australian economies certainly caused large-scale and long-term modification of the Australian environment and to suggest otherwise is 'to deny their place in Australia's ecological history' (Kohen 1995: 137). Whether these adaptations of economy and law were 'improvements' or not, the fact remains that the environmental impact of Indigenous Australian economies had not, over 50,000 years, rendered them at the time of European colonisation anything other than sustainable and successful.

Scientists such as James Kohen (1995) and Jared Diamond indicate that Australian economies could not have relied on the yields of agricultural land use – the risk would have been prohibitive and unnecessary:

> Rather than depending on a few crops that could fail, they minimised risk by developing an economy based on a great variety of wild foods, not all of which were likely to fail simultaneously. Instead of having fluctuating populations that outran their resources and stared, they maintained smaller populations that enjoyed an abundance of food in good years and sufficiency in bad years.
>
> (Diamond 1997: 309)

Had the English understood or been curious about the economies and laws of the Indigenous peoples of the lands that they sought to colonise, they may have learned the potential problems of introducing their own young and foreign economy and property law. They may have learned that economies are limited by the material conditions of their place of origin. However, the colonists did not perceive the differences between their economy and those of the peoples they colonised as products of geophysical contexts but of cultural contexts. More importantly, the colonists did not perceive differences as differences but as levels in a universal hierarchy. At the time Australia was colonised, the twin ideological forces of Christian theology and Enlightenment philosophy articulated the same vision of the unity of all humankind: 'Christianity was adamant that all humans were descendants of common ancestors and this belief had survived increasing contact with non-Christian peoples' (Gascoigne 2002: 148). Enlightenment philosophy similarly advanced the ideology of monogenism, indeed it was the condition of the possibility of progress and civilisation:

> Enlightenment thinkers of the late eighteenth century were generally inclined to explain human varieties in terms of evolutionary development. Hence the view that human society went through different phrases, the ultimate goal of which was the development of a society remarkably like that of the theorists of the Enlightenment.
>
> (Gascoigne 2002: 148)

Captain Watkin Tench wrote in his account of the journey of the First Fleet to Botany Bay and the first 4 years of settlement that Aborigines were 'children of the same omniscient paternal care' and that 'untaught, unaccommodated man, is the same in Pall Mall, as in the wilderness of New South Wales' (cited in Gascoigne 2002: 148). The idea that Pall Mall man was biologically the same as Australian wilderness man meant that the differences between the English and Indigenous Australians could not be explained by differences in adaptations to local environmental conditions. Rather, the differences between them could only be explained by degrees of *cultural progress*.

Because the colonists 'did not recognise these different but complex and highly functional sets of ways of living together and living with the land, they could claim that Australia was a *terra nullius*' (Hodge 1999). Degrees of culture could explain differences between peoples' economies and laws in terms of points on a scale. At the lowest point was savagery and at the highest point was civilisation. The differential term, culture, could be measured by proximity to nature. Thus 'savages' or 'natural races' stand in the 'most intimate relations with Nature' if not indeed 'in bondage to Nature' (Ratzel, cited in Head 2000: 36). Locke had said this in 1689 when he said that the savage was not 'removed from the common state Nature placed it in' (cited in Fitzpatrick 1992: 82). If nature were something from which people should be removed, then culture was something to which people should aspire: 'The conception of "natural races" involves nothing anthropological or physiological, but is purely one of ethnography and civilisation. Natural races are poor in culture' (Ratzel, cited in Head 2000: 36). The 'primitive' embodies nature by contrast to the 'citizen' who embodies culture.

At the centre of the legal discourse of *terra nullius* was the ideological juxtaposition of nature and culture and the privileging of the latter term. As Kerruish observed of *terra nullius*, it is certainly 'ill informed, instrumental and justificatory in its function but also containing European ideas of savagery and civilisation. Such ideas, coming out of a particular culture, prefer their own, misunderstand other cultures, other ways of living in a landscape' (Kerruish 2002: 281–282).

The English perspective of 'ways of living in a landscape' was that agriculture was the logical end point of cultural development. Palaeontologist David Horton described the view thus: '[S]ocieties evolve, and eventually they evolve into agricultural societies, and then comes civilisation' (Horton 2000: 59). Locke went so far as to claim that the entire purpose of law and the state was the protection of property, implicitly as the means to define civilisation: 'The great and chief end, of Men uniting into Commonwealths, and putting themselves under Government, is the Preservation of their Property' (cited in Fitzpatrick 1992: 84–85). As Fitzpatrick points out, the regime of property was increasingly conflated with law because in the experience of the English, the joint arrival of agriculture and property and their combined articulation of a highly developed cultural order:

> requires a complex and more intense regulation than the episodic assertions called for in the nomadic state; what is required is an explicit, permanently sustained ordering that is law. In the result the paradigm of law corresponds to the property relation.
>
> (Fitzpatrick 1992: 84)

The idea that private property was the signifier of civilisation was contemporaneous with the colonisation of lands and peoples in Australia and British North America. Culture could be signified not only by agriculture and private property in England, but also by colonial expansion. The colonist, like the private proprietor, was enlightened and cultured. The assessment of uncultured people was their wont of enlightenment: property and law. In 1840 the *Adelaide Chronicle* remarked that:

> The marks of civilisation, and consequent improvement, are everywhere visible, both in town and country – but the natives of the land remain unimproved, unenlightened, and almost as savage as we found them.
>
> (cited in Gascoigne 2002: 162)

As the author points out, in asserting British sovereignty, claiming Australia a *terra nullius* and imposing a foreign economy and property law, the English relied on several markers of cultural progress. Land use was one, literacy another. But the things that were regarded as markers of cultural progress were, in fact, indicators of specific geophysical and ecological contexts. None of the 'marks of civilisation' was developed independently of geophysical and ecological contexts. Land uses and husbandry derived from Eurasian plants and animals, metallurgical knowledge, guns, steam engines and germs were 'the end products of 10,000 years of development in Eurasian environments' (Diamond 2005: 321). Importantly, none of those markers was appropriate for survival in foreign countries:

> Europeans have never learned to survive in Australia or New Guinea without their inherited Eurasian technology. Robert Burke and William Wills were smart enough to write, but not smart enough to survive in Australian desert regions where Aborigines were living.
>
> (Diamond 2005: 321)

The problem was that although a different (and non-hierarchical) perspective on differences between indigenous and non-indigenous economies and laws was available, it was the perception of the colonists that mattered because they had a 'monopoly on evaluation' (Weaver 2003: 135). The contact between the British and the Indigenous peoples of Australia and British North America was not a dialogue:

> The technology of law that colonisers introduced through sovereignty over frontiers exclude the habitat and social practices of first peoples, although those peoples had resolved conflicts and determined relations with respect to territory prior to contacts with Europeans. A one-way flow of concepts meant that when first peoples were approached about ceding property rights, even by scrupulous, sympathetic, and linguistically adept colonial agents, the parties bargained across a cultural abyss.
>
> (Weaver 2003: 140)

In Australia, the Indigenous people's interests in land were excluded from the development of colonial property law. In British North America, too, 'the First Nations lay totally outside this dialectic' even though 'their property claims (were) seen as collective use-rights to particular territories or natural resources' (Girard 2005: 122).

4.2.3 Waste and cultivation

Cultural progress was an abstract idea but it was not, apparently, an empty claim. Cultural progress was thought to be demonstrated and measured by relation to the state of nature that surrounded any given society. Cultural progress could be seen. Viewed as a landscape, improved and exploited land evidenced the labour of a society of advanced culture. Unimproved land to the contrary 'was indicative of sloth and mismanagement' (Gascoigne 2002: 71) and indicated a 'backward' or 'primitive' culture: 'The most repeated justification for occupying frontier lands turned on a single word – waste: the waste of land, the waste of water, the waste of native labour' (Weaver 2003: 149). Colonists claimed repeatedly over a very long time (arguably to the present day) that the Indigenous peoples were insufficiently industrious because they did not improve (meaning cultivate) the land and left it to waste.

The colonists' conflation of improvement with a highly specific form of cultivation is an important one to note. Biologist James Kohen argues that by the time of the British colonisation of Australia in 1788, Aboriginal land management practice had effected significant transformation of the landscape (Kohen 1995: 127). Indeed, he says that by this time it would have been impossible to 'revert to an "unimproved" environment' and that 'the balance and distribution of species had been altered by Aboriginal involvement, most obviously by the use of fire' (Kohen 1995: 207). At what point is the human impact on the non-human environment regarded as improvement, or as management, or as exploitation? Kohen defines land management as the use of land 'without any long-term deterioration' whereas he defines exploitation as the use of land that 'involves long-term degradation to the detriment of the environment' (1995: 125). Using this distinction, he says: 'Aboriginal people were land managers, not exploiters' (1995: 128). But were Aboriginal people improvers of land?

The English idea of 'improvement' cannot be regarded as a general category encompassing a number of possible systematic human land use practices. If so, the idea of improvement could not have been used to the effect it was in the rationalisation of colonisation. In Australia, the Aboriginal use of fire as a technique of land management, for example, was observed by the colonists from the outset of colonisation. Colonist Edward Curr wrote that there was an:

> [I]nstrument in the hands of these savages which must be credited with results which it would be difficult to overestimate. I refer to the fire-stick . . . he tilled his land and cultivated his pastures with fire.
>
> (cited in Boyce 2009: 23)

Indeed, the effectiveness of Aboriginal land use practices was sufficient for the purposes of colonial pastoralists. Aboriginal 'improvements' to the land functioned not only as the basis of the Aboriginal economy but of the colonial economy of Van Diemen's Land:

> Aboriginal burning regimes were most cost-efficient than the labour-intensive cultivation of introduced grasses, and as a consequence the latter was virtually unknown until the 1830s. Early pastoralism relied on Aboriginal techniques, but in areas where Aborigines has been dispossessed, the British were forced to set the country on fire themselves.
>
> (Boyce 2009: 103)

As the colonists learned as soon as they endeavoured to apply the land use practices of their homeland in Australia, there were actual and substantial physical reasons why they may not work: 'Over much of Australia the environment simply did not allow the development of the kinds of farming and herding practices which had developed in other parts of the world' (Kohen 1995: 128). Those reasons were physical in nature: rainfall, aridity, flooding, climate, soil, hydrology and so on. And yet despite the contradictions of experience and physical conditions, the idea of improvement persisted on the basis that improvement was not, necessarily, actual. The insistence on the idea of improvement as cultivation was irrational because within a short time it was widely understood to be non-viable. The appeal of the idea of improvement to the English was that it did not have to be discernible in application and reality – its power was precisely its mythic proportions and its political convenience.

The landscape of unimproved land, in the English sense of being uncultivated, was perceived as wasteful and wasted. The literature of colonists well demonstrates the dominance of the ideology of landscape and the twin poles of productivity and waste (Tully 1993). The lands of Australia and North America were often described in negative terms as waste. Importantly however, the landscape was not described as hopelessly or forbiddingly wasteful, but as ripe with potential to sustain the project of colonisation:

> Picturesque landscapes are described in such a way as to invite colonisation; once a colony is implanted, however, the land is then constructed according to the 'gloomy, melancholy and monotonous' paradigms of description. The 'whitewashed buildings [which] bore outward testimony to the cleanliness and regularity of the inhabitants' stand in opposition to the gloomy forest.
>
> (Ryan 1996: 80)

Australia was considered 'an awful contrast to that beautiful place of England' (cited in Young 2000: 1). The eucalyptus trees were regarded as 'a forest in rags' (cited in Young 2000: 1). As depressing as the Europeans apparently found the Australian landscape, they likened it to the former commons of England and believed fundamentally in its capacity for 'improvement', that is intensive agricultural production. The land needed to be 'rescued from a state of nature' (Gascoigne 2002: 71). Describing Australian lands as a wasteland opened them to the possibility of change and the demonstration of superior cultural evaluation and relations to land. In 1840 *The Australian Miscellany* praised recent improvements to 'trackless wastes of barren lands' that 'became the scene of industry and plenty' (cited in Gascoigne 2002: 70).

Cultivation and improvement were not simply a matter of the earth's imagined potential; they were a matter of human duty. In the same way that the commons had made way for enclosure in the interests of national prosperity and progress, foreign lands had to make way for cultivation in the interests of empire and civilisation. De Vattel wrote in *The Law of Nations* in 1760 that land belongs not to nations but 'to mankind in general; destined by the Creator to be their common habitation . . . and to derive from it whatever is necessary for their subsistence, and suitable to their wants' (cited in McRae, Nettheim and Beacroft 1991: 76–77). It was thought that those nations whose population exceeded their resources, however, could legitimately claim the lands and resources from other places if its inhabitants were not sufficiently exploiting their land. By extending the argument that humans bore the burden of responsibility for cultivating the land *as* humans, de Vattel asserted that it was the right and duty of all people to improve nature by cultivation. Those who did not observe their duties were, therefore, less entitled to the goods of life because they disobeyed what he believed were the laws of human necessity:

> But when the human race became extremely multiplied, the earth was no longer capable of furnishing spontaneously, and without culture, sufficient support for its inhabitants; neither could it have received proper cultivation from wandering tribes of men continuing to possess it in common.
>
> (De Vattel, cited in McRae et al. 1991: 76–77)

The rationale of the law of colonisation was thus identical to that of private property. When Captain Cook described Aborigines as 'hav(ing) no fixed habitations but move from place to place like Wild Beasts in search of food', he encapsulated the sense in which Australia was a *terra nullius* (cited in Horton 2000: 30). Certainly people lived there, but their economy was imagined to be inferior and thus undeserving of the land. Land had the potential for improvement (beyond that already recognised) and all people had a duty to cultivate its fruits. Waste was the ideological condition of both these developments. Waste signified opportunities which if not seized were forfeited:

> At almost every point, the practice of agricultural improvement undermined Aboriginal society. For the Aborigines, the arrival of the Europeans with their strange animals was an invasion of their hunting lands and a grave interference with the water supplies so essential to life. For the Europeans it was the transformation of 'waste lands' into productive use, as Providence intended.
>
> (Gascoigne 2002: 153–154)

In British North America, the ideas of waste and cultivation also motivated the colonists in their project to create and keep private property. Historian John Weaver describes the sense of urgency and competition that accompanied the great land rush in eighteenth-century American history. The notion that waste signified opportunity was felt strongly: 'Astute landhunters knew that if they failed to seize land quickly others would scoop it up' (Weaver 2003: 88). He quotes George Washington in a letter he wrote in 1767:

> Any person ... who neglects the present opportunity of hunting out good lands, and in some measure marking them for his own, in order to keep others from settling them, will never regain it.
>
> (cited in Weaver 2003: 88)

The circulation and application of improvement theory in British colonies indicated the ubiquity and relevance of the Enlightenment precept – progress: 'Progress meant a willingness to accept change for future advantage and a confidence that the application of reason would ultimately mean a better world' (Gascoigne 2002: 10). Improvement theory applied to various aspects of daily life: agriculture, education, religion and criminal punishment, for example. However, the dominant and most tangible form of improvement was in intensive agricultural cultivation. Most of the colonial literature dealing with agriculture refers repeatedly to the concept of improvement (Gascoigne 2002: 10; Weaver 2003: 27). The reason was because, as discussed in earlier, 'improvement and property rights have had a reciprocal association since the Enlightenment' (Weaver 2003: 27).

4.3 Trading place

> Particularly in those colonies where all unalienated or 'waste' land belonged to the Crown, the government could, through the regulations it adopted, exercise a profound influence over the progress of settlement, the pattern of land utilisation, the structure of land ownership, and the rate of economic growth. Consequently there was a very close and fundamental correlation between the way in which the British government discharged its responsibility for the administration of the Crown lands and the extent to which individual colonies could be made to satisfy British requirements.
>
> (Burroughs 1967: 1)

The appropriation of land was the means and the ends of British colonisation. Property law was thus, from the outset, the key technology of the entire colonial project. In North America, 'royal instructions from 1755 to 1774 to the governors of new crown colonies expressed a vague idea of betterment. They censured the large proprietary grants of the past. Henceforth governors were to grant land to parties in proportion to an ability to cultivate it' (Weaver 2003: 25). Instructions issued to successive governors of colonies in Australia 'envisaged cultivation by gangs of prisoners on Government farms and by time-expired convicts and free settlers on their own smallholdings' (Burroughs 1967: 2). Grants of land to private individuals and to British-based companies were intended to complement rather than compete with the landholding of the British Crown. Unlike in the market economy of England, land in New South Wales was not alienated by sale until the 1830s. Nevertheless, the assumption and annexation of lands in Australia as well as in British North America were intended to constitute self-sufficient colonies, in accordance with the desires and needs of an alien economy and polity back in England.

4.3.1 Land grants

Several colonies of British North America were created by large land grants to 'commercial enterprises run by London-based companies or by individual proprietors' (Freyfogle 2003: 50). The grants of land were over vast tracts of land in these instances: ranging from 200,000 acres to the Ohio Company in 1748, for example, to 20–30 million acres to the Vandalia Colony from 1768–1772 covering the region south of the Ohio River from near Pittsburgh to the Kentucky River (Weaver 2003: 105). In Upper Canada, 1.3 million acres were granted to the Canada Company in 1826 while in Lower Canada, the British American Land Company purchased Crown reserves in the eastern townships of about 850,000 acres (Weaver 2003: 220). Charter colonies were created by a grant of land from the Crown to a company that would then grant rights to individuals. In addition to the right to grant land, the companies had rights to govern the land provided the laws were not repugnant to those of England (Springer 1986: 32). The Crown grant to the charter companies of Massachusetts Bay, Plymouth, Rhode Island, Connecticut and New Haven were in fee simple and were free of feudal dues other than a share of the profits of gold and silver mined from the lands.

In the early nineteenth century in British North America, land was also granted to 'common people' pointing to 'an effectual democratic insurgence' (Weaver 2003: 12). Land was also granted to 'loyal subjects' (Weaver 2003: 26) in reward for service to years of war in the late eighteenth and early nineteenth centuries. In both cases, it was the idea of improvement that was used to legitimate the dispossession of land from the first peoples. The appropriation and redistribution of land was tied to the grantees' 'ability to cultivate it' according to the *Terms for Land Grants in New Colonies* in the *Royal Instructions to British Governors, 1670–1776* which were carried out by the governors of Georgia, East Florida, West Florida, Quebec and Nova Scotia (cited in Weaver 2003: 91). As discussed earlier, the right of the Crown to grant land over and above the right of the first people to do so was confirmed in *Johnson v McIntosh* (1823). The land-granting system depended on the prohibition (initially unofficial) against land transactions between first peoples and individual colonists. Thus, regardless of how the land granting systems may have diverged in their operation across various colonies, they were all contingent on the dispossession of first peoples and all designed to encourage 'improved', literally 'profitable' land use: 'All landholders were potential land producers – that was axiomatic on frontiers' (Weaver 2003: 106). Land grants were thus a way of reaffirming the sovereignty of an alien English power because proprietary interests in land could only derive from the Crown.

The ideas that uncultivated land was wasted and that 'improved' and profitable land validated the British appropriation of foreign lands were similarly maintained in Australia. Yet, whereas in British North America, Indigenous interests in land were considered usufructuary and there were negotiations between governments and individuals and first peoples, in Australia the Crown failed to recognise any Indigenous interests in land. In Australia, the land-granting system was the primary form of conveying property from the colonial authority to private individuals until alienation of Crown land by sale replaced land grants in 1831. Official sales of lands were permitted prior to this, but rarely and only according to particular conditions. Grants and even promises of grants were sold only between private individuals (Campbell 1994: 6). In any case, 'all other interests originated in Crown grants' (Edgeworth 1994: 403). The grants were 'intended to create a group of small landholders who could sustain the colony by producing food crops' (Lane 2000: 5). The various sizes of the land granted related to 'the amount of capital brought into the colony by the petitioners, or their military rank, or presumed social worth. Each governor introduced variations. Social rank and favouritism generally influenced their actions' (Weaver 1996: 985). This early colonial system of official land distribution explicitly married law and politics, which although different from social relations organised by the property in England, maintained the same connection between property and status.

The early governors of New South Wales were authorised to grant land of the Crown in accordance with 'Instructions of the Colonial Secretary' regarding the qualifications of grantees, the acreages to be made available and not insignificantly the conditions on which grants were to be made (Campbell 1994: 2). But while the process was 'local', the logic and ideology underlying it were not. The conditions of grants conveyed the imperative of agricultural improvement of land, the requirement of the payment of quit rents, the prohibition on alienation for a fixed period (Edgeworth 1994: 404) and 'the reservation to the Crown of rights over minerals, water and rights of way' (Edgeworth 1994: 403). In this way, property in colonial New South Wales linked private landholding to the service of imperial policy. In formal terms, it operated against the ideology of private property and was arguably more protective of the rights of the sovereign than the private individual who was, as in England, constructed as a landholder rather than a landowner. New South Wales could not be regarded as having applied the spirit of modern English property law while 'Crown ownership of natural resources was seen to be essential given the paramount need to control development and maximise revenue in its colonies' (Edgeworth 1994: 410). But, practically speaking, the agricultural improvement required by the conditions of land grants ensured that the earliest departures of Australian land law remained grounded in the ideology and natural economy of English property law. The land use was, even at this early time, identical between them. The realisation of improvement theory was differently effected in the English 'garden' than in the Australian 'desert' but nevertheless stemmed from the same beliefs, concepts and aesthetics.

In 1792, Governor Phillip granted land to 'deserving' convicts, to James Ruse for 'experiment farm' at Parramatta that he had been working since 1789 and to ex-marines. In 1793 land grants were extended to officers of the New South Wales Corps: 'To every non-commission officer one hundred acres, and to every private man fifty acres' (Historical Records of Australia 1925: 124–128). Convict labour was made readily available to work the land of this latter group of grantees: 'All the civil and military officers may as such be allowed two convicts each, to be maintained out of the public stores for two years' (Historical Records of Australia 1925: 441–442). Not surprisingly, the larger areas of land owned by officers combined with their access to convict labour made this group of colonists almost completely responsible for transforming the economy of New South Wales from struggling subsistence to 'successful agriculture with the ability to export produce' (Linn 1999: 9). It also meant that this class of landowners was responsible for transforming the landscape of New South Wales from the earliest days of colonisation. The deployment of free or cheap labour and the free grant of land certainly were at odds with the operation of the private property market in England. But, again, despite this divergence, the ideology of labour that the convicts put into practice was strictly an alien ideology intricately tied to an alien theory of property.

Directives to successive governors of New South Wales were to develop agricultural economy to the level of self-sufficiency and beyond to the service of the British Empire. In 1803, Colonial Secretary Lord Hobart wrote to Governor King that:

> The improvement and extension of the agriculture in the country already settled is an object of the first importance, not only as affecting the subsistence and resources of the inhabitants in general, but as it regards the employment of the convicts now under your charge, or who may be sent hereafter.
>
> (cited in Gascoigne 2002: 74)

By 1819 the export of wool from New South Wales to Britain was so significant to the economies of both the colony as well as to Britain (Gascoigne 2002: 82) that the ideology of improvement was adjusted to accommodate the debate about whether pastoralism constituted sufficiently sophisticated land use as compared with agriculture. The theory of improvement was never separate from the idea of limitless economic growth and development. The production and accumulation of wealth was associated with the sophistication of economic activity and the degree of exploitation of the land (Gascoigne 2002: 69). Thus while the system of free grant in New South Wales demonstrated an unambiguous divergence from English land law, it cannot be said to be local, because it functioned within the economy of empire and the ideology of the English Enlightenment.

In 1824 by Imperial Act of Parliament, the Australian Agricultural Company (AAC) was founded and was granted 1 million acres of land in New South Wales 'under unusually liberal conditions' (Buck 1994: 131). The Act provided 'for granting certain power and authorities to the company to be incorporated by charter ... for the Cultivation and Improvement of Waste Lands in the Colony of New South Wales and for other purposes relating thereto' (cited in Buck 1994: 131). As was the case in British North American charter companies, the AAC was empowered to grant land in accordance to the principles of its charter and to ensure the economic self-sufficiency of the colony. In 1826 63,710 acres of land was granted to 38 private individuals, 'the smallest grant of which was 320 acres and the average grant was almost six times this size' (Ashton 1987: 22). The British colonisation of Australia was a project of expansion in a very physical, territorial sense. Certainly agricultural production was needed to sustain the colony, but territorial expansion was disproportionate to the colonial population and their needs. Territorial expansion exceeded the needs of an ideally self-sufficient colony: it generated imperial economic wealth and secured the political sovereignty of the 'parent' country against the sovereignty of rival nations, but most necessarily against the Aboriginal nations.

Colonists, emancipated convicts, free settlers or officers, were 'permitted to enter into possession of a tract of land of the Crown with an assurance that they would receive a formal grant of it' (Campbell 1994: 4). This practice created difficulty for newly arrived governors who were required to pursue and formalise the promises of grants made by their predecessors. Governor Brisbane complained in 1822 that he had:

> discovered that Major General Macquarie [his predecessor] had been exceedingly liberal in his promises of land:- so much so, that, exclusively of those he had himself been enabled to perfect, there remained a balance of unexecuted grants to the amount of 340 thousand acres.
>
> (cited in Campbell 1994: 4)

Indeed, during his office, Macquarie transformed the nature of land ownership in New South Wales. He granted 162,000 hectares of land while previous governors had jointly granted only 72,900 hectares. The distribution of land by free grant departed radically from the distribution of land in England where in addition to the vast landholdings of the long-established landed class, a class of landholding mercantile professionals was strengthening and land itself had become a major part of the market economy. In colonial New South Wales by contrast, the distribution of land through free grant, often a result of imperial patronage, arguably undermined market forces (Gascoigne 2002: 62–63). This was precisely the situation criticised by proponents of utilitarianism.

Jeremy Bentham, in his criticism of the colony of New South Wales in 1803, had linked free land grants to the unreformed and corrupt excesses of colonial government: 'Until the 1820s, the governor was the sole executive and legislative authority in the colony. It was a government founded on overt military power' (cited in McMichael 1984: 82). Governors 'had powers to establish courts to try breaches of the regulations they themselves had decreed' (Gascoigne 2002: 41). Bentham argued that these powers were unconstitutional because they were inconsistent with the representative and responsible government of separation of powers. He wrote that the colony was 'Star Chamber-out-Star-Chamberized; legislature and judicature confounded and lodged together, both in one and the same hand' (cited in Gascoigne 2002: 41). Despite constitutional reforms in 1823 that limited the executive authority of the governor, namely by the establishment of the New South Wales Legislative Council and a supreme court, the government of the colony remained unrepresentative because although the council was constituted of 15 members by 1828, the governor nominated them. Nominated members were invariably wealthy settlers representing the interests of pastoral capitalists:

> The reforms of the 1820s rationalised, rather than liberalised, the colonial regime. In spite of concessions allowing wealthy settlers an advisory role, the British state retained its authority in those areas that vitally concerned the creation of a colonial periphery – namely, the disposal of land and convict labour. The colonial state continued to be an autocratic regime under imperial authority. In other words, the British state maintained a mercantilist political structure that served the imperial division of labour (premised on transported labour).
>
> (McMichael 1984: 84)

In the 1820s Edward Gibbon Wakefield criticised free land grants and transported labour on the basis that it 'smacked of the use of government favouritism and monopolies to distort the workings of a free market' (cited in Gascoigne 2002: 63). He called the existing manner of transporting convicts 'shovelling out of paupers' and argued for more organised migration based on the suitability of migrants for colonisation (cited in Gascoigne 2002: 62). New South Wales, he claimed was a place where:

[T]he colonial members of the governor's council . . . have been deeply
interested in the misgovernment of which they shared the profits, in
the shape of contracts, undue supplies of convict labour, and immense
grants of land.

(Wakefield, cited in Gascoigne 2002: 65)

The relationship between land, law and politics seemed far closer in colonial
Australia than in England and seemed a departure from the Enlightenment
ideals of civilised government and utilitarian social progress. Arguments
against free grants of land and against convict labour from Bentham and
Wakefield combined with their proposals for the systematic and regulated
alienation of colonial wastelands ultimately influenced the imperial government to discontinue free grants in 1831 (Gascoigne 2002: 64). The Imperial
Land Act 1831 authorised the sale of Crown land by public auction at a
'sufficient price of 5s. an acre and the expenditure of the proceeds financed
the emigration of British labourers' (Burroughs 1967: 3). After this Act was
passed and immigration was encouraged under the Wakefield system, 'a
period of intense commerce in land took place' (Lane 2000: 6).

In Van Diemen's Land, the grasslands were alienated rapidly by Crown
grant. Between 1804 and 1831, when free land grants ended, a little under
2 million acres were given away (Boyce 2009: 146): 'By 1831, when the new
Ripon land regulations (which introduced the sale of crown lands) came
into effect, almost all the profitable land had been granted' (Boyce 2009: 146).
As in British North America, the Crown's instructions and conditions
attached to the land grants 'reflected the British government's land policy,
instructing the governor to make "a grant of land in proportion to the means
of bringing the same into cultivation" ' (letter of 1827 cited in Boyce 2009:
148). However, Boyce points out that due to the constraints of geography and
climate that cultivation was a long time coming and in the meanwhile, the
colony maintained a 'kangaroo economy': 'The contest for control of the
major resources of this far-flung outpost of the empire was by no means
resolved, and the securing of food supplies for the island's thousand or so
European residents far from guaranteed' (Boyce 2009: 60).

As had occurred in New South Wales, in Van Diemen's Land, too, not
long after the granting of 350,000 acres of land to the Van Diemen's Land
Company in 1826, a land market developed. The company was granted an
effective monopoly of land in the northwest corner of the island (Boyce 2009:
202). Yet, arriving 'comparatively late on the scene' the company was forced
to search for its lands in the forests. The company's surveyors eventually
'found the open country they were looking for' yet this land was not naturally
open but were 'Aboriginal hunting grounds created over many generations'
(McFarlane cited in Boyce 2009: 202). The anthropogenic landscape change
was either not recognised or not evaluated as 'improvement' because despite
the unambiguous displeasure of the local community, the company persisted

and acquired possession and title by brute force. Several colonial records indicate sustained and widespread killing of the local Aboriginal people during the company's process of dispossession and acquisition of this land (Boyce 2009: 202–205).

The lie to the logic of 'improvement', however, was that regardless of whether the colonists couldn't or didn't understand Indigenous economies and land use practices, they were prepared to alter their understanding of 'improvement' to accommodate and legally recognise entitlement to land based on non-agricultural land use practices in non-Indigenous communities. In Van Diemen's Land, visiting officials lamented that there were no fences and not enough European grasses growing. Boyce writes that land clearing, manuring and crop rotation were uncommon until the 1830s (2009: 107). Whatever the practice on the ground, the ideology of improvement-as-cultivation persisted and prevailed. However, in prevailing, it quietly accepted pastoralism and, later, forestry, in the place of agricultural land use practice as the most profitable 'improvement' of the land. From 1840 onwards the colony experienced an economic recession broken only by the 'west-coast mineral boom of the 1870s' (Boyce 2009: 228). In England, the idea of improvement manifest in land use practice was almost exclusively agriculture, but in the British colonies the idea was manifest less in agriculture than in pastoralism, forestry and mining. The project of colonisation revealed the purpose of the idea: improvement was not wed to any particular kind of land use at all, but to surplus production, commercial profit and the growth of British economy: 'The non-Indigenous relationship to land is to take more than is needed, depleting ruwi and depleting self' (Watson 2002: 256). Indigenous Australian economies and land use practices were denigrated and ignored, not because they weren't effective and long standing – they were used by the colonists themselves in the early decades when the land use practices of their homelands proved difficult, less efficient and non-viable. Indigenous Australian economies and attendant land use practices were denigrated and ignored because they did not abstract the land as a commodity and therefore would not contribute to the British economy: 'Our relationship to land is as irreconcilable to the western property law system, as it is to fit a sphere on top of a pyramid' (Watson 2002: 257).

4.3.2 Land markets

Alienability, or the right to transfer land by sale or other means, was, in the eyes of the American revolutionaries, the defining and distinguishing feature of American property law. Describing property law as feudal and emphasising restrictions on its alienability was a complaint against imperial authority. Yet, the contradiction of the claim was that the so-called democratisation of property in the colonies was not so far removed from developments in English property law. Certainly, the influence of the feudal doctrines of tenure and estates remained powerful in England and the idea that land ownership was essentially a form of landholding from the Crown was technically accurate in England. Even so, the agrarian, industrial and scientific revolutions of seventeenth- and eighteenth-century England were made possible in large part by the weakening of the feudal character of English property law such that the commercial nature of real property transactions was regarded as inevitable (if threatening to the landed aristocracy). In British North America, as in Australia, the idea that land grants, and (later) the alienability of land, made those polities more democratic was a powerful one. Thus, no matter that the triple principles of private property, exclusive possession and alienability derived from England – the developing narrative of nationalism in the British colonies overlooked its intellectual, English origins (Alexander 1997: 84–85).

The system of alienating Crown land through free land grant in colonial New South Wales evidenced alien concepts of land and law. British sovereignty was the first condition of both these modes of acquisition. Land could be neither granted nor sold were it not already exclusively possessed of a sovereign: private or public. The system of free land grants, as Bentham and Wakefield had remarked, were based on political favour and that related land law to the hierarchical class structure of English society. The assignment of free or convict labour to landholding officers marked 'the rise of landed property with all its imported prestige, privileges and rights', which was 'inextricably bound' with rising mercantile activity and a merchant class (Ashton 1987: 16). The operation of land law in colonial New South Wales at this time was certainly different from the operation of private property law in England, but the capital economy and social structure it produced was not. The subsistence of the colony even from the earliest years was never more important than individual profit: a point well demonstrated by the monopoly of wheat production and trade during the interregnum period between Governor Phillip's departure in 1792 and Governor Hunter's arrival in 1795. Landholding officers rapidly increased their wealth and status through monopolising the production and sale price of wheat. The capital gains of officers also allowed them to use their land for grazing and pastoralism. Although small settlers such as emancipated convicts and free migrants were numerically predominant in the colony, their landholding was limited to 60 acres or less and they lacked the acreage and capital to graze animals. The officers produced wheat not to share with the colony but to sell to the colony, at considerable profit. Land and its resources, regarded as commodities, from the earliest days of colonisation were part of an alien capitalist economy.

Contrary to utilitarian critiques of land grants undermining market forces, land grants were commonly bought and sold. The sale of land grants and land permits evidenced the prevalence of alien concepts of private property and economy of commerce: 'Despite restrictions of transfer a thriving land market grew up' (Lane 2000: 5):

No less than four fifths of the lands in Sydney and Parramatta were then held under occupation permits. These permits were commonly bought and sold. Nearly every town allotment, Governor Brisbane reported to the Secretary of State on 3 September 1823, had 'been purchased from some obscure individual, who had exercised the right to sell, under an old verbal permission to occupy, given him by a magistrate or the surveyor'.

(Campbell 1994: 6)

With this land market already in place, the introduction of alienation of Crown land through auction in 1831 saw a further 'explosion of enterprise' (Lane 2000: 7). Thus, while land law in colonial New South Wales clearly exhibited distinct and specific modifications to suit colonial politics and economy, the concepts and operation of those politics and economy were not local. The nascent land market in Australia evidenced not simply an English heritage, but the augmentation of England's capitalist economy.

Purchasers were required to buy a minimum of 640 acres (Ashton 1987: 22) and were offered allowances for keeping convicts (Lane 2000: 7). The idea that the sale of land was conditional on a *minimum* size indicated that although market forces were instituted by the systematised alienation of Crown land, the context in which that market operated was entirely different both geo-graphically and politically to England. The sale of land was imagined to be, in the same way that land grants had been imagined, part of the British colonisation of an alien country: central to the populating and exploiting of 'new' lands. The larger size of land deemed appropriate for grants also reflected the adjustment of evaluation of land to suit the potentially larger productivity of Australian lands corresponding to its larger land mass: 'In Australian conditions the massive quantity of land was made to serve as alternative to the generally better quality of British land: country where agriculture was marginal could be put to use to pasture stock' (Gascoigne 2002: 76). The size of land grants also indicated the idea that land was available in abundance, a consequence of the discourse of *terra nullius*. The idea of abundance and the discourse of *terra nullius* thus carried substantial consequences in the economic evaluation of land.

The alienability of land at the centre of the developing colonial economies rendered land a tradeable commodity. Although legal historians have argued that the property laws of British colonies were sooner or later sufficiently distinctive from the laws of the homeland as to be different from them, the alienability of land in those colonies was precisely, and above all, what made those laws English and alien. Indigenous land laws and epistemologies were very different from those of the newcomers: emphasising communal rather than individual rights and inalienability rather than alienability of land. Alienation in Aboriginal economy was based on exchange rather than accumulation (Muecke 1992: 47).

4.3.3 Land grab

Land markets coexisted with land grants and then ultimately replaced them. One effect of the land market was the formalisation and legitimisation of another process of land acquisition: the land grab (Weaver 2003). In this process, land was seized legally or illegally and either settled or sold on, thus creating, formalising and capitalising on the title. In British North America, the process was known as *landhunting* and was characterised by fierce competition. It was understood that landhunting was a rare and commercial opportunity to access and acquire resources for not much more than the effort of 'finding' them. George Washington wrote in 1767: '[A]ny person . . . who neglects the present opportunity of hunting out good lands, and in some measure marking them for his own, in order to keep others from settling them, will never regain it' (Washington, cited in Weaver 2003: 88). Landhunting was, like land grants and the land market, the transformation of land that had been possessed by communities in perpetuity into land that would be possessed by potentially numerous different and individual interest holders over variable periods of time with the singular purpose of improvement. Weaver writes that 'within three generations, during the nineteenth century, some of the best land in these locales (America, Australia, New Zealand and South Africa) was secured, surveyed, apportioned, registered, and drawn into finance capitalism' (Weaver 2003: 89).

The land grab was the micro level of colonisation, that is, it was the application of English concepts of land ownership and land use by private individuals. Often these individuals would defy the 'limits of settlement' imposed by imperial authorities and simply claim land for themselves in the name of 'first occupancy' or 'improvement', terms the authorities would recognise, although not always immediately: 'In the estimation of governments in charge of frontiers, invocations of improvement absolved landhunters, squatters, and speculators' (Weaver 2003: 86). This explains why the practice of cattle grazing was not considered contrary or unacceptable as a form of land improvement. The possession of land and population of it with large numbers of livestock was consistent with the legal definition of modern property. Grazing was a physically obvious activity that substantiated claims to 'exclusive possession' was motivated largely if not solely for the purpose of improvement and commercial profit: 'Grazing devoured territory, more so than labour-intensive forms of landhunting associated with felling trees, pulling stumps, ploughing, and planting' (Weaver 2003: 279).

In New South Wales, the land grab was known as *squatting*. Squatting there was so widespread and commercially successful that it acquired sufficient political clout to effectively challenge conventional English notions of unlawful occupancy:

'Squatting', initially referring to the illegal occupations of Crown land by landless men of ill-fame who preyed on others' livestock, achieved social legitimacy as land-owning graziers advanced their flocks into unsettled districts en masse.

(McMichael 1984: 135)

Squatters and the rise of the pastoral industry in New South Wales arguably represent one of the most significant and distinctive developments in Australian legal history. More importantly, pastoral squatters and the laws that accommodated their property interests left an indelible trace in the Australian landscape. Various accounts of Australian history, legal, economic, sociological, geographical and ecological, unanimously acknowledge the distinctiveness of pastoral squatting in Australia. Legal historian Bruce Kercher claims that squatters 'were the most audacious breakers and makers of law in Australian history' (1995: 118). John Weaver presents the history of the 'pastoral invasion of the continent' as unique among the less remarkable histories of squatting in other 'neo-Europes', particularly on the North American frontier (1996: 982). Property historian Andrew Buck (1994) ties the rise of pastoral squatting to the unique evaluation of land in colonial New South Wales as a mere means to support the wool industry, which by the mid-nineteenth century had collapsed the distinction between real and personal property in Australian law. Paul Gascoigne's history of the influence of Enlightenment ideology on the colonisation of Australia (2002) observes the initial contrariety and later integration of pastoralism within the ideal of progress achieved through agricultural improvement. Peter Burroughs (1967) and Phillip McMichael (1984) each relate the squattocracy to colonial politics and to the contradictory imperatives of imperial policy: economic profitability and agricultural ideology. Nancy Wright shows that the vast landholding of squatters was the critical issue over which the first election in New South Wales was fought (Buck and Wright 2001: 105). Paul Ashton (1987) analyses squatting within the context of land use and demonstrates the way in which the pastoral industry contributed to the degradation of the Australian natural environment. Ann Young (2000) also situates pastoral squatting within the environmental history of Australia, explicitly tying law and order to materiality:

The first major development of agriculture came after the 1830s, as squatters moved out from the established settlements. This expansion into previously unsettled areas was anarchic and uncontrolled, and its impacts were devastating.

(Young 2000: 35)

Squatting was initially, until and including the 1820s, an activity limited to the coastal regions of New South Wales within an area formally known as 'the limits of location'. Settlement was officially limited to this area for two reasons: first, to ensure that the alienation of land would be controlled and certain: 'Land distribution should have been an orderly process under which it was surveyed before having been placed in private hands' (Kercher 1995: 119). Second, a fixed area of settlement was prescribed so that a concentrated population of yeomen would work an agricultural economy, resembling the English economy and social organisation:

> For the colonial authorities civilisation was closely linked with concentration of settlement as farming communities could develop within the sound of church bells and within reach of schools and the forces of law and order.
>
> (Gascoigne 2002: 76)

Yet despite the early decision to encourage small farms and close settlement, the materiality of Australian land, soil quality, climate and rainfall, made this policy non-viable. Farmers of smallholdings could not sustain cropping much beyond subsistence levels and thus could not successfully impose their alien economy onto Australian lands. They claimed that 'British land policies were entirely inappropriate in a country that was much more suited to pastoralism than farming' (Kercher 1995: 120). Farmers began to occupy tracts of land beyond that of which they had been granted (if granted land at all) to graze animals. Sheep farming proved particularly profitable: 'Gradually and reluctantly it was conceded that the future of the colony lay with larger estates, which, increasingly were devoted almost exclusively to pastoral activity' (Gascoigne 2002: 76). Thus, although the shift from agriculture to pastoral grazing appears to be a form of adaptation of colonial land use practice and land law to local conditions, it was not. The shift from agriculture to pastoralism was based fundamentally on the introduction of Eurasian animals, the non-indigenous practice of grazing itself and the commercial and alien economy that it supported.

Squatters linked their practice of fine wool production to the idea of improvement by arguing that the sale of fine wool made a positive contribution to the economy and character of New South Wales: 'Pastoralism was the saviour of the colony of New South Wales, they claimed, and the way it could turn from the disgrace of convictism to respectability' (Kercher 1995: 120). Furthermore, and more importantly in terms of eventual official acquiescence to squatting, the economic benefits of pastoralism could potentially extend to Britain: 'The authorities in London came to view the Australian continent as a valuable wool-producing region which could relieve British manufacturers of their existing dependence on foreign supplies' (Burroughs 1967: 2). In 1819, the Colonial Commissioner of Inquiry, J.T. Bigge, reported that the future of the colony lay in the pastoral industry rather than in small-scale agricultural farming. Bigge recommended that 'the rearing of sheep and cattle, on an extensive scale' be encouraged (cited in Ashton 1987: 40). Pastoral squatting was described and encouraged in terms of imperial interests.

The official endorsement of large-scale pastoralism and the consequent adjustment of imperial policy regarding the ideal forms of land use and economic production effectively changed the legal status of squatting. Whereas squatting was technically trespass in law, the squatters had sufficient political leverage via their mercantile significance to influence land policy in their favour:

> The colonial and imperial governments gave into this pressure and mass disobedience of the law . . . the governments of the 1820s responded by allowing them to graze their stock on Crown land under a ticket of occupation. This allowed them to take their stock wherever they wished, but it did not mean that they acquired title to the land.
>
> (Kercher 1995: 121)

The extent to which squatting was not only accepted, but strangely legitimised, differentiated Australian property law not only from English law, but also from colonial counterparts such as North American law. Even so, this distinctive and remarkable rise of pastoral squatting in Australia in the 1820s 'was infinitesimal as compared with the migrations of the Heroic Age of the thirties' (Rae-Ellis, cited in Weaver 1996: 984). The notion that squatters were heroes evidenced a frontier mentality particular to foreign people in 'new' lands. The changed status of squatters on account of their mercantile significance demonstrates the prevalence of a system of commerce alien to Australia until the arrival of the colonists.

From the 1830s squatting expanded dramatically beyond the official limits settlement and included such a vast number of people and from socially diverse backgrounds, that squatting 'diluted the clear social hierarchy dominated by the pastoral gentry' (McMichael 1984: 87). Social structure was so affected by squatting that Governor Gipps distinguished Australian squatters from their American counterparts 'who are generally persons of mean repute and of small means, who have taken unauthorised possession of patches of land'. In New South Wales, by way of contrast, squatters he said, were among:

> the wealthiest of the Land, occupying with permission of Government thousands and tens of thousands of acres; Young men of good Family and connexions in England, Officers of the Army and Navy, Graduates of Oxford and Cambridge are also in no small number amongst them.
>
> (cited in McMichael 1984: 85)

Significantly, the very definition of squatting was undone and recreated in the Australian context: squatters in Australia seemed to have 'eradicated the liabilities of illegal occupation' (Weaver 1996: 983). This was despite the fact that the licences were intended to force squatters to 'at least recognise the title of the Crown' (Lane 2000: 7). Either way, the new definition of squatting and its 'elevation to respectability' (Weaver 2003: 76) was distinctively Australian. Importantly, however, because this distinctive development depended utterly on the squatters' 'connexions in England' it perpetuated the link between class and property apparent in English property law.

Squatting licences were 'created ad hoc in response to a situation which was well beyond the control of the administration' (Lane 2000: 7). Squatters were licensed to run an unlimited number of animals over an unlimited area of land for 10 pounds a year. A squatting licence was not designated to any particular piece of land, in part because there were little means by which to resolve boundary disputes in the absence of surveyed boundaries and a land registry. Fencing was expensive until the introduction of wire in the 1860s and so squatters developed alternative semiotics for boundaries: 'By the early 1840s, bounds might be tied into trees that had been ringbarked or marked with a carved symbol, ploughed furrows, piles of rock, and heights of land separating watersheds' (Weaver 1996: 1000).

The squatters' practice of bounding land superficially resembled the practice of land transfer that preceded cartography and the registration of titles in England (Pottage 1994: 364–374). But English land transfer law in that period relied on a 'local sense of place' (Pottage 1994: 366) in which landmarks used to measure boundaries were not created to be boundaries 'according to external standards of proportion and orientation' (Pottage 1994: 366) but rather were recognised according to a local knowledge of land. This knowledge was articulated in terms of 'the images which local culture superimposed upon the landscape' (Pottage 1994: 365). The question of identifying the bounds of land, therefore, 'could be addressed only by someone who was sufficiently familiar with this local sense of place' (Pottage 1994: 365).

In Australia, by contrast, the semiotics of boundaries between squatters' runs, although neither fenced nor surveyed cartographically, could not be said to be expressions of a local knowledge of the land nor part of a local cultural narrative of place. Rather, this alternative 'pioneer' semiology was the direct function of establishing externally recognisable marks 'of proportion and orientation' motivated only to avoid and to resolve disputes over exclusive possession of the land. The question of identifying the bounds of land was never imagined to be addressed by a local, or indigene of the land. It was a pre-existing expectation that the question would be resolved by an 'objective' account both in measure and in person, external to the place itself. 'Evidencing land ownership' to establish exclusive possession, if temporary in the form of licensing, was what the squatters' landmarks were about (see Pottage 1998a). The measure and process of proving land ownership were adjusted in the Australian context of squatting to proving the possession of a licence, yet this change was only an adjustment, a modification of English legal traditions rather than a departure from them. Squatting licences bore an uncanny resemblance to modern English land law: providing unrestricted enjoyment of lands in exclusive possession.

Boundaries and fences meant the same thing in England as they did in New South Wales. The signifier, 'fence', and the signified, 'boundary of exclusion', was a code common to both property regimes. But the code and the form of property that recognised boundaries and fences were not universal. Local Indigenous peoples had no reason to recognise and respond to boundaries and fences because the meaning or of that code, 'exclusion', did not exist in and was repugnant to their property regime:

> Agricultural improvement had been based on the move to enclosed lands, which undermined traditional patterns of common ownership. So, too, in Australia land use was based on notions of exclusive owner-ship, which left little or no role for sharing the land with its original inhabitants.
>
> (Gascoigne 2002: 154)

Legal historian Bruce Kercher argues that the concept of property articu-lated by squatting licence legislation departed radically 'from English notions of land holding' and yet he acknowledges these new concepts were ones that 'the colonial judges and London let past the repugnancy test' (1995: 121). This admission that the legislation was both potentially repugnant to and approved by English law well demonstrates the way in which the greatest differences and departures of colonial property law from English law were legitimated by English authority to serve English interests.

The ideology of Enlightenment and its insistence on agricultural improve-ment and close settlement evident in much early imperial policy and colonial regulation of property failed to identify and respond to the substantially differ-ent local geographical and climatic conditions in its colonies. Consequently, the idea of improvement and its attachment to property law was constantly undermining the actual progress of the colony by failing to adapt theory to practice. The legal recognition of squatting in New South Wales was in many ways the pragmatic, economic recognition that the idea was unsuited beyond the physical conditions of its origins: 'Ultimately, Australia was too large and too arid to be ever fully improved in the way of Europe where human activity overshadowed almost the entire landscape' (Gascoigne 2002: 83). Governor Gipps wrote to the colonial secretary in 1840 regarding the legitimacy of pastoral squatting:

> As well might be attempted to confine the Arabs of the Desert within a circle, traced upon their sands, as to confine the Graziers or Woolgrowers of New South Wales within any bounds than can possibly be assigned to them: and as certainly as the Arabs would be starved, so also would the

flocks and herds of New South Wales, if they were so confined, and the prosperity of the Country be at an end.

(cited in Gascoigne 2002: 83)

The connection between squatting and property law by all accounts was the growing commercial economy in Australia and particularly its dependence on the production and supply of wool: 'By 1840 some 20 per cent of British wool imports came from Australia and 50 per cent by 1850' (Gascoigne 2002: 81). But where did land fit into this equation and how did it affect property law? Two key pieces of legislation provide insight into the cultural value of land in the colonial regime of property.

First, the Waste Lands Occupation Act 1846 (UK), which was brought into operation in 1847, granted squatters property rights more closely approximating proprietorship than ever before. The act provided for established squatters to take up 14-year leases without competition at 10 pounds per annum rent for each station, with a capacity of carrying 4000 sheep. The leases included the option to purchase freehold title to the property for one pound per acre at the conclusion of the lease period and offered compensation for improvements made to the property. The legislation gave squatters superior rights than those they had enjoyed under licensing, which had denied proprietorship by permitting only usufruct rights to property: 'Leasing implied attachment to an area; licensing did not' (Weaver 1996: 994). The legislation was criticised as 'locking up the land' for the benefit of large-scale pastoralists at the expense of small landholders (Buck 1995: 158). Kercher elaborates the meaning of 'locked-up land' thus: '[T]he legislation meant that large squatters would tie up thousands of acres at minimal cost calculated by reference to the number of animals a run could support' (Kercher 1995: 122). Under this act, squatters enjoyed the rights of private property to exclusive possession since 'the underlying conception of property that these developments reflected was perfectly in accord with their desire to treat land as a tradeable commodity' (Buck 2001: 53). The unlimited enjoyment of the land and their insistence on evermore exclusive and alienable possession indicated a commitment to the principles of private property theorised and developed in England. The alienability of property was present among colonists from the outset of colonisation.

The second significant development in Australian property law at this time passed by the New South Wales Legislative Council in 1843 was the Liens on Wool Act, which allowed a pastoralist to mortgage a woolclip while still 'on the sheep's back'. As Buck acknowledged, this legislation 'raised the issue of just what property was in a colonial context' (1995: 156) and 'was changing the meaning of property in colonial Australia' (1996: 97). In relation to the question of identity of Australian property law, Buck argues that the legislation indicated that 'the social and economic context of New South Wales was substantively different from its metropolitan parent' (1994: 137). How were these differences understood and articulated at the time? Lord Stanley, Secretary of State for the Colonies, understood the Australian law to be so radically different from English law as to be repugnant to it. He insisted that the legislation be repealed or else disallowed (Buck 1994: 136). Lord Stanley's criticism, however, was said to misunderstand the nature of property in Australia and was opposed successfully. A select committee established to inquire into the operation of the act conducted the following interviews in 1845. The first respondent is lawyer, Hastings Elwin:

> Q: Here, sheep, cattle and horses are the principal property?
> A: Sheep pre-eminently.
> Q: Without them the land would be of no value whatever?
> A: None.
>
> (cited in Buck 1995: 156–157)

The second respondent is Leslie Duguid, Managing Director of the Commercial Bank. When asked about the status of sheep, cattle and horses in the colony he replies:

> They form, in my opinion, the 'real property' of this country. You have said sheep, cattle and horses ... I would rather restrict my opinion to sheep and wool.
>
> (cited in Buck 1995: 136–137)

Such unequivocal statements convinced the committee that land was not the basis of the regime of property in New South Wales and it concluded that:

> Sheep, cattle and horses should possess all the incidents of fixed property in England; that it is sound policy not to curtail those incidents, directly or indirectly, but to give them their fullest scope; and that any state of the law which should prevent the freest use of them, would be an unwarrantable interference with the rights of property.
>
> (cited in Buck 1995: 137)

Pastoral squatting and the mortgage of wool represent the apotheosis of English concepts of land use. Land had become so irrelevant in the reality of the now more correctly called 'property market' that it was valued precisely by the extent to which it was limitlessly exploited by the pastoral industry. With land irrelevant to property in New South Wales, property as a concept had now become utterly dephysicalised.

Pastoralists reconciled the Enlightenment preference for progress with their non-agricultural commercial interests by describing animal husbandry and the production of wool in terms of improvement. Experiments with cross-breeding sheep and importing 'quality breeding stock' were regarded by

Tasmanian colonists in 1818 as vital to 'improving the breed of this useful animal' (cited in Gascoigne 2002: 84). Furthermore, improvement extended from sheep to people and, in accordance with the logic of Enlightenment, contributed to a yet more civilised culture 'the employment of the convicts in the management of sheep in New South Wales, may be highly conducive to their moral improvement and reform' (Bigge, cited in Gascoigne 2002: 84):

> Larger sheep and finer fleeces were instances of the possibilities of progress, as techniques of experimentation endorsed by the Scientific Revolution yielded economic and social benefits. The humble sheep was a motor of change: turning waste lands into profitable ventures, improving convicts into honest workmen and dispossessing the Aboriginal population.
>
> (Gascoigne 2002: 85)

The licences and later leases of squatters represented a substantial departure of property law in New South Wales from English land law in doctrinal terms. But the difference between the economic value of land in Australia and England was not more than a variation. Property law in the colony of New South Wales protected the same economic values of land and natural resources as commodities and maintained the same principles of their regulation: the right to alienate the property and the right to exclude others from it (and its profits). Colonial property law encouraged the expansion and assumption of vast tracts of Australian lands and protected the rights of colonists, particularly squatters, to enjoy that land without restriction. Indeed, the conditions or restrictions on which squatters were granted land related to minimum size of land and the minimum number of stock required grazing thereon. The number of sheep in New South Wales increased from 99,487 in 1820 to 13 million in 1850 (Gascoigne 2002: 36). Overstocking and consequent soil exhaustion devastated Australian lands: 'Erosion as a result of overgrazing increased the bare areas, so that less rainfall seeped into the soil and grasses did not grow well in the drier soil conditions' (Young 2000: 42). Environmental historian Ann Young claims that 70% of land degradation in the semi-arid and arid areas of Australia happened in the first 20 years of settlement of those areas (Young 2000: 35). Property law was fundamental to the existence and continuation of an alien and dominant form of land use in the colony of New South Wales: pastoralism.

As with land grants and the subsequent land markets, the land grab was also a process characterised by the juxtaposition of abstract ideas and material limits. Although the idea of improvement that rationalised and motivated the land grab was originally wed to the ideal of agricultural land use, the material capacities and limits of the lands themselves often rendered those uses difficult. In New South Wales, these limits led to the rise of pastoralism. But in other climates and geographies, not even pastoralism could provide an acceptable alternative land use practice to agriculture. Back in the northern hemisphere both agriculture and pastoralism proved difficult in Canada:

> There were environmental limits to grazing, and brutal winters, like those that gripped the Canadian prairies, checked drovers. In Canada, ranching was confined to southern Alberta and the arid valleys of central British Columbia. Because of its harsh climate and isolation, the Canadian prairies were spared the pastoral squatting that often sped frontier occupation.
>
> (Weaver 2003: 110)

Even in the lower North American colonies, pastoralists, or grazers as they are there called, 'often miscalculated or lacked sufficient information when selecting ranges and runs' (Weaver 2003: 278). In these cases, the remedy was simply to move on. In some climates, 'aridity pushed landhunting' where as in others 'poor drainage and cold winters in the mountains forced pastoralists to move for the good of their sheep' (Weaver 2003: 279). In both instances, the drive for surplus production and profit and the genuine or wilful misunderstanding of alternative land use practices 'helped make the land rush unstoppable' (Weaver 2003: 90).

4.4 Maladaptation

> The common law has proved immensely strong. It crossed the Atlantic and reached the antipodes, and it has flourished in all its homes. But it came to those homes among the cultural baggage of emigrants. No society has reached out to choose it.
>
> (Milsom 2003: 19)

The property laws and land use practices in British North America and in the British colonies of New South Wales and Van Diemen's Land developed in ways that distinguished them from English property law and land use practices (McLaren et al. 2005). Yet, these laws and practices were based firmly and unequivocally on English enlightenment ideas of progress and improvement and on the English capitalist economic practices of surplus production and commercial profit. Land grants, land markets and the land grab were not merely legal and economic creatures, events and processes. Grants, markets and the taking of land were physical in their implementation and effect. The material or biogeographical impact of English law and economy in distant lands was apparent from the earliest days of their colonisation and continue to be so.

Whether the English were simply trying to make themselves feel at home by making alien lands more like their home (Dunlap 1999: 19) or whether they were simply trying to secure control of sufficient natural resources to sustain and grow the English economy, the fact remains that the law, property law, transformed foreign lands into particular kinds and patterns of landscape.

Conventional analyses of property law, or land law as it was then known, usually compare property using a horizontal analysis, in other words by comparing one property law in one jurisdiction or period of time to another property law in a different jurisdiction or period of time. The results of these analyses help us understand the differences between property laws in terms of degrees of their sameness and difference from each other in an anthropocentric sense. However, if we use vertical analysis, we compare the relationship between the property law and its effect on landscape change in one place or period of time, to another property law and its effect on landscape change in a different place or period of time. The results of this type of analysis help us understand the differences between property laws in terms of the relationship between land law and the land.

A vertical analysis of the property laws of England and its colonies reveals that the relationship between the laws and the lands were the same. It also reveals that in the lands that were then colonised by England, the law was not adapted to the land, rather, the land was adapted to the law. Modern English land law and the land uses that it facilitated and protected in the period of the British Empire were not borne of respect and response to specific and local geographical and climatic capacities and limits, but in spite of them. It is in this sense that the law reveals itself as having failed to adequately adapt to materiality and it is therefore in this sense that modern property law can be understood as 'maladapted'. The chapter now concludes with a brief account of one obvious example of the maladaptation of land law to land in British colonies: the production of food and subsequent land degradation in Australia and North America.

4.4.1 Australia

The first example of maladaptation was the failure of the English to develop local methods and sources for living in the foreign lands they colonised without recourse to the physical and metaphysical resources of their home of origin:

> White English colonists did not create literate, food-producing, industrial democracy in Australia. Instead, they imported all of the elements from outside Australia: the livestock, all of the crops (except macadamia nuts), the metallurgical knowledge, the steam engines, the guns, the alphabet, the political institutions, even the germs. All these were the end products of 10,000 years of development in Eurasian environments.
>
> (Diamond 1997: 321)

Having left their homeland, the British encountered difficulties obtaining and maintaining supplies of food when they colonised other lands. In the early years especially, they lacked an understanding of the different local food sources, rainfall patterns, climate and soil conditions. The new arrivals also brought with them strong cultural preferences for certain food sources and methods, namely agricultural and pastoral food production, which were mostly not available or easily viable in the lands they colonised. Without fresh supplies sent from England, survival was not guaranteed. The 'difficulties encountered and the privations endured' in colonial New South Wales for example, were 'reminiscent of much of the early history of the American colonies' (Wadham and Wood 1957: 9).

'Fear of famine prevailed' in the early years of the colony of New South Wales (Wadham and Wood 1957: 10). John White, Surgeon-General of the First Fleet that arrived in New South Wales, wrote in April 1790:

> much cannot now be done, limited in food and reduced as the people are, who have not had one ounce of fresh animal food since first in the country; a country and place so forbidding and so hateful as only to merit execration and curses.
>
> (quoted in Boyce 2009: 3)

As White's letter reveals, the colonists attributed food shortages and instances of starvation in the young colony to the land itself rather than to their own unfamiliarity with its geographic conditions and resources and to their lack of hunting and gathering knowledge and experience. Governor Phillip was so convinced of the inadequacy of the land to yield sufficient food to sustain the colony that he wrote: 'No country offers less assistance to the first settlers than this does ... a regular supply of provisions from England will be absolutely necessary for four or five years' (cited in Gascoigne 2002: 71).

Food shortages, crop failures, the constant threat of starvation and the importation of food, flora and fauna indicated the inability of the colonists to adapt and attach themselves to new and different lands and to learn from the first peoples and their long successful economies. The difficulties that colonists encountered trying to make the land adapt to their economy perpetuated their perception of the wildness of these lands and the need to civilise and improve them. In New South Wales, the local flora was condemned as 'too contemptible to deserve notice' (Captain Tench, cited in Gascoigne 2002: 72). Without developing knowledge of the food sources and methods that were already locally available to enjoy and to learn and without ploughs and horses to recreate their British agricultural economy, starvation 'daunted the settlers and left them feeling isolated and abandoned at the end of the earth' (Jeans, cited in Young 2000: 1). Palaeontologist and climatologist Tim Flannery claimed that, in New South Wales, 'starvation

was ubiquitous, with several convicts actually dying from want of food'
(1994: 348):

> Viewing the new world of Australia through the filter of agricultural
> improvement shaped by alien British experience could also be distorting.
> It was symptomatic that they made almost no use of Aboriginal know-
> ledge of the land ... hence the irony of explorers dying in areas that
> could support Aboriginal tribes.
>
> (Gascoigne 2002: 99)

With survival in question, it was necessary to adapt. However, adaptation
was initially limited to rationing the original English food supplies and then
to rationing supplies in the intervals between the arrivals of further supplies
from home. Dependence on supplies was so significant that it constrained
the colonists' travel and exploration possibilities: 'Explorers still saw the
environment as an obstacle to overcome rather than a potential resource on
which to depend' (Boyce 2009: 3).

However, the colonists were not discouraged by their difficulties in obtaining a secure food source, neither were they discouraged by the imagined
'hostility' of the land. The English had faith in the rectitude of the ideas of
improvement and progress and, most importantly, in their own ability to
realise those ideas: 'The continent they had taken to be their own could be
moulded to meet their needs. For all the strangeness and harshness of the
landscape it was amenable to improvement' (Gascoigne 2002: 9). The logic
of improvement theory was the basis for their difficulties with becoming
independent of the food sources and methods of their homeland. The logic
of improvement turned on the universal appropriateness of food production
for all human economies (in place of hunter-gatherer food sources), as well as
on the universal amenity of all land to improvement. The universalistic and
universalising logic of improvement theory lacked, and rejected, a sense of
locality and place: neither land nor land use was regarded as things that were
locally specific.

Difficulties encountered by the colonists in developing and establishing
food sources were never regarded as instances of the need to better adapt
their economic practices, rather, they were regarded as encouragement to
persist. The soil of the coast of New South Wales has low phosphate levels
which render it unsuitable to agricultural and pastoral land use practices
(Shaw 1990: 2). But the colonists did not know this and seemed unwilling
to learn it through harsh experience and thus they persisted in their efforts
to grow sheep there notwithstanding the ongoing failure (Boyce 2009: 3).
With time, the coast of New South Wales became known not as the place
where the colonists had failed to adapt their economic practices to different
geographical conditions, but as the place known for the 'relative poverty of
their soils' (Wadham and Wood, 1957: 9). To the southwest of the colony

of New South Wales, en route to what is now the Australian capital, Canberra, colonists both cultivated crops and grazed animals on their farms but the ratio was 1:4 (Shaw 1990: 2). The preferred land use practice was the grazing of sheep and cattle because this was the practice offering the greater profit, which was the ultimate purpose of the 'improvement' of land. Over 60 years after the foundation of the Australian Agricultural Company, the power of the idea of improvement had not waned and was officially promoted again by taxes on 'unimproved' land. In 1884 the South Australian government imposed a tax on 'unimproved' land in order to release under-utilised or unproductive land for agricultural use (Ashton 1987: 30). New South Wales followed in 1885. However, imperatives of property law and taxation notwithstanding, agricultural production in New South Wales did not exceed domestic consumption until 1898. Western Australia imported over 14 million pounds' worth of agricultural produce until 1906 (Ashton 1987: 32).

An interesting counterstory to that of starvation and struggle is told by historian James Boyce in his history of Van Diemen's Land. There, within the first year of the colony, 'a dramatically different encounter with the Australian bush began' (Boyce 2009: 4). The climate, soil quality, fresh water supply and rainfall of this island, combined with the different socioeconomic backgrounds of the colonial population, made for a different colonial economy. Boyce argues persuasively that the 'economic and cultural backgrounds' of the convicts were not homogenous and that indeed, Britain's poorest were often those who had lived, until their transportation, in pre-industrial communities with different skills and values relating to land ownership and land use (Boyce 2009: 6–9). In the two decades that preceded the arrival of free settlers in Van Diemen's Land, the land was shared rather than fenced and privatised and an economy based on hunting took hold. The advantages of the colonists on this island compared to the colonists on the Australian mainland were twofold: they brought dogs with them from England, which could be used to hunt very effectively as no other dog had been introduced to the island and the local fauna were thus highly vulnerable to them (Boyce 2009: 24); and the community was prepared to postpone and even abandon ideals of improvement and agricultural food production to embrace the local food source: kangaroos. As Jared Diamond reminds us, societies will, given time, select the most efficient economy of resources. Hunter-gatherer economies move to production economies when it is more effective and efficient to do so in terms of the relationship between time, effort and output (Diamond 1997: 365). Similarly, in Van Diemen's Land, we see that an ostensibly production-based economy moved to a hunting-based economy when that proved more effective and efficient. Indeed, the early colonists seemed to retain elements of the production economy, but only to supplement the primary food source, kangaroo. The governor of the colony himself accepted the need for this shift in response to ongoing and substantial malnutrition, illness and death in the colony. The governor 'took a momentous policy decision' in 1804 by ordering the first government purchase of kangaroo meat to replace the 'poor quality imported fare' and save the colony from collapse (Boyce 2009: 44): 'A large cash market for kangaroo was immediately created, and, in direct consequence, the foundation for a new society was laid' (Boyce 2009: 44). By 1806, however, the supply of kangaroo meat was reduced and near exhausted by unsustainable hunting practice (Boyce 2009: 53). Official instructions and colonial authorities ultimately encouraged and compelled English land use practices in place of a hunting economy. The colony's economy shifted to wool production and then to forestry despite early attempts to adapt the economy of the colony to the land itself.

Agriculture, the pastoral industry and forestry affected enormous degradation of lands in all Britain's Australian colonies. The necessary clearing of lands in all these land use practices, or more properly these industries, led to the depletion of soils, soil erosion and loss of native flora and fauna in New South Wales. In the colony of Van Diemen's Land, overgrazing and weeds degraded the grasslands, erosion was noted by colonists within years of their arrival and local native fauna such as the emus and kangaroos became 'nearly extinct' (Boyce 2009: 249). These were the direct consequences of the imposition of an alien land law and land use practice. Geoffrey Bolton's ecological history of the colonisation of Australia titled a chapter on land clearing 'They Hated Trees' (Bolton 1981: 37). Tim Flannery tells us that Australian colonists regarded timber resources as abundant and almost inexhaustible. He cites the professional opinion of Commissioner Frye of the New South Wales public service in 1847 that the 'Big Scrub of northern New South Wales could not be cleared in five or six centuries.' Flannery continues dryly: 'Clearance of the Big Scrub began in earnest in the 1880s, and by 1900 it was all gone' (1994: 360). Tree felling was needed for agricultural development, for building, for fuel, for furniture and for gold mines. Cutting trees down supported the colonial economy and the discourse of private property encouraged this activity because human agency in the natural environment was thought to legitimate entitlement to property. Even so, the extent of tree clearing was extravagantly wasteful and the effects were irreversible:

> The woods, like other elements of the landscape, such as grasses, soils and waters ... were swept away in the pursuit of improvement, development and progress as then understood ... the prodigality was matched only by the ignorance and misperception of the extent of the wooded endowment of the continent.
>
> (Williams, cited in Young 2000: 18)

One method of land clearing was ring barking. This technique involved cutting away the bark in a ring around a tree trunk and its branches in order to kill the tree or just the affected part. It was effective and cheap and was used from the outset of the colonisation of Australia (Ashton 1987). This method was particularly popular with pastoralists and agriculturalists and as more and more land was annexed by the colonists, the landscape gradually but dramatically transformed. Another method was fire, particularly where the trees were very long established and their roots very difficult to remove. In Western Australia, the State Agriculture Bank 'which financed most wheat-belt settlers, recommended ringbarking and fire as the cheapest and speediest ways of reducing forest to sheep paddock and wheat field' (Lines 1991: 147). In 1873 the first Secretary of Agriculture in Victoria, A.R. Wallis, argued for the need for remedial action and technical education in agricultural matters. In Goulburn, not long after colonisation, 'concern was expressed for increasing scarcities of timber' (Ashton 1987: 26). 'By the 1890s, over a quarter of the forests extant in New South Wales a century earlier had been destroyed. The environmental consequences . . . were to be immense' (Ashton 1987: 33).

It is important to observe the connection between property law and these changes to the landscape. Property law made purchases and grants of land conditional on 'improvement' and yet these improvements were not evaluated with a view to the medium or long term. The focus of these grants and purchases was the 'now' and the improvements were expected to begin immediately without need of consideration and analysis of local conditions. Even on occasions where the conditions of grant and purchase were partially and even completely ignored in preference for more profitable land use practices, the fact remains that the landscape was altered and often permanently. The instances in which the idea of 'improvement' failed outright and/or led to visible environmental degradation were not considered sufficient to question or subvert the rectitude of the idea, because other, vast, tracts of land were available, abundant and cheap. Instances of the failure of the idea and condition of improving unimproved wastelands were thus, officially, ignored: 'On exhaustion, the ground was either abandoned for fresher fields or left "fallow" and unattended' (Ashton 1987: 26). One commentator of the time, a witness to a commission established by the South Australian colonial government, remarked in 1875 that the logic of the land law determined this result:

> So long as virgin soil is to be had at one pound an acre, so long will the average South Australian farmer prefer to spend the money in the purchase of new land, rather than in the improvement of what has been impoverished.

> (cited in Ashton 1987: 24)

Once colonists in Australia rejected the land laws and economies of local Indigenous peoples, then abandoned early hybrid economies that combined food production with hunting and then embraced completely surplus agricultural, pastoral and forestry production – the physical consequences were impossible to undo. In the words of biologist, James Kohen wrote 'populations which adopted agriculture as their economic base no longer had the option of returning to a hunting and gathering lifestyle, which by definition has a lesser impact on the environment' (Kohen 1995: 127). Certainly all human economies, by definition, modify the environment in which they function. However, the environment responds differently to different economic pressures – some take short periods of time to recover and replenish, others take long periods of time, several human generations and others take so long they are incalculable and/or permanent. The impact of modern property law and the idea of improving and transforming land into commodities for commercial profit left from the period of colonisation to the present remains clearly one from which it would take many generations to recover, given the opportunity to do so.

4.4.2 North America

As in Australia, the early period of the British colonisation of North America was characterised by difficulties in the identification and securing of local food sources and locally viable economic practices. The colonists depended on imports and gifts from first peoples to begin with and consequently, this period is referred to in the literature as the 'starving period' (Ball and Walton 1976: 102). Agricultural improvement was pragmatically set aside and the colonists adopted a hunter-gatherer economy depending on hunting and fishing wild fauna and collecting local natural food stuffs and eventually combined this with subsistence levels of crop cultivation in open lands (Ball and Walton 1976: 102). As in Van Diemen's Land, private property and the idea of improvement had not entirely replaced the pre-industrial property relations experienced by many colonists in their homeland and the earliest period of North American colonisation contains numerous examples of common landholding for subsistence agricultural food production (Banner 1997). However, by the eighteenth century, the British colonies of North America were almost entirely self-sufficient in conventional and mostly private land use practices and a food production economy. Certainly, there are records of imports in this period from the West Indies and southern Europe, but these were often alcohol and non-food items.

Food production in this period was almost entirely for domestic consumption rather than export (Mancall and Weiss 1999: 22, 36). Indeed, exported agricultural products such as wheat and bread constituted only 14% of exports with other natural resources constituting the majority such as furs etc. (Klingaman 1971: 554). The colony of New England, however, relied heavily on imported food as the soil was 'rocky' and the climate 'harsh' and 'rust disease' threatened crops (Klingaman 1971: 563). Even in fertile lands such as Chesapeake in northeastern America, the colonists of Virginia and Maryland had to adapt their English preferences and methods for locally suited foods and production processes. The forest of ancient trees that covered the land had to be cleared before the soil could be prepared for agriculture and the root systems of the trees were enormous and made removal difficult and slow (Carr 1992: 276). The colonists chose to 'accept a new diet' and grow 'Indian corn by Native American methods that did not require plowing' (Carr 1992: 276). As a consequence of their adaptation, Carr writes 'food was never again a serious problem' in the colony and indeed corn was the primary source of nourishment in the colony. However, Carr qualifies the point by noting that hunger and malnutrition did continue, but not over long periods of time (Carr 1992: 276). The colonists also followed the local Indigenous people's methods of growing beans and peas and supplementing their diet with fresh meat from wild foods. As in Van Diemen's Land, the colonial economy here also included the hunting of deer and fishing. The pragmatism of colonists in North America also explains their ready embrace of the grazing cattle in many places where agriculture was less profitable: 'On frontier after frontier, plans for compact agrarian settlement crumbled under hooves' (Weaver 2003: 275).

Historian John Weaver details numerous and substantial instances of land degradation from colonial land use practices in North America but notes that the climate and geography of Upper Canada protected it from the degradation that accompanied the otherwise universal grazing practices of other colonies. The mountains, the cold and the numerous lakes limited the areas in which grazing could permanently affect the landscape. In the arid parts of North America, small landholdings invariably led to landscape degradation because 'too many people and too much livestock' were allowed and encouraged 'into fragile ecological zones' (Weaver 2003: 13). Where soils were degraded beyond productivity, colonists advanced further inland. In Virginia, some landholders left their lands because of 'the soil depletion that accompanied tobacco growing' (Weaver 2003: 97). As the quality of soils degraded, graziers needed to increase the quantity of their landholding to support the same head of cattle and so the scale of degradation increased also. However, in the late nineteenth century when 'new' land was scarce or non-existent, colonists had fewer choices in how to respond to the problems caused by their overstocking of the land. In California, ranchers eventually 'carried out voluntary slaughters to preserve the native grasslands' (Weaver 2003: 277). Such actions demonstrate that the colonists themselves, given the opportunity of time, recognised the ways in which their land use practices were maladapted to actual geographical conditions.

The problem was that although colonists could and did reflect and learn from the relationship between their land laws, their land use practices and the change to the lands themselves – the urgency that seemed to characterise the colonial imperative prohibited that opportunity or at least reduced it. Weaver eloquently captures some colonists' reflections and laments which are worth extracting here in full:

Late in life a few early settlers could reminisce and even reflect about the ecological damage their efforts to improve had brought. Some old pioneers were nostalgic about the worlds that they had encountered and had worked to seize and change in a short time. They and their children were the last to know lakes, forests, marshes, and grasslands before all was 'improved.' Upper Canadian Charles Durand remembered in 1897 the 'beautiful sea salmon' in Burlington Bay – gone by the 1830s. South African William Collins listed the splendid birds that he knew at Bloemfontein in the 1850s. 'Where are they now?' 'I may as well out with the truth' admitted Australian grazer Edward Curr, 'it is to regret the [passing of the] primitive scene, the Black with his fishing canoe, the silence, the gum trees.' Blacks, reeds, and bellbirds are gone.

(Weaver 2003: 90)

The sentiment of loss is clear but what is significant is that the colonists learned within their own lifetimes the importance of aligning land use practice with the specific capacities and limits of the lands themselves. In other words, these are records of the maladaptation of modern property law and its improvement imperative to foreign lands the world over. Blame is not important; it is the lesson that matters: 'Although they appear foolish in hindsight, they were in reality only terribly maladapted' (Cook, cited in Flannery 1994: 355).

4.5 Conclusion

Accounts of the development modern property law in Australia and North America often remark on the variety and innovation of rights and remedies tailored to suit specific colonial contexts. They do so to distinguish the property laws of England's colonies from each other and from those of the imperial English authority. In the context of significant socioeconomic differences, these varieties and innovations help us understand the relationship between property law and culture. By extending our analysis of property law to include the terrestrial context of significant geographical and climatic differences, these varieties and innovations point not to legal and cultural differences. Rather they highlight the ingenuity of the colonists in achieving common intellectual, economic and cultural goals notwithstanding vastly different geographical and climatic conditions.

It is important to situate property law within the physical context of the 'natural' environment to better understand its pivotal role in anthropogenic landscape change. Where and when property law is not local in its origin, development or application, it may well prove to be maladapted when assessed in material terms. The manifestations of English ideals that were encoded in colonial property laws assumed a local character but that did not mean that they were derived from adaptations to local environmental conditions. Environmental changes in Australia and northern America caused by colonial land use practices demonstrate the ubiquity and power of an alien regime of property that facilitated an alien economy. The primary value of land in that economy was abstract: the security of individual liberty and wealth. The abstract logic that separated the world into the distinct categories of nature and culture was particular to the colonists, not to the Indigenous peoples it dispossessed and colonised. The colonists' rejection of the economies and land laws of the Indigenous peoples that had developed over long periods of time and that were often appropriate to local physical conditions made possible the introduction of the abstract principles of private property law.

Modern English property law separated persons from things in legal doctrine, in legal practice and in the landscape itself. The detachment of people from place at the basis of modern property law made possible the prescription, regulation, and prohibition of different types of land ownership and land use without reference to the specificity and variability of land itself. Despite its lack of attention to the land, modern English property law transformed the landscape not only of England but of other countries across the globe. Sensibility to land 'is a product of economic structure and working relations with the earth' (Fitter 1995: 9). The property laws of the English colonies were neither responsive to nor sustainable within different and diverse geographical and climatic conditions and consequently they can be seen to be maladapted.

Chapter 5

Conceptual developments

> Political revolutions aim to change political institutions in ways that those institutions themselves prohibit.
>
> (Kuhn 1996: 93)

> However unreal social reality was becoming under the fetish of the commodity it was also actual. The logic of the thing-thing conception is a totalisation. It is not the totality.
>
> (Kerruish 1999)

5.1 Introduction: dephysicalisation

Theories of property have contributed enormously to both the creation of modern property law and to its development to the present day. Theories of property have informed and influenced legal practitioners and law teachers for centuries. For this reason, it is important to understand how the theories of property have developed the person/thing paradigm of people–place relations since the time of Locke. In the nineteenth and twentieth centuries, the person–thing model of property relations was rearticulated as a person–person model by eminent scholars. Yet the logic of 'dephysicalisation' contained in the person–thing model remained central to the person–person model, thus perpetuating the abstraction and alienation of people–place relations and maintaining the irrelevance of land to property relations. But what, precisely, does dephysicalisation mean?

In legal theory, 'dephysicalisation' means the removal of the physical 'thing' from the property relation and its replacement with an abstract 'right'. Dephysicalisation describes the shift from the person–thing model of property to the person–person model of property that is thought to have started in the late eighteenth century with the work of English legal philosopher Jeremy Bentham. This definition of dephysicalisation is usually referred to in the context of legal concepts and processes, rather than as an important part of the broader paradigm of people–place relations that characterises Anglocentric culture. As the previous chapters have argued, however, dephysicalisation can be traced back further, to the marriage of entitlement to property with the improvement of land and the work of Locke. Bentham did not invent the idea of dephysicalisation, he merely restated it. He argued that it was only unlearned people who confused the legal category of 'thing' with the physical thing itself, suggesting that the dephysicalisation of 'things' was by then well established. The significance of Bentham's work to theories of property law is that he argued, against Locke and Blackstone, that entitlement to property is not vested in natural rights or natural law, but in positive law. By Bentham's time, the idea that the 'thing' of property, such as land, was an object, whose defining characteristic was that it was an abstract, legal right possessed by the person or subject, was already accepted.

The first section of the chapter presents the contributions of Jeremy Bentham, J.S. Mill, Wesley Hohfeld, Kenneth Vandevelde and C.B. Macpherson to the person–person theory of property. For both Bentham and Mill, property was described in terms of its use value, as an instrument of an idealised state and economy. Bentham and Mill conceived of property as part of the positivisation of law and utilitarian political theory. Both theorists define property as a relation between persons rather than between persons and things. The point of having a property right is not, therefore, the 'thing' attached to the right, it is the having of a 'right' against the 'rights' of all other persons. The use value of property, between persons, is the precursor of the exchange value of property theorised by Hohfeld, Vandevelde and Macpherson. Hohfeld qualifies the legal relativity of property rights between persons, while Vandevelde and Macpherson emphasise the political possibilities and consequences of dephysicalised property rights. Both the use value and the exchange value of property advanced by these theorists present property relations as relations between persons, and thus as exclusively sociopolitical relations. This idea of property therefore eclipses place – property relations have become entirely about people.

The next section of the chapter, 'Thing–thing property', presents a critique of the dephysicalisation of property and of the person–person model of property. Economic philosopher Karl Marx argued that modern property relations are better described as thing–thing relations than person–person relations. He argues not that modern property relations accounts for 'things' in a physical sense, but in the sense that 'things' are commodities. Marx removes the 'person' from the property relation because, he argues, people themselves have become objectified and commodified. In a world without people and without place, Marx says, there are only 'things'. Marx critiques dephysicalisation as a three-stage process that abstracts, inverts and fetishises physical reality. French philosopher Jean Baudrillard also presents property as a relation between things, rather than between persons. For Baudrillard, property does not have use value, exchange value or commodity value – property has only a symbolic value. Property, he says, participates in a semiotic economy. The paradigm of nature/culture is meaningless in Baudrillard's theory of property because there is no real world, no physical realm, only a world of signs and simulation of that world. To Baudrillard, property points to the absence of any external reality beyond the signs of culture.

Contemporary English legal scholars Kevin Gray and Alain Pottage also consider property in terms of a semiotic economy, in which the sign value of property protects the illusory sanctity of law as an institution. Their critique of property challenges not merely the legal category of property, but more significantly, the foundation of law itself because the illusiveness of property subverts the constitutive foundations of law's authority. While Gray's theory contemplates the legal instantiation of property as an economy of symbolic illusions, Pottage critiques this economy and the very concept of dephysicalisation itself. What emerges from the very different work of Gray and Pottage is the idea that property is now so abstract, that it is meaningless. Whether property is theorised as being power, capital, wealth, commodity or symbol, the starting point is the same – property is always a metaphor for something else.

The conclusion of contemporary property theory, that property is elusive and indeterminable and that reality has been commodified and symbolised beyond being, does open up other questions. What happened to the 'real' in property? What is the physical 'reality of commodification'? (Best 1994). The second and third chapters of this book attempted to address the first question, the next chapter attempts to address the second question. This chapter locates the concept of dephysicalisation within the current theories of property law and argues that theory plays an important part in maintaining, by rationalisation, the modern paradigm property law and its separation of people and place.

5.2 Person–person property[1]

5.2.1 Positive property: Jeremy Bentham

Jeremy Bentham profoundly influenced modern law and property in the Anglophone world by conceiving of property as a creation of law, rather than as a material thing. The origin of property, he said was cultural, not natural. As Bentham stated, property 'is metaphysical, it is a mere conception of the mind' (1978: 51). Bentham rejected the natural rights theory of John Locke and William Blackstone, for whom property relations took place in a state of nature and which were relations between persons and things. The problem with Locke's idea of property in specific terms, Bentham argued, is that it

---

1 Parts of this section were first published in 'Restoring the "real" to real property law' in *Blackstone and His Commentaries: Biography, Law, History*, edited by Wilfred Prest and published by Hart Publishing in 2009. They are used here with kind permission.

'overlooks so many other valuable subject matters of possession, namely power, reputation and condition in life' (Postema 1986: 174). Blackstone, by way of contrast, and to a limited degree:

> [W]idened the range of property discussed at a time when most discussions of property were restricted to land, interests in land and money in so far as it was to be regarded as a debt that could be charged against the debtor's land.
>
> (Sokol 1994: 297)

Nevertheless, Bentham regarded Blackstone's work as a 'striking example of the inability of the common law to provide adequate definitions of property' (Sokol 1994: 287). This was in part due to the definition and division of property into the categories of the 'real' and the 'personal', which Bentham argued was an obsolete structure inherited from and particular to the feudal context, in which land was the locus of both the means to life and power. The problem in this division as he saw it was that such an historical definition of property failed to account for the changed economy, in which land no longer functioned as the sole source of wealth and power and had thus become anachronistic and irrational. From Bentham's perspective, Blackstone had not only upheld this 'irrational' division of real and personal property, he had also hierarchised it by privileging real property (Sokol 1994: 294) over other forms of property. And indeed the need to reform property law to account for growing forms of wealth holding was the basis of Bentham's submission to the 1828 Real Property Commission (Sokol 1994: 287).

In his submission, Bentham proposed a unified system of property law that would encompass 'newer proprietary rights such as shares in companies and copyright' (Sokol 1994: 287) and that would ultimately 'take its place in the civil law, forming part of a code of law coherent in all its part and comprehensible to all' (Sokol 1994: 300). Significantly, the agenda of the Commission itself was to promote efficient management and security of land title following the enclosure movement, which had 'made precarious many traditional rights in common land' (Sokol 1994: 290) and had begun to challenge the adequacy of the common law to enforce this programme (see Brown and Sharman 1994). Responsive to the 'needs' of law at the time, this Commission belonged to a changing operation of law as a 'scientific administration' of positive principles. The reforms of the Commission, Bentham hoped, would form 'a universal jurisprudence' to 'provide the necessary concepts of rights on which to base the rational utilitarian system of property law' (Sokol 1994: 300). Bentham had criticised the inadequacy of the common law for its inconsistency and confusion of the categories of real and personal property in his critiques of Blackstone (Sokol 1994: 292). But the common law property regime was unsatisfactory to Bentham not merely because it was outdated, but because it vested law's legitimacy in nature.

Bentham's critique of natural rights in property was part of his broader radical philosophy of legal positivism and utilitarianism: 'Bentham, conceiving himself as the Newton of the moral world, combined law's completeness with its limitless sovereignty in the prospect of an eventual attainment of total and "certain order" ' (Fitzpatrick 1992: 57). The impact of Bentham's philosophy on the development of modern property was twofold. First, his rejection of the person–thing relation in Blackstone's natural rights theory of property produced the notion of property as a person–person relation. Second, the proposed integration of the distinct bodies of personal property and real property into one broad body of property rights, according to the person–person model of property, transformed the locus of social wealth from land, to law or legal right. In effect, what Bentham's theory of property achieved was the separation of land from the idea of property and from the body of law itself by 'elevating' the entire basis of property from natural rights to cultural rights: 'Bentham anticipates the modern tendency to regard all rights secured to an individual by law as "a species of normative property belonging to the right of the holder" ' (Hart, cited in Postema 1986: 174). To Bentham, the function of law was to protect the security of the individual citizen and the government by protecting the institution of property rights (Postema 1986: 175). The integration and codification of real and personal property into a positive scheme of private property rights Bentham argued was the means by which to achieve such a 'civilised society'. The expansiveness of Bentham's idea of property proposed that 'all forms of social interaction available to human beings except political relationships and institutions fall under the concept of property' (Postema 1986: 174).

In Bentham's time, the economic and legal primacy of the category of real property was diminishing and so law could no longer be conceptually dependent on 'any exterior reality' (Fitzpatrick 1992: 56) for its authority. The particularities of reality had to be rejected or incorporated into a universal model of law that would transcend place (Fitzpatrick 1992: 56). Bentham's property was law and the law was property: 'Property and law are born together, and die together. Before laws were made there was no property; take away laws, and property ceases' (Bentham 1978: 52). Both law and property were cultural, and thus dephysicalised, Bentham argued, they existed only as abstract logical forms.

Bentham's claim that there is no property in and through nature does not undermine the logical bases of Locke and Blackstone. The anthropocentric logic of the nature/culture paradigm that constructed the physical/metaphysical and body/mind dualisms, for example, is deployed by each theorist to rationalise the authority of their particular concepts of property. Nature was always culture's *other*. For Locke, nature had replaced God and natural rights therefore replaced divine rights. Bentham's idea of positive law replaced Locke's whole notion of transcendent authority with rational immanence. Bentham's theory of law did not need to appeal to either God or (by parallel) nature, because it was self-legitimating and guaranteed by positive institutions and processes. Nevertheless, the instrumentalist view of nature was common to both theorists. Bentham, like Locke, conceived of nature as something to be cultured: 'Who has renewed the surface of the earth? Who has given to man this domain over nature – embellished, fertilised, and perfected?' The answer, of course, is the 'beneficent genius' and 'security' of law (Bentham 1978: 56).

Bentham's theory of property separates people and place, defining people and culture in opposition to land and nature. So did Locke and Blackstone. Bentham's difference from his predecessors is that the instrumentalist value of nature of his theory of property is not defended, it is assumed. For Bentham, the subordination of nature to culture is already accepted whereas Locke had linked the subordination of nature to law's agency. In Locke's theory of property, property was the abstract sign or signifier and place was the reality that was signified. But Bentham's theory of property abstracted place even further – by removing place from the equation altogether. There was only one part of the property equation – property. All that property signified, according to Bentham, was property:

> In other words, the sign is not experienced as arbitrary but assumes a real importance. As a consequence, the material reality that the sign was commonly supposed to point to crumbles away to the benefit of the imagination, which is no more than the over-accentuation of psychical reality in comparison with material reality.
>
> (Kristeva 1991: 186)

The object, or 'thing', of real property, land, is erased by Bentham's insistence that it represents nothing at all, except the abstract 'right' to which it is attached. Nature, the physical realm is concealed by the 'self-sufficient determination of positive law – the law posited by the sovereign' (Fitzpatrick 1992: 54). This is precisely the conclusion of Bentham's positivist programme. The meaning and origin of law is entirely self-referential.

To say that 'property is entirely a creature of law' (Bentham 1838: 308) is to argue that 'the origins of property *just are* the origins of law' (Postema 1986: 184). By asserting the omnipresence of law/culture and the absence of nature, Bentham 'brings to light, that which ought to be hidden' (Freud 1990: 345) – the question of the origin of the authority of law: 'The question and the quest are ineluctable, rendering irresistible the journey toward the place and the origin of law' (Derrida 1992a: 192). This question of origin subverts Bentham's idea of property precisely because, being vested in positive law itself, property is without origin. Bentham approaches the question thus:

What is it that serves as a basis to law, upon which to begin operations . . .
Have not men, in the primitive state, a natural expectation of enjoying
certain things, an expectation drawn from sources anterior to law?

(Bentham 1978: 52)

His answer is that there was and remains a 'savage' and 'very limited' form
of possession outside the law but that it is 'miserable and precarious'. Indeed,
these very 'physical circumstances' are so dire that they necessitate or give rise
to law:

A feeble and momentary expectation may result from time to time from
circumstances purely physical; but a strong and permanent expectation
can result only from law.

(Bentham 1978: 52)

For Bentham, the origin of the law is the happy and inevitable miracle of
civilisation. Indeed the 'force and origin' of Bentham's law derives 'purely
from its intrinsic being' (Fitzpatrick 1992: 55).

After briefly celebrating this rupture from nature, Bentham's Cartesian
focus shifts swiftly from the abject physical condition at the origin of law, to
its beneficial abstract consequences. Bentham's movement from the real to
the abstract enacts the 'scheme of elevation' (Derrida 1992a: 193) that Freud
described in his account of repression at the origins of morality:

The scheme of elevation, the upwards movement, everything that is
marked by the prefix *super* is here as decisive as the schema of purifica-
tion, of the turning away from impurity, from the zones of the body that
are malodorous and must not be touched. The turning away is an upward
movement. The high and the pure, are what repression produces as the
origin of morality, they are what *is better* absolutely, they are the origin
of value and the judgment of value.

(Derrida 1992a: 193–94)

Bentham's property seems to turn away from the primitive possessions
hidden in a cave and the 'impenetrable forests, sterile plains, stagnant waters
and impure vapours' of 'savage nature' to the 'healthy and smiling' 'cultivated fields' of 'peace and abundance' (Bentham 1978: 56). But Bentham's
movement conceals, rather than departs from, the physical realm. Nature is
not somewhere else; it is covered over by law. Bentham's repression of nature
forgets the ground on which it stands: 'The law, intolerant of its own history,
intervenes as an absolutely emergent order, absolute and detached from any
origin' (Derrida 1992a: 194). Denying its 'terrestrial dimensions' (Fitzpatrick
1992: 55), Bentham's theory of dephysicalised property endows his concept
of law with 'the qualities of a fable' (Derrida 1992a: 199), which deconstruct
the possibility of his a-historic positivism. Bentham's theory that property is

a dephysicalised relation between persons demonstrates that the paradigm of modern property law is, as Karl Marx called it, the 'illusion of jurisprudence' (Marx 1975b: 142).

5.2.2 Utilitarian property: J.S. Mill

J.S. Mill's idea of property had a moral purpose that required the alienability of the physical, as advanced in Bentham's positive theory of property. Mill's *Principles of Political Economy* (1878) expresses the idea that the absence of place in property permits the priority of the state and its economy. But Mill's theory of property differs from Bentham's in that Mill's property has a physical function, even if it has no physical value. Mill's utilitarianism does not erase 'things' from the equation of property because things have a use value that depend on their physical attributes as a 'thing': 'When the property is of a kind to which peculiar affections attach themselves, the compensation ought to exceed a bare pecuniary equivalent' (Mill 1978: 97). Mill admits here that real property exists as a distinct category of property in its physicality and particularity, yet he simultaneously asserts that this real property right can be alienated and exchanged, like other property rights.

In his critical reflection on the state of private property, Mill casts grave doubt over the 'discretion of a class of persons called landlords who have shown themselves unfit for the trust' of the community that 'has too much at stake in the proper cultivation of the land' (1978: 97). Mill's idea of a proper use of the physical as 'a railroad or new street' is a morally qualified utilitarianism, defined socially rather than individualistically. Importantly, Mill's better and morally sound use of place transforms its very physicality or thingness into a semi-real, semi-abstract space or meta-place, the predominant function of which is to carry the common public citizen to and from their particular private places. The lack of physical particularity in public spaces, such as roads and railways foreshadowed in Mill's thesis, anticipates and avails the cultural development of dephysicalised property in the following centuries.

Mill's acknowledgment of the physical remains based on morality not nature. Nevertheless, it remains quite different to Bentham's radical eclipse of the category of real property. For Mill, nature is valued utterly in the pragmatic terms of its function in the utilitarian project and thus all private property is secondary to the needs of public property and the sovereignty of state:

> Landed property is felt even by those most tenacious of its rights, to be a different thing from other property . . . [but] the claim of the landowners is altogether subordinate to the general policy of the state. The principle of property gives them no right to the land, but only a right to compensation for whatever portion of their interest in the land it may be the policy of the state to deprive them of.
>
> (Mill 1978: 97)

Yet Mill's prioritisation of public property over private property is consistent with Bentham's positivist scheme of property rights because the physical
loss of property as a thing, as *realty*, can be neutralised by compensation or
purchase and thus can participate in the grander economy of the state and
security of its citizens.

Mill's economy of property stops short of a complete commodification of
the physical realm. For him, the function of compulsory acquisition, for
example, is not as part of a monetary economy, but rather as part of a
political, explicitly utilitarian, programme. It is the utility, not the profitability, of the land that matters. Certainly the utilitarian economy and the
monetary economy of property both construct nature as the negative *other* of
the law, but where Mill's theory of property attributes a *negative meaning* to
nature, Bentham's theory of property makes nature *meaningless*.

5.2.3 Property rights: Wesley Hohfeld

A consequence of the dephysicalisation of property was that the concept of
property itself 'became infinitely expandable. The result was that during the
1880s and 1890s a variety of new property interests for the first time received
recognition by American courts' (Maurer 1999: 370). Courts 'began to define
property as the right to value rather than to some thing' (Vandevelde 1980:
333). The subsequently augmented body of property rights had been relativ-
ised according to liberal and utilitarian ideals of social organisation. Since
the distinction between real and personal property rights was eroding, determinations of what constituted a legitimate property right varied from case to
case (Vandevelde 1980). According to Kenneth Vandevelde (1980: 333), such
indeterminacy of property was the reason for, as well as the context of, the
property theory of American legal scholar Wesley Newcomb Hohfeld.
Hohfeld contributed two essays to the growing controversy over the
definition of property law in 1913 and 1917. Hohfeld was concerned to clarify
and simplify the concept of property that was subject to considerable change
in the legal practice of his time. His main point is that property law weighs the
'aggregate of abstract legal relations' rather than deferring to 'figurative or
fictional' categories of property according to distinctions between physical
things (Hohfeld 1913: 24). Property was no longer defined absolutely, by
categories of 'real' or 'personal' things, because these 'things' were now, as
'things', meaningless. Instead, property was defined as relative, that is, by
relating the rights of persons to each other.

Hohfeld did, however, provide a theory for the slowness with which these
changing concepts were received into society more generally. Where Bentham
and Mill were concerned to prescribe particular social structures and values
around the idea of dephysicalised property, Hohfeld sought to revise and adapt
the language of law to those prescriptions in order to correct and stabilise the
'unfortunate tendency to confuse and blend' the true and definitive model of

dephysicalised property (Hohfeld 1913: 20). To this extent, Hohfeld's essays provide an excellent discussion of the disjuncture within the discourse of property between what he classifies as 'legal and non-legal' conceptions of property. In so doing, he articulates a set of basic property rights, described as 'the lowest common denominators of the law' which are believed to define the regime of modern or 'new' property (Hohfeld 1913: 58). The common feature of these rights was that they were all legal relations between persons rather than between persons and things. In a statement that is strikingly similar to a statement by Bentham on the definition of property, Hohfeld states that:

> [T]he term 'property', although in common parlance frequently applied to a tract of land or chattel, in its legal signification 'means only the rights of the owner in relation to it'. It denotes a right over a determinate thing.
>
> (Hohfeld 1913: 22)

Australian legal scholar Margaret Davies has observed that Hohfeld unequivocally buried the significance of the physical to the meaning of property: 'The cornerstone of (his) analysis of property was the notion that rights *in rem* (against the world) are in essence a multitude of rights *in personam* (against a person)' (Davies 2007: 43). For Hohfeld, rights between persons constituted the entire property relation. People–place relations were simply irrelevant to property in legal discourse. Any thought to the contrary, Hohfeld argued was 'fallacious'.

The consequences of the Hohfeldian view of property were both legal and cultural. From the legal perspective, if the property relation excludes the physical completely in so far as the 'thing' is irrelevant to it, then property relations 'may have become indistinguishable from contract and tort' (Lametti 2003: 338). From the cultural perspective, the dephysicalisation of property is equally radical because property, being 'utterly devoid of content' (Lametti 2003: 339) no longer prescribes or regulates people–place relations as a specific and important relationship concerning law. Having excluded the 'thing' from the property relation, it was no longer possible or necessary to differentiate between property concerning a vast tract of land, the DNA of a plant, a body of groundwater or hedge funds. And if the concept of property 'includes everything, does it mean anything?' (Seipp 1994: 30).

5.2.4 Political property: Kenneth Vandevelde and C.B. Macpherson

American lawyer and legal scholar Kenneth Vandevelde wrote an article in 1980 that makes much of Hohfeld's work in the development of what he terms the 'new property' (1980: 330). And indeed Hohfeld provides one of the clearest statements of modern property available. But Hohfeld's conception of property was not new; it restated and crystallised the concept of dephysicalised property that Bentham and Mill had theorised within their theories of positivism and utilitarianism. Vandevelde overlooks the influence of these theorists and their indelible traces in the writing of Hohfeld. He posits Hohfeld as an exponent rather than as a contributor to the theory of dephysicalised property. This omission is particularly notable given the explicitly political focus of Vandevelde's thesis and the explicitly political nature of the work of Bentham and Mill. Vandevelde instead structures his thesis into a juxtaposition of two parts: the 'old property' of Blackstone and the 'new property' of Hohfeld. He draws from this contrast his central point that the shift from natural rights in property (person–thing) to dephysicalised rights in property (person–person) is a movement toward an unbridled politicisation of property and hence the destruction of law. Hohfeld's significance to Vandevelde's thesis is twofold. First, Hohfeld's articulation of property as abstract legal relations clarifies the person–person model that firmly locates property law within the realm of social politics. Second, Hohfeld's qualification of those relations or rights as relative rather than absolute and ordered, supports Vandevelde's thesis that the evaluation of property was indeterminable by recourse to a fixed structure or hierarchy of absolute categories. So far as property was:

> reconceived to include potentially any valuable interest, there was no logical stopping point. Property could include all legal relations . . . (so) if property included all legal relations, then it could no longer serve to distinguish one set of relations from another.
>
> (Vandevelde 1980: 362)

Vandevelde argues that because property was no longer finite and absolute, it was indeterminable: 'This century long evolution resulted in an inability of property concepts to settle controversies and legitimate the results' (1980: 330). The 'explosion of the concept of property' meant that property, as a distinct category of law, had become meaningless. The consequence of this development bears a profound impact on the legitimacy of law, Vandevelde argues: '[T]he destruction of meaning in the concept of property destroyed the concept's apparent power to decide cases' (1980: 363). The courts' response to this crisis in meaning could no longer derive from any specific logic of property law, as it did not exist, but only from 'overt recourse to political goals' (Vandevelde 1980: 330). Property *as* law he concludes thus 'came at the price of the courts' legitimacy' (1980: 366). Vandevelde, drawing from American jurisprudence concludes that in this way, property was ultimately 'what the law said it was' (1980: 364).

The increasing rise of dephysicalised forms of property according to the economic demands of capital combined with the courts' subsequent abandonment 'of the myth of judicial neutrality' through recourse to a relativist rights discourse, destroyed the authority of law (Vandevelde 1980: 330). Vandevelde measures the loss brought about by the dephysicalisation of property not in physical terms, but in terms of a metaphysical form, an idea of government. His critique of property is based on a theory of political justice and social order. The loss of the physical in the 'new' dephysicalised equation of property is therefore immaterial to his anthropocentric critique. Dephysicalised property subverts Vandevelde's ideal of positive law. Vandevelde's theory of the politicisation of property finds dephysicalisation problematic because the 'government of law' has descended into the 'government of nine old men' (1980: 367). The increased power of the market and politics to make law (see Unger 1976: 198) erodes the legitimacy of law. The specifically dephysicalised form of property Vandevelde identifies is both part and product of this erosion.

The historical development of property law from Blackstone to Hohfeld via Bentham and Mill indicates the shifting evaluation of nature and physicality from a negative other to outright irrelevance. The link that Vandevelde draws between the growing predominance of dephysicalised forms of property in law and the increased economic significance of non-physical forms of wealth points to the increasingly symbolic value of land. Land was no longer thought to be the source and expression of economic success. Power and wealth were increasingly produced and maintained symbolically. While Mill arguably revived the physical if only for its alienable use value in his theory of property, by the time of Vandevelde, it had vanished altogether.

While Vandevelde laments the meaninglessness and subsequent sociopolitical danger brought to law by the dephysicalisation of property, another political theorist sees dephysicalised property as an opportunity to reform social organisation. Canadian political philosopher C.B. Macpherson (1973) critiques the modern function of private property from the perspective of the democratic tradition. Reading modern property relations in terms of exchange value (person–person), Macpherson, however, sees the process of dephysicalisation as a result of the conquest of the 'scarcity' that had informed earlier theories of property. Macpherson not only presents a different account of the reason for dephysicalisation of property, he also presents a different account of the consequences and opportunities it brings to bear on society. Approaching a time of 'material plenty' Macpherson describes modern property as 'an individual right . . . an individual share in political power' (1973: 37).

Importantly, Macpherson acknowledges that the precondition for the idea of property as the right to power is the (belief in the) abundance of nature as a resource. As long as nature is a resource and is unlimited or constrained as a utility, the right to property-as-power functions, in a manner similar to that according to Adam Smith and utilitarian theorists, not simply as the right to the means to life: but the right to the means to the 'right kind' (Macpherson 1973: 38) of life:

> Property has always been seen as instrumental to life, and justified as instrumental to a fully human life. In the circumstances of material plenty, which we now envisage, the relative importance for a fully human life, of a merely sufficient flow of consumables will diminish, and the importance of all the means to life of action and enjoyment of one's human capacities will increase.
>
> (Macpherson 1973: 38)

Of course, the abundance of property only makes sense if it is exchangeable and abstract, if, in short, it has lost all sense of its specificity. As a political theorist, Macpherson like his predecessors, maintains an anthropocentric approach to property, hierarchically coupling metaphysical/physical, human/non-human. His idea of life is constructed by the contrast between a basic existence in a state of nature and a sophisticated lifestyle in a mature polity. For Macpherson, the economy of nature, or the physical realm, is unquestionably inferior to the economy of culture, the metaphysical realm. If property were wealth for Smith and utility for Bentham and Mill, it was a 'consumable' for Macpherson. Macpherson's ideal economy served as the condition of the evolution of human society beyond the physical realm and the constraints of biological necessity. Place and its 'products' for Macpherson exist only in so far as they are consumed as the basis of the 'right kind of society'.

Macpherson in his utopian vision views dephysicalised property rights, between persons, as being rights, which when properly exercised, offer not only meaningful relations between persons but also a 'fully' meaningful and 'free' life for all persons. Thus in 'retrieving property in line with a reconstructed polity' (Bowrey 1993: 175), Macpherson abstracts the physical into an ideal world of consumption that can then be transcended.

Vandevelde and Macpherson describe a contemporary culture of property in which the status of physical things, most obviously land, has been eroded. The wealth and wellbeing of humans they argue, are determined by property relations through which physical things are consumed not out of necessity, or for their use or exchange values, but so that we may transcend the constraints of materiality and thus attain the abstract ideals of Vandevelde's meaningfulness and Macpherson's social order. The implicit contention of Vandevelde's and Macpherson's theories of property is that the physical realm is the antithesis of meaning and order. This 'highly instrumental view of nature consisting of capital assets – as resources – available for human exploitation . . . is viewed as a necessary pre-requisite to emancipation and self-realisation' (Harvey 2000: 125). In the ideal worlds of Macpherson's self-realisation and Vandevelde's emancipation, the importance of property lies not in physicality, the land, the thing or *realty*. The importance of property lies in what it represents – its abstract political right. The economy of representation in this equation of property has been inverted. Originally, the property right signified the 'thing'. Now the physical 'thing' signifies the property right.

The contemporary theory of property advanced by Vandevelde and Macpherson is one in which the metaphysical meaning, or the signification, of property is more important than the physical 'thing' that is signified. This is the slippery logic of illusion and fetish according to which property signifies no thing at all – an absence. The following section traces the critiques of the concept and institution of dephysicalised property and its signification of absence.

5.3 Thing–thing property

The model of thing–thing property relations is not a development of the concept of dephysicalised property neither is it a concept of rephysicalised property. It is a critique of the concept of dephysicalisation and the model of person–thing and person–person property relations. Central to this critique is the interpretation of dephysicalisation as a process of objectification. According to critiques of dephysicalisation, the concept not only objectifies the 'thing' of property relations, but also the 'person' and ultimately law itself.

The work of the German political theorist Hannah Arendt and the German economic philosopher Karl Marx speaks directly to the abstraction of the physical world, or nature, advanced by Bentham and Hohfeld and apparent in the work of Vandevelde and Macpherson. Importantly, Arendt and Marx include 'persons', or people, within their understanding of nature rather than separating people from nature. Arendt and Marx argue that abstraction is a process of commodification and consumption. Their work situates the concept of dephysicalisation within the broader context of the material and the ideological sustainability of modern property law.

The section then turns to the theory of French philosopher Jean Baudrillard by way of introducing the connection between dephysicalisation and illusion that contemporary theorist Kevin Gray draws and Alain Pottage interrogates. Gray and Pottage approach the idea of the meaninglessness of property as a question of discourse and signification. Although their emphases and conclusions are different, they are both concerned with the difficulty, if not the impossibility, of ever defining what property *is*. Both theorists relate this failure of meaning directly to the dephysicalisation of property. In this way, their work does not posit different or newer ideas of what property is or should be. Superficially, their works mark an increasing awareness and discomfort with the idea of property-as-symbol and with the exhaustion of the values of use and exchange within property discourse. Nevertheless, contemporary property theory most often describes and repeats the paradigm of modern property law rather than interrogates it. Gray's piece is perhaps the best example of this. His theoretical analysis of the meaninglessness of property is by no means obscure or irrelevant to the development of property law. It is precisely this theoretical material that is relied on by the judiciary and by legal educators. The dephysicalisation of property is not, therefore, exclusively theoretical or ideological, it is practised and taught – constructing an unreal reality that is 'as real as real can be' (Kerruish 1999).

5.3.1 Consuming property: Hannah Arendt

Arendt is concerned with the sustainability of dephysicalised property relations. She interrogates the possibility of an unreal reality and in so doing challenges the anthropocentrism of the property theories of Vandevelde and Macpherson. Arendt directs her attention to the person–person model of property and the mutual exclusivity of metaphysical human culture and physical non-human nature. She uses the word 'with' to relate these so-called oppositions, linking the terms together as the 'condition of human life'. Her definition of 'human life' extends beyond the limited political sphere of Vandevelde and Macpherson:

> Without being at home in the midst of things whose durability makes them fit for use and for erecting a world whose very permanence stands in direct contrast to life, this life would never be human.
>
> (Arendt 1958: 135)

Arendt argues that the concept of dephysicalisation is both ideologically and physically unsustainable. She warns against its trajectory toward the commodification of property because the 'explosion of the concept of property' that Vandevelde had argued destroyed the authority of law (Vandevelde 1980: 362) she says has material consequences also. Arendt cautions that the commodification of property 'harbours the grave danger that eventually no object of the world will be safe from consumption and annihilation through consumption' (1958: 132). She argues that the erasure of the physical is a departure from the home of 'being'. Echoing the moral utilitarianism of Mill whose theory of property retained a trace of the physical world for its utility, Arendt argues that 'the man-made home erected on earth and made of the material which earthly nature delivers into human hands, consists not of things that are consumed but things that are used' (1958: 135). The distinction between the property theories of Mill and Arendt is that the agency of nature is negated in Mill's view, whereas Arendt's theory asserts the agency of nature within the vital and mutually defining, person–thing relation.

The sustainability of dephysicalisation concerns Arendt because she views nature as the condition of human life, rather than something that can or should be transcended:

Painless and effortless consumption would not change but only increase the devouring character of biological life until a mankind altogether 'liberated' from the shackles of pain and effort would be free to 'consume' the whole world and to reproduce daily all things it wished to consume. How many things would appear and disappear daily and hourly in the life process of such a society would at best be immaterial for the world, if the world and its thing-character could withstand the reckless dynamism of a wholly motorised life process at all.

(1958: 130)

Arendt's theory presents the real or physical world as inescapable and necessary, but also as enabling rather than constraining and inhibiting. Arendt's critique of dephysicalised property revisits Marx's thesis that the emancipation from labour is emancipation from necessity, which she argues would 'ultimately mean emancipation from consumption as well, that is from the metabolism with nature which is the very condition of human life' (Arendt 1958: 130). Through this alternative approach, Arendt anticipates environmentalist critiques of the property discourse on the basis of their commodification of the physical world. Nevertheless, far from presenting an ecocentric critique of property, Arendt's concept of property still applies the nature/culture dualism of anthropocentric logic, separating humans from non-humans, people from place. Where she departs from the dominant theory of property is that she collapses the hierarchy of the couple, presenting nature as the condition of human life. In this way, Arendt's radical concept of property presents the interactive dependence of culture on nature, and thus argues powerfully against the notion of the cultural transcendence of nature.

5.3.2 Property as fetish: Karl Marx

The idea of an unalienated relationship between people and nature was central to Marx's philosophy of property (Harvey 2000: 126), it was also central to his critique of capitalism and modern property law. Analysing the liberal economy of the nineteenth century, Marx's work is by no means recent and yet it remains strange, even threatening, to law.[2] Marx's ideas of fetish and inversion provoke an interrogation of the purpose of property law, which illuminate and even undermine the authority of that law. They do this by bringing questions of meaning and of logic to the positive discourse of law that seeks to control and define property in terms of its facticity rather than

---

2 Property scholars often follow the tradition of Locke and Marx in addressing the notion of alienation in dephysicalised property in terms of labour. This book does not pursue the question of labour in property. The Marxist critique of alienation is however valuable in thinking through the separation of people and place through property law. See, for example, Dickens (1996).

its normativity. Although the contemporary theories of Gray and Pottage do not take up the ideas of inversion and fetishism directly, their focus on the production of meaning and the functionality of logic in property law echo Marx's themes of fetish and inversion.

The idea of abstraction is an important part of Marx's critique of modern property. Abstraction explains the historical development of the dephysicalised forms of property that Bentham had envisaged. Rather than material things such as land having intrinsic value, as particular and unique places, the demands of changing forms of wealth created quantitative values of land, as spaces or areas (Pottage 1994: 361–384). The quantitative evaluation of a thing, or object, standardised the thing according to other objects, which allowed their comparison and trade. The 'new' forms of property that Bentham was concerned the law should protect to the same degree as 'old' forms of property, such as land, therefore, needed to be comparable and measurable against land, as well as against each other, in order that trade in the newer forms of property could flourish. This process of comparison and measurement effectively dissolved 'the concrete and the particular' (Best 1994: 44) of place. Marx speaks of this change as a movement from qualitative value to quantitative value (Marx 1978: 93). Quantitative value was signified by money. The uniformity of the language of money, which standardised the evaluation of things, became its own logic so that things or objects could only be spoken of, related and exchanged in terms of that language. For Bentham, such abstraction through standardisation and commodification of land was positive for property law because it positivised law.

Marx, however, attended to the normative aspects of commodification, particularly to the means through which abstraction was produced and legitimised. The self-sufficiency and circularity of the language of quantitative evaluation of property could ultimately produce meaning without any reference to 'reality'. In trading stocks and finance capitalism, 'money is made out of money, profit is made through the manipulation of figures with no apparent connection to the commodity world already abstracted from social relations and activity' (Best 1994: 44). As 'real' property and social wealth shifted from land to capital, the physical specificity of place ceased to be part of legal discourse. This allowed the category of 'real' property to untie itself from physicality such that the evaluation of 'things' became an independent logic from the precursor logics of use and exchange. 'Life is lived only in the abstract' because the physical had been 'transcended' and the concrete and particular dissolved (Best 1994: 43–44).

The 'dawn of abstraction' (Best 1994: 42) brought about by dephysicalised forms of property was read by Marx as a form of cultural as well as physical, or natural, loss. Marx's ecological concern was that the dephysicalisation, abstraction and alienation of natural and social realities were inherently unsustainable. Perceiving the materiality of nature and the materiality of human society as organically bound, the process of commodification, he argued, threatened not just a way of life, but life itself: 'Man lives on nature – [this] means that nature is his body with which he must remain in continuous interchange if he is not to die' (Marx 1975a: 276).

Considered against the contemporary idea or theory of biodiversity (see, for example, Takacs 1996), Marx's critique of quantitative evaluation and its abstraction of materiality profoundly disturb modern legal theories of property. This criticism of dephysicalisation, taken seriously, could revalorise real property as a distinct and prior category of law because it suggests that law itself is founded and constituted by materiality. Marx's notion that the abstraction of reality 'turns [subjects and objects] into abstract entities, strips away their unique characteristics and reduces them to a numerical expression' (Best 1994: 44), implies that dephysicalised property law merely administers and enforces an 'economic calculus'. The positivisation of law consequent on the dephysicalisation and commodification of reality makes law itself part of that abstractness. Law seems merely another mechanism for the production, signification and exchange of commodities. As such, the legitimacy of law, which derives precisely from its exteriority to that signification, is undermined. Marx's idea of abstraction directly and specifically confronts the strangeness of dephysicalised property as something that undoes the foundational and authoritative logic of law.

The second key part of Marx's critique of dephysicalised property is his account of what he calls the process of *inversion*. This process, he says, occurs between the abstraction of reality and the fetishisation of that unreality. It is central to Marxist and later to poststructuralist critiques of linguistic, libidinal and logical economies. Modern property relations, Marx says, are between things, not between individuals. Put simply, inversion for Marx is the 'triumph of the economy over its human producers' (Best 1994: 43). The conventional view of property relations is that although there are two terms, the subject (person) coupled with the object (thing), one term is thought to dominate the relationship – the 'person' or subject of property. In economic terms, that hierarchical relationship was articulated as the person's (or subject's) exploitation of the things (or objects) of nature. As described earlier, the person–thing model of property relations was displaced by the person–person model. Marx's counter-reading of that change is that modern property relations are more accurately described by the model of thing–thing. Marx argues that the dephysicalisation of the object or thing has not removed it from property relations at all. He says dephysicalisation has actually commodified both the subject (person) *and* the object (thing). Only quantifiable and standardised objects Marx says exist in this economy:

> Forced to sell his or her labour-power to survive, 'the worker sinks to the level of commodity and becomes indeed the most wretched of

commodities', reduced from the status of qualitative individual to mere exchange value in the form of labour power.

(Marx, cited in Best 1994: 43)

The alienation of the modern worker from nature is to Marx the 'loss of human reality': 'The increase in the quantity of objects is accompanied by an extension in the realm of the alien powers to which man is subjected' (Marx 1978: 93).

The third important aspect of Marx's critique of modern property is his theory of the phenomenon of fetishisation. This theory combines his ideas of abstraction of reality, alienation from nature and inversion of subjects and objects. Marx argued that the conventional basis of modern property, its labour, had been overtaken by the fetishistic logic of the commodity. According to Marx, because the dephysicalisation of property commodifies people as well as place, the purpose of property is therefore neither for people nor their environment, but for the profit or commodity itself (Kerruish 1999). Marx's critique of this economy is not that it exists but that it grows to dominate all social relations: 'Before capitalist society, commodity production existed, but always marginally in relation to other activities' (Best 1994: 43).

By fetishism, Marx means that 'things', abstracted from their physical value, and inverted as commodities, mysteriously acquire lives of their own and come to dominate the lives of their makers (Kerruish 1999). The fetish value of the 'object' or 'thing' of property is greater than its use or exchange value, because it hides the physical conditions of its production. Marx compares the force and illusion of religious and superstitious attitudes to the transcendence of the fetishised object of property in positive legal discourse:

> Fetishism describes the way in which markets conceal social (and we should add geographical) information and relations . . . This was Marx's agenda: to get behind the veil, the fetishism of the market, in order to tell the full story of social reproduction through commodity production and exchange.
>
> (Harvey 2000: 232–233)

Marx's objective was to unveil the 'illusion' and retrieve the knowledge of the physical conditions of economic production.

Marx's critique of modern property asks how property relations are lived and sustained in the material terms of the physical world. He suggests that the (un)reality of the commodity culture is excessive and impossible because it is physically unsustainable. Marx's ideas of concealment, illusion and impossibility are taken up explicitly by both Gray and Pottage through reference to the language and the logic of modern property relations. To better appreciate their analyses, it is worthwhile considering Baudrillard's idea of simulation, which couples Marx's theory of fetishism with structuralist theories of social semiology.

5.3.3 Property as symbolic exchange: Jean Baudrillard

Baudrillard's *Symbolic exchange and death* distinguishes modern and postmodern societies by their relation to commodities (1994: 8–12). According to Baudrillard, modern societies are 'organised around the production and consumption of commodities' whereas postmodern societies are 'organised around simulation and the play of images and signs' (Baudrillard 1994: 8). Baudrillard calls this fetishised economy of signs 'simulation'. In this economy of signs, meaning is made despite the absence of any 'earthly referent'. In hyperreality, 'the object is absorbed altogether into the image' (Best 1994: 51):

> The commodity form has developed to such an extent that use and exchange values have been superseded by 'sign value' that redefines the commodity primarily as a symbol to be consumed and displayed.
>
> (Best 1994: 41)

In contemporary property relations, he says, the primary function of the object or thing is not to signify its physical and material value as a thing for use or exchange. Instead, it is to signify or represent the symbolic value of the thing of property. The dialectic of subject–object, person–thing 'implodes' (Best 1994: 51) because property rights do not signify any physical reality and because physical reality does not exist. Reality is produced by the appearance of itself:

> Abstraction today is no longer the map, the double, the mirror or the concept. Simulation is no longer that of a territory, a referential being, or a substance. It is the generation by models of a real without origin or reality: a hyperreal. The territory no longer precedes the map. Henceforth, it is the map that precedes the territory . . . it is the map that engenders the territory.
>
> (Baudrillard, cited in Best 1994: 50)

For Marx, the phenomenon of fetishism described the way in which markets conceal the conditions of the production of commodities. The semiology of property functioned only as long as the physical was signified as irrelevance and absence, pointing to the omnipresence of law and culture. For Baudrillard, however, in the economy of simulation there is no reality behind the veil of the fetish. The reality is the veil. Whereas in modern property relations, the signifier 'property' had signified the use or exchange of a thing as a resource, in postmodern property relations, the signifier 'property' signifies only itself. The thing in postmodern property discourse 'is represented as the rule of law. It is invested with the qualities of objectivity, impersonality (represented as neutrality) and universality' (Kerruish 1999).

The collapse of the dialectic of subject–object, which had founded positivist, utilitarian and political rights-based theories of property, brings us to a theory of property law as little more than the signification and administration of a property market. The rise of the property market and the increasing importance of the proprietary interests of abstract legal entities such as corporations, indicates the end (or the repression) of earlier (instrumentalist) values of property, particularly the utilitarian and exchange values of the physical. Contemporary property theorists define property as nothing more than the abstract signification of the property right itself. The work of Pottage, Harvey and Gray point to the decreasing significance of the private interests of individuals. In the place of these interests are the abstract interests of corporate institutions. Property law, as the guardian of such institutions, protects the interests of neither persons nor things. Instead, property protects its representation, as an institution.

A good example of the semiotic economy of property law is the standard description of property relations in contemporary real property law textbooks. These accounts ascribe to property law immense importance as the primary legal institution that structures the market economy. Land functions just like any other commodity, students are told, it carries no distinguishing, particular 'physical' features. Strangely, acknowledgment or homage is made to the 'traditional' physical significance of land as property in order to authorise modern 'developments' along the trajectory of dephysicalisation:

> In the twentieth century land has not only continued to serve its traditional role in the production of wealth and in the provision of shelter, but has increasingly become an independent commercial commodity to be bought and sold in the same manner as many other investments.
> (Neave et al. 1999: 429)

The 'traditionally' real and physical significance of land in property law is described as part of an evolution of property. According to this account, a survey along this linear development finds that physical property traditionally valued for use and exchange, 'shelter and wealth', has not been absented or diminished but rather improved into an abstract and thus more malleable species of property. The institutional aura of property in the market culture is the focus of contemporary theorisation of property and jurisprudence broadly. Indeed, 'some would say that *the* major institution in the emergence of the modern law and modern private property is the land market' (Kerruish and Bowrey 1999: 143). But what does it mean to speak of property as an institution? How and why does the 'institution' of property reproduce the dialectic of person–thing, subject–object and real–abstract? These are the questions directly explored in the writing of English property theorist Alain Pottage.

5.3.4 Critiquing the person/thing paradigm: Alain Pottage

In 'Instituting property' (Pottage 1998b: 331), Pottage works through these questions via a review of two recent mainstream works in property law.[3] Both theorists, he argues, approach property as a socio-legal institution without saying how and what that is, as though the signifier connected to the signified. His central point is that neither the term 'property' nor 'institution' is immediately meaningful today and particularly no longer in the undefined sense in which those theorists deploy the terms. Thus he argues, their theories of property as a socio-legal institution do not account for the normativity and facticity of property relations, and use the language of property as though it were clear and meaningful, whereas, he says, it is not.

Pottage approaches contemporary property law as an historically specific discourse that constructs and is constructed by its social culture. He argues that analyses of the 'constructive interpretation of social practices and expectations' that constitute legal principle are absent from these two theorists' works and that, instead, they present property as an institution because they take legal principle to be already 'descriptive of society'. Pottage claims that to speak of property as an institution, without qualification or situation, is an empty and dangerous claim that avoids and conceals the conditions of property and of the rule of law. The 'hollow resonance' of fetishised property produces the sense of 'law's foothold in the factual world, while at the same time closing off the very historical and sociological investigations of the facts which would make that foothold seem less plausible' (Pottage 1998b: 331).

On the one hand, Pottage's critique suggests that behind the claim that property is an institution is nothing at all, that it is simulated: an idea that 'promises more than it can deliver' (1998b: 331). Yet, on the other hand, it is precisely the unexamined 'thing' behind the institutional flag, waved by these property theorists, that motivates his critique. The simultaneous presence and absence of property apparent in Pottage's critique is precisely the uncanny *un*reality that characterises contemporary property discourse. In lifting the veil of the 'institution', he brings into focus the disjuncture between the theory and practice of property. The practice of property disrupts and yet is strangely disguised by the conventional economy of signification that modern property constructs. Property law increasingly augments the 'rights' of abstract corporate bodies (also regarded as 'institutions') as the most 'real' or

3 A review article of Harris (1996) and Penner (1997).

compelling interests warranting the protection of the law. Pottage directly confronts the degree to which the modern corporation disables the conventional person–thing paradigm of property:

> If individual interest cannot be taken as the basic unit of analysis, so that the corporation cannot be seen as an aggregate of individuals, what other units are available? Can the corporation, which is not a thinking, feeling, being, be a coherent unit of analysis? To answer to these questions leads the analysis away from the model of scarcity, and towards an understanding of social processes which cannot be mapped on to 'real' persons and things.
>
> (Pottage 1998b: 339)

But what is significant about this postmodern shift in the subject(ivity) of property posed by the corporation is that the paradigm of person–thing remains not only theoretically, but practically, part of the vocabulary of property law. So while the shift in the practice of property law 'dissolves the category of property as a category of social analysis by dissolving its basic theoretical components', the dissolution itself is peculiarly disguised. For this reason, Pottage argues that to speak of property as an institution is to point to the difficulty of that reality and to actively maintain the strange unreality of contemporary property.

For Pottage, the problem with property is more than the anachronism of its theory set against its practice. It is not only that property theory is 'out of step' (Arendt 1992: 25) with property culture. Pottage claims that the dephysicalisation of property makes property strange because this process, which 'has so decisively overtaken the conditions in which property categories were formed', fundamentally ruptures the logic of property (Pottage 1998b: 110). The failure or dysfunction of its logic therefore presents a crisis in its ability to mean. The dephysicalisation of property has arrested meaning because 'the vocabulary of property is animated by operations which cannot be described in terms of that vocabulary'.

Pottage directly critiques the contemporary operation and validity of the subject/object vocabulary of modern property theory in his article, 'Persons and things: an ethnographic analogy' (2001: 112–138). Here he examines recent anthropological work specifically with regard to the logical and economic structures of different paradigms of property. Approaching property this way, Pottage offers property theory the depth he argues is missing from the mainstream theories he had earlier reviewed:

> The 'facts' apprehended by Harris and Penner remain facts as they are fictionalised by legal categories. These categories impose an oversimplified model of 'society' and its components. Where a sociological or socio-theoretical perspective reveals a complex fabric of discursive roles

and representations, property theory offers only a simple ontology of persons and things.

(Pottage 1998b: 337)

The theoretical framework of both person–thing and person–person models of property relations present the individual person as the subject of property law. Pottage's critique of this framework is based on the changed function of property law. Whereas for Blackstone, Bentham and even Hohfeld, property law protected the rights of subjects, as individual persons, for Pottage, property law protects the rights of abstract entities and organisations, such as corporations. Following Kelsen, Pottage argues that to speak of a property right as protecting the interests of a person is to obscure the function of that right as the protection of a particular economic value:

If the subjectivity elicited by subjective right is merely an instrument for the realisation of legal or economic objectives, the subject soon dissolves into the insubstantial shadow of the right. That was Kelsen's point in suggesting that the category of the 'real' subject was logically or strategically necessary, but experientially empty.

(Pottage 2001: 120)

The admission that the subject/object framework of modern property is meaningless or 'empty' does not indicate that property no longer exists, but rather that its existence is symbolic rather than substantial. The function of contemporary property law is to maintain the *appearance* of the modern logic without the economy of that logic. In doing so property law 'amplifies an ambivalence in commodity logic in which "things and persons assume the social form of things"' (Strathern, cited in Pottage 2001: 120). Again it is clear that this understanding of property as a thing–thing relation is not equivalent to its rephysicalisation. On the contrary, Pottage's critique of modern property, following Marx, regards dephysicalisation as the abstraction of persons and things alike. The problem, he argues, is that the 'legal boundary between persons and things, rather like that between nature and culture, is no longer self-evident' (Pottage and Mundy 2004: 2). In a world where property rights are claimed in human tissue, gametes and embryos by pharmaceutical corporations, Pottage sees the boundary or division between persons and things as little more than a semantic exercise that the law has taken up: 'Humans are *neither* person *nor* thing, or simultaneously person *and* thing, so that law quite literally *makes* the difference' (Pottage and Mundy 2004: 5).

5.3.5 Instituting illusion: Kevin Gray

English legal scholar Kevin Gray published an oft cited article 'Property in thin air' in 1991 which recalls Marx's critique that the paradigm of modern property law is 'the illusion of jurisprudence' (Marx 1975b: 142). Gray's article is devoted to exposing the strange lack of clarity around the idea of property. Positioning his own perspective outside this common opacity, Gray solves the problem and identifies the culprit. In one crystalline sentence, Gray identifies contemporary property not as an historical development but as a misunderstanding: 'Property is not theft – it is fraud' (Gray 1991: 252). The point is that property is not something but the lack or absence of that thing. If property were about theft, then it would be about the *possession* of a thing. But the association of fraud and property conceptualises property as a symbol or sign of a thing where really there is nothing. In law as in regular usage, fraud is 'advantage gained by unfair means, as by false representation of fact made knowingly' (Macquarie Dictionary 1992). If property is fraud, then it is a representation of unreality and the law is the agent of that (mis)-representation. The point of this comparison highlights the role of property in the culture of simulation that Baudrillard had theorised. Fraudulent representation, like simulation, breaks the connection between signifier and signified, representation and referent.

Opening with the seemingly radical admission that property is 'mere illusion', Gray seeks to avoid replicating the scholarly tradition of 'sidestepping' the 'unattainable quality inherent in the notion of private property'. Gray exposes the unfixedness, the subtleties and the variations of property. Our relation to property, Gray argues, is a relationship of desire, of lack. We are 'beguiled' and 'seduced' by its appearance. But it is only an appearance. The implication is that 'in reality' property does not exist.

'What constitutes the "propertiness" of property?' (1991: 259) Gray asks. Having travelled the ideas of visual trespass and physically non-excludable resources from moral and legal perspectives, Gray reaches his conclusion headed ' "Property" is a relative concept'. Here he insists that defining property is impossible because it is a dynamic un-thing (1991: 295–296). The reason that property is an illusion Gray says, is because it is not 'itself a thing' but a 'concentration of power over things' (1991: 299). Property is not real it is abstract: a signification of a complex power relationship. Gray's inquiry is a bold admission of 'deep scepticism about the meaning and terminology of property' (1991: 305). His concern suggests that the elusiveness of the concept of property is part and product of its moral function and operation. Property 'in all its conceptual fragility, is but a shadow of the individual and collective human response to a world of limited resources and attenuated altruism' (Gray 1991: 307). Property has changed from a person–thing relationship, to the illusion or fantasy of the thing.

5.4 Conclusion

Both modern and contemporary property theories abstract the physical and insist that property signifies something else and possibly nothing at all. Whether a thing is a resource, a utility, or a sign of a commodity, it is intrinsically immaterial in property theory. Describing property as an illusion, as something determined only through an economy of signs, undermines the role and rule of law as an objective and original body of logic. The available role of law then is either to defraud its 'subjects' or to pragmatically administer and maintain the competing interests of the market. Either way the weakening of the rule of law present fundamental challenges to mainstream fetishised representations of property law: 'The corporate system has taken the place of the institution of private property in the economic organisation of capitalism' (Kerruish 1999).

Furthermore, because as Vandevelde, Macpherson and Gray have argued, property relations are relations of power, to speak of property-as-illusion is to conceal the very real, material consequences of the distribution of that power (see Cotterrell 1986). Land, for example, remains actually possessed even if it is exchanged and alienated in abstract terms. Thus while the idea of property-as-illusion is theoretical, it enacts that idea *physically*, that is, in a way that is neither abstract nor meaningless: 'However unreal social reality was becoming under the fetish of the commodity it was also actual' (Kerruish 1999). There are material consequences of the theory of dephysicalised property:

> 'Things' may be intangible; they are no less created as things by conceptualisation and exchangeability. It is certainly a consequence of the dynamic of wealth that forms of property less-connected to wealth creation than to use in everyday life tend to be seen as consumer goods, to be protected by consumer rather than property law, or in the case of Aboriginal ideas of property to be virtually unprotected and increasingly seen as non-proprietary.
>
> (Kerruish 1999)

Chapter 6

Placelessness in contemporary practices

Scientists have not generally needed or wanted to be philosophers. Indeed, normal science usually holds creative philosophy at arm's length.

(Kuhn 1996: 88)

[S]cience students accept theories on the authority of teacher and text, not because of evidence. What alternatives have they, or what competence? The applications given in texts are not there as evidence but because learning them is part of learning the paradigm at the base of current practice.

(Kuhn 1996: 80)

6.1 Introduction

Dephysicalisation, the contemporary legal expression of the nature/culture paradigm, is not just a theory – it is a practice. The theory that property is an illusion is practised and materialised by the ownership, use and management of land. The theory, practice and pedagogy of property law, say that place is irrelevant. That irrelevance is tangibly evident. Land ownership is strongly related to land use. It is important therefore to consider the concept of dephysicalisation that defines modern property law in terms of both the ownership and the use of land. In the eighteenth to nineteenth centuries, as discussed earlier, to encourage industrial-scale agricultural and pastoral productivity, the British Crown used the mechanism of dephysicalised property to transfer land to private individuals and companies in her colonies through land grants, the facilitation of land markets and the encouragement or admission of landhunting/squatting. At the beginning of the twenty-first century, over 60% of the land in the United States is privately owned (Lubowski et al. 2006: 35) and over 63% of the land in Australia is privately leased or owned (Australian Bureau of Statistics 2000). The majority of privately owned land is used for agriculture and grazing. 60% of the Australian land mass is used for agriculture (Australian Bureau of Statistics 2000). Fifty-two percent of the US land mass is used for agriculture and 35% for grazing (Lubowski et al. 2006: 35). What this means is that well over half the land mass of these two nations is held or owned by farmers. How these landowners (or landholders)[1] relate to their land is irrelevant to property law. Precisely because property law excludes the physical world and its systems from its discourse, another area of law has become increasingly and rapidly important in regulating land use and ownership – environmental law. Environmental law starts where property ends, not as a different set of values about place, not even as a law about place, but as a quarantined section of law that addresses problems and disputes concerning the physical aspects of land ownership that property law does not accommodate. Where property law determines who owns the land, environmental law determines the ways in which that ownership can and cannot be manifest. Dephysicalisation is not therefore simply a theorist's concept, it is a paradigm of people–place relations that lawyers practice, pedagogues repeat and landowners make real. Theorists claim property is an illusion, but the land and its many systems, are real.

Lawyers and legal educators, like scientists, generally distance themselves from philosophy or, more specifically, from legal theory. Their principal concern is practice. The separation of theory from practice is dichotomous rather than differential and, like other dualisms, the terms are hierarchically related. Also like other dualisms, the distinction is blurred and transgressed. The claim that practitioners and pedagogues often make that theory can be set aside or that it does not inform the practice of law is as contentious as the claim that theory is law's thinktank while practitioners are mere administrators. The various theories of property-as-thing, as-commodity, as-fetish and as-illusion presented in the previous chapter all point to the profoundly dephysicalised culture of contemporary real property law and the diminished value of place or nature. The relationship between theory and practice is not unilateral. Theory neither leads nor reflects the practice of law; they work together as legal discourse. Similarly, law neither leads nor reflects the socio-political practice of property ownership; they too work together as a cultural discourse. Cultural discourse prescribes, regulates and enables cultural practices, which, in relation to property law, transform land into landscape and ecologies into economies. This chapter explores how the theory of dephysicalisation, which underpins the paradigm of modern property law, is practised and taught.

Legal and cultural discourses both describe property as a relation between persons, or between the relative rights of persons. The second section in this chapter, 'Legal practice', explores two ways in which legal discourse protects

---

1 In Australia, the doctrines of tenure and estates mean that land is held of the Crown. Significant agricultural and pastoral land is leased from the Crown. The term landholder is, therefore, used to be more precise but the term landholder will be used predominantly in the chapter for the sake of convenience.

and perpetuates the notion of dephysicalised property in the practice and pedagogy of law. In legal practice, property is regarded in terms of 'rights' that are always exchangeable and alienable. The objective of courts is to measure competing rights against each other rather than to explore questions pertaining to the physical contexts of land use. The loss, taking or acquisition of property by governments is also debated not in terms of the loss, taking or acquisition of actual, physical property, but of the right to the commercial benefits of property. The underlying idea of property in these cases is property as a commodity, the loss of which is compensable because a commodity is fungible. The thing of the property relation in these cases, the land for example, has no intrinsic value. Anglophone courts pronounce the places over which disputes are fought to be irrelevant to their decisions. In cases such as *Yanner*,[2] *Newcrest*[3] and *Lucas*,[4] courts swiftly transform disputes about physical land use practices into disputes over abstract property rights.

The section then briefly explores the way in which property is defined and taught in law schools. The dominant line of legal education is that, with the exception of the law of native title and Indigenous people's property interests, place is largely irrelevant and absent from the paradigm of property law. Land is presented to law students principally as an object of property relations between persons. Indeed, it is only if and where the history of colonisation and dispossession of Indigenous people's lands and property rights are taught that concepts of place emerge at all. However, these lessons can essentialise Indigenous people's relations to place and cast people–place relationships in terms of the nature/culture paradigm, which denies the integrity and connectivity of Indigenous laws and relationships with 'country'. Such a perspective on Indigenous property laws and relations prohibits (predominantly) non-Indigenous law students from understanding the dependence of 'culture' on 'nature' and thereby repeats and affirms the paradigm of placelessness in modern property law: 'The frog's illusion is in not seeing its own vulnerability, that it is the same as all the other animals, contained by laws of creation and affected in the same thirsty way when wells run dry' (Watson 2002: 266).

The third section, 'Cultural practice', explores how some cultural discourses maintain and others challenge the concept of dephysicalised property law through the lived experience of proprietorship and custodianship of land. The section begins by exploring the way in which land ownership and land use practices are invariably expressed in terms of the strict vocabulary of people: the rights of proprietorship. Farmers' associations and property

---

2 *Yanner v Eaton* (1999) 201 CLR 351.
3 *Newcrest Mining (WA) Limited v Commonwealth* (1997) 190 CLR 513.
4 *Lucas v South Carolina Coastal Council* 505 US 1003 (1992).

rights lobby groups represent the interests of a small but powerful group of proprietors and lessees. What property is, to them, is a right to own and enjoy property-as-commodity, which includes a right to be compensated for the loss of that commodity. The relationship between such proprietors and their lands is principally determined by the commodity value of that property. Expressions such as 'battling the land' (Linn 1999) that appear to admit the physical into cultural discourse are directly connected to the value of land as commodity. The land is 'battled' to release its marketable goods. In Australia, for example, farmers are the iconic 'Aussie battlers'. In the United States, property developers battle for their 'right' to either develop or be compensated in terms of freedom and citizenship. These different cultural identities are an unequivocal expression of their function, as individuals, in an equation of property. Their ownership depends on their ability, as proprietors, to appropriate, subdue and turn profit from physical things as commodities.

Against the dominant cultural discourse of ownership as proprietorship and entitlement to profit, dissident voices, Indigenous and non-Indigenous, describe ownership as a responsibility rather than a right. Importantly, their perspectives emphasise the role of knowledge in the law and ethics of ownership. For them, and in different ways, the notion of losing property means losing place, something that is incompensable because it is not an abstract right but a real and physical relationship within a network, or ecology, of life. Non-Indigenous landowner Bob Purvis offers a critique of the dominant discourse and practice of dephysicalised property in relation to the pastoral industry. In interviews with landscape scholar Jim Sinatra, Purvis refers to the maladaptation of Australian property law as being responsible for the 'destruction of this country' which he says affects him 'deeply' (Sinatra and Murphy 1999: 67). Non-Indigenous farmer Peter Andrews offers a critique of dephysicalised property in the context of land use also; in particular, he critiques farming practices that he regards as destructive: 'Farmers go out, clear their land, plough it up and believe that's the right way to farm, the right way to increase production. The reality is it's the way to stop production' (Andrews 2006: 7). For both Purvis and Andrews, ownership requires responsibility for using the land in a way that observes, understands and responds to the particularities of the land itself. Specifically, both farmers speak about the need to read the land in terms of its existence as a network of systems and relationships rather than as a blank slate.

Paddy Roe, Aboriginal Australian lawman and guardian of the Lurujarri Trail in Western Australia, provides an example of resistance to the dominant discourse of ownership and dephysicalised property. Roe describes ownership as being a part of the land. For Roe, the paradigm of modern property law is effectively 'killing this country' – which he says means also 'killing the people. We all go down together' (Sinatra and Murphy 1999: 11). The mutual relationship between people and place is also articulated by native title claimants. Significantly, the law abstracts this physical relationship into a matter of cultural identity. While the relationship between people and place is important to the cultural identity of Aboriginal communities, as the custodians express this relationship, it is also about the *health of the land* itself. One of the subversive questions posed by native title cases is whether property, or ownership, affects the land itself or whether it is only a contest of rights between people and cultures. Yorta Yorta woman Monica Morgan argues that the latter view misunderstands the importance of the relationship between property and place. She says that if the local Indigenous knowledge about place and 'protecting country' is not sought, understood and acted on then everyone, Indigenous and non-Indigenous, will 'lose' because no human community and law can live independently of place (Weir 2009: 148). Ownership for Morgan and Roe is articulated in terms of a mutual and reciprocal economy of responsibilities for 'country' rather than a unilateral economy of rights in land and its 'resources'.

Together, legal and cultural discourses of property reproduce and put into practice the concept of dephysicalisation. The paradigm of nature/culture expressed by modern property law is not, however, universal in space and time. This chapter attempts to demonstrate its contingency on particular and con-tested practices. Specifically, the chapter focuses on the relationship between property and place in terms of entitlement, responsibility, knowledge and connectivity.

6.2 Legal practice

In the whole of Australia, for example, there are only one or two aca-demic teachers of real value in real property, in contracts or in torts, yet there are about seventeen law schools. One finds a number of law schools without a single member of staff capable of teaching equity. There are, to be sure, multitudes of academic homunculi who scribble and prattle endlessly about such non-subjects as criminology, bail, poverty, consum-erism, computers and racism. These may be dismissed from calculation: they possess neither practical skills nor legal learning. They are failed sociologists.

(Meagher, cited in Bates 1984: 181)

Teachers of 'real value in real property' according to Roderick Meagher, QC, are teachers who provide law students with sufficient knowledge of property to practise law. He juxtaposes and prioritises 'practical skills (and) legal learning' to a theoretical or 'sociological' skills base. In doing this, he draws on a familiar opposition between theory and practice, theory and reality. It is in the practical sphere or in reality, Meagher would argue, that one would expect to find definitive and current concepts of real property. The real business of law takes place in the courtroom and it is here that the values of real property are found and managed. Maureen Cain (1994) and

David Sugarman (1994) take up this point, but from very different perspectives, in their work on lawyers, business and social order. Cain presents the power of legal practitioners to define law as a licence to create law's truths rather than as a genius's access to truth:

> Lawyers are translators – that is their day-to-day chore. They are also *creators* of the language into which they translate . . . To think for the first time, a debenture share, say, is a creative act . . . It is in this sense that lawyers are conceptive ideologists.
>
> (Cain, cited in Sugarman 1994: 119)

If we agree, in part, with Meagher, Cain and Sugarman that the practice of law is also the location of its realities and truths, then to better understand the 'real value' or ideology of place in real property law, we should look to the decisions of the courts and especially the highest courts. The contemporary definition of real property as 'elusive' and 'meaningless' must achieve its authority in the courtroom. How do the US Supreme Court and the Australian High Court define real property? What are the values of property articulated in their definitions? What relationships between people and place do they recognise and legitimate? The discourse of property as 'rights' that dominates contemporary jurisprudence is evident in the discussion of the following case law. The cases also demonstrate the struggle of the courts to connect property to the physical world.

6.2.1 Practice of law

Legal scholar Brad Sherman has argued that intellectual property in plants and botanical innovation highlights the dysfunction of the concept of dephysicalised property in contemporary legal practice. Modern patent law, he observes, removes or 'decontextualises' the invention from its material conditions to facilitate the tradability and commercial benefit of that invention (2008: 565). The problem with the separation of the invention from its material conditions, in the case of plants and botanical innovation, is that this is not, actually, possible. Sherman says that a more accurate and viable approach is one in which the 'plant inventions' are regarded in the context of the 'informational and material environments in which they are generated' (2008: 565). The reason for this, he says, is that:

> [T]he environment is not something that is simply external to the object. Instead the environment enters the constitution of the entity: it is folded into and becomes part of the object in question.
>
> (Sherman 2008: 565)

From a biological perspective, the obviousness of this point is clear, but the fact that it is made for lawyers and legal scholars, in one of the most eminent law journals in the Anglophone world, indicates the extent to which materiality is neither the source nor the condition of modern property law. The ubiquity and power of the paradigm of placelessness and the concept of dephysicalised property is sufficient for the scholar to explain to fellow scholars and practitioners precisely how and why patents in plants (as decontextualised objects) are problematic.

A case that well demonstrates the way in which the concept of dephysical-ised property has become central to legal practice is the Australian High Court case of *Yanner v Eaton*.[5] In 1994, the appellant, Murrandoo Yanner, a member of the Gunnamulla clan of the Gangalidda tribe, using a traditional harpoon, killed and took two juvenile estuarine crocodiles from Cliffdale Creek near the Gulf of Carpentaria, Australia. Yanner held neither a licence nor a permit under the Fauna Conservation Act 1974 (Qld) to do so. Con-sequently, he was charged with breaching s 54(1)(a) of the Act, which pro-hibited a person taking, keeping or attempting to take or keep prescribed species of protected fauna without a licence. Yanner argued that being a traditional owner of the land, he was entitled to exercise his native title right to hunt without a licence, on the basis of s 211 of the Native Title Act 1993 (Cth). Section 211 provided that the law did not prohibit native title holders from carrying on activities that were otherwise prohibited by state law where those activities were for non-commercial and communal needs and were an enjoy-ment of native title rights and interests. The respondent argued that Yanner's native title right had been extinguished by s 7(1) of the Fauna Conservation Act, which states that 'all fauna . . . is the property of the Crown'.

The question before the Australian High Court was whether the Fauna Conservation Act was subject to native title rights. In answering this question, the meaning of the word 'property' in the Fauna Conservation Act, which was not defined therein, became the subject of judicial analysis (at 365–368). The court decided by a majority of 5:2 that Yanner was entitled to exercise his native title right to hunt without licence otherwise required by state law. The decision was taken with direct reference to the question of the definition of 'property'. Both the majority and the minority judgments deployed the theories of property discussed in the previous chapter.

Gleeson CJ, Gaudron, Kirby and Hayne JJ turned first to Bentham, stating that: 'Property does not refer to a thing; it is a description of a legal relation-ship with a thing. It refers to a degree of power that is recognised in law as power permissibly exercised over the thing' (at 365–366). Like Bentham and Hohfeld, their Honours note that 'false thinking' about property mistakenly takes property itself to be a 'thing'. To emphasise the point they quote English legal scholar Kevin Gray (1991: 299) repeating the idea that property

---

5 *Yanner v Eaton* (1999) 201 CLR 351.

is a 'legally endorsed concentration of power over things and resources' (at 366). Their honours note that 'Bentham recognised this long ago' (at 366). But they go further, saying that although property is '[u]sually . . . treated as a "bundle of rights" . . . even this may have its limits as an analytical tool or accurate description' (at 366). Their Honours recognise and quote Gray's point that 'the ultimate fact about property is that it does not really exist: it is mere illusion' (at 366). Consequently, the majority decided that because property is elusive, its meaning unfixed, it is impossible to simply assume the meaning of the word 'property' in the legislation and so it must be analysed.

Gummow J also recognised and quoted Hohfeld's point that the word 'property' is 'a striking example of the inherent ambiguity and looseness in legal terminology' (at 388). Gummow J also argued that because the meaning of 'property' is unclear in the legislation, it 'then becomes a question of statutory or constitutional interpretation' (at 389). Gummow J 'interprets' the meaning of property with regard to Hohfeld's definition that 'property comprised legal relations not things, and those sets of legal relations need not be absolute or fixed' (at 389). His interpretation of the term 'property' is consistent with the concept of dephysicalised property in which property is the 'aggregate of legal relations' (at 389).

On the basis that the meaning of 'property' is not fixed in law and that the legislation itself does not specify its meaning, the majority argued property is a right that can only be defined 'without preconceptions about the intention with which certain words are used' (Lane 2000: 17). The majority held that, while the crocodiles were the property of the Crown as set out by the Act, 'property' did not mean full beneficial ownership to the exclusion of all others. They thus rejected the contention by the respondent that the Fauna Conservation Act had extinguished the native title right to hunt exercised by Yanner.

The minority also reach their conclusion directly by reference to the definition of 'property'. But McHugh and Callinan JJ, in separate judgments, explicitly rejected the analytical approach adopted by the majority in finding their definition of property. McHugh J says that property is neither elusive nor unfixed. Furthermore, he says, statute law is not open to interpretation: 'Words in legislative instruments should not be read as if they were buildings on a movie set – structures with the appearance of reality but having no substance behind them' (at 376).

Just when it seems the actual physical world of land or relationships to land will make an appearance in the High Court, it does not. The potential for a new view is undermined at the moment of its very opening. Property, McHugh J says, is power. Power to alienate a thing and exclude all others from it. In other words, as the respondents contended, property means full beneficial ownership: 'Property . . . describes a relationship between owner and object by reference to the power of the owner to deal with the object to the exclusion of all others, except a joint owner' (at 376).

Callinan J repeats the positivist approach of McHugh, but even less elaborately. For Callinan J, the meaning of property in the Act is 'ordinary and natural' (at 406). His bluntness is noteworthy: 'The Act uses the word "property" without qualification. If something less than absolute ownership were intended then an appropriate qualification in that regard could be expected to have been expressed' (at 404).

Absolute ownership is something English law never gave under the doctrines of tenure and estates and in the context of the overlapping rights of equitable interests. Callinan J disregards the long and complex history of property's qualifications in English law in order to exclude yet more qualifications of ownership, in this case, native title interests. Callinan J defines property through reference to broader cultural discourses of individualism and freedom, but he conceals his cultural attachments beneath a veil of positivism. His recourse to techniques of statutory application seemingly alleviates the need to analyse the meaning of property. Callinan J echoes the concerns of Vandevelde, that the abstractness or looseness of the meaning of 'property' makes it a political choice and thus undermines the authority of the rule of law. Unlike Vandevelde, however, Callinan J does not seem to recognise that his own 'choice' of law is political because his positivism conceals a mythology of property unsupported in the historical development of law. While he may believe this saves law from politics and social relations, in fact, this approach avoids confronting the construction of property law as relative rights.

Australian barrister Patricia Lane argues that *Yanner v Eaton* is a radical development in property law: 'The decision highlights the new analysis of rights and interests in land that is required as a result of recognising rights derived from traditional Indigenous connection' (Lane 2000: 17). The novel aspect of the case is not, however, its definition of property. Property remains in this case what it has been since the time of Bentham – abstract rights. The 'new analysis' is perhaps an acknowledgement that property regulates and prescribes social order and that this order has been (slightly) modified. Whether the 'new analysis' of property rights draws the court into an inappropriate political process, as Vandevelde and Callinan J might have argued, the 'new analysis' does not engage the court in an evaluation of non-Indigenous values or relations to land. Rather, it translates real and in this case physical traditional Indigenous relations between people and place, into abstract legal rights.

Australian legal scholar Lisa Strelein notes that in this case 'the High Court returned to the spiritual aspects of Indigenous people's connection to the land' (Strelein 2009: 47). She quotes Gummow J (at 382): 'The conduct of the appellant is inadequately identified in terms of the statutory definition of "take" and its components such as "hunt". What was involved was the manifestation by the appellants of the beliefs, customs and laws of his community.'

The oppositional logic of metaphysical/physical at work here separates, rather than integrates spiritual and economic practices. The totemic significance of the crocodile to Yanner exceeds the neat bifurcated categories of people–place relations as either economic or spiritual. His Honour regards the expression of Yanner's actions as 'taking' and 'hunting' as inadequate perhaps because these are physical activities that often have only economic significance attached to them and perhaps because of a narrow interpretation of the significance of economic practices. To view Yanner's actions as a manifestation of 'beliefs, customs and laws' elevates them to the metaphysical realm. *Yanner v Eaton* maintains the core anthropocentric value of property law – that property is not about things and the physical world – and if it is about the physical world then it is only for metaphysical reasons. Certainly the case does indicate the willingness of courts to 'recognise' 'new' forms of property and 'other' relationships of property, but it nonetheless converts these into its preexisting and Anglocentric discourse of abstract rights. The 'real business' of property law, as these cases demonstrate, is that property is a 'loose' matter of choosing between rights, not practices and relationships.

In *Yanner*, the court concealed questions of place and land use beneath the veil of statutory interpretation and a struggle to discover the technical meaning of property itself. Conveniently, questions of place and land use were easily elevated to questions of abstract rights in the realm of culture. But in other case law the task of absenting questions of place and land use can be more difficult because the dispute over the property right in question is not between different cultural values of property but between different 'natural' or environmental values of property. An increasingly large body of case law specifically debates questions of the 'natural' or environmental value of property. These are the cases that deal with claims to compensation for the acquisition or taking of property rights by rights holders where their right has not been acquired or taken in the legal terms of title, but in the economic terms of land use.

Across the English-speaking world, increasing environmental regulation of land use on privately held land is debated in terms of the economic and political value of property. The values of property as profit and as liberty dominate both scholarly and popular literature on 'regulatory takings'. The public and private dualism is redrawn in these disputes, invariably framing the analysis in terms of cost allocation. The difficulty with the public/private framing of such disputes is that it maintains the unilateral dynamic of people–place relations that is embedded within the idea of property as right. Because people–place relations in modern property law are regarded as one-way flows of profits from things to people, a 'cost' to the rights holder without 'compensation' contradicts that dynamic. Modern legal discourse does not countenance the possibility of reciprocity between people and place, much less obligation or responsibility of people to place. The public/private frame converts responsibility into a one-off cost, which is then allocated and paid, rather than learned and practised as part of an ongoing relationship with and in place.

Property law excludes place from its discourse because it claims to regulate the ownership of the right, not the use of the thing over which that right is exercised. Yet as *Yanner* showed, property law does regulate land use, even if it frames those questions in terms of ownership and translates people–place relations and land use practices into entitlement and rights. Environmental law, by contrast, defines itself as the regulation of land use (Farrier, Lyster and Pearson 1999: xii). Even so, it denies that it directly prescribes how to use the land; rather it resolves disputes by recourse to administrative law:

> Environmental law sets up legal frameworks within which public officials decide between competing uses of land. The law hardly ever tells them what decisions to make and rarely tells them that they *must* exercise the powers which they are given to protect the environment.
>
> (Farrier et al. 1999: xii)

Like property law, environmental law regards the natural environment anthropocentrically, 'seeing the environment as a "resource" to be used by human beings' (Farrier et al. 1999: 1). The core difference between the two separate areas of law is that private property protects the rights of owners with regard to their land-as-property, while environmental law limits those rights, as particular uses of land-as-environment. As such there are tensions between property law and environmental law. English legal scholars Sean Coyle and Karen Morrow argue that:

> The belief that the powers and rights of an owner to use land in prescribed ways might be *inherently* subject to community-directed obligations to nurture and protect the natural environment is a direct challenge to the assumption that the terminology of rights is the appropriate one to use to describe the complex relationship of property between persons and land.
>
> (Coyle and Morrow 2004: 10)

Australian legal scholars, Farrier et al. note that because the function of private property often requires the 'development' and sometimes the 'destruction' of the natural environment, it clashes with the objectives of environmental law. Once the government has transferred Crown land into private ownership it becomes 'politically more difficult to regulate land use' because it is 'likely to be confronted with demands from owners that their "private property" rights should be respected' (Farrier et al. 1999: 10). Private property rights are considered fundamental rights in cultural and legal discourse: 'Rights-talk is embedded in our legal, moral and political culture' (Coyle and Morrow 2004: 10). Property and environmental laws are not therefore different and equal laws; they are ordered by the priority of property rights:

> The issue of how to persuade or require private landholders and lease-holders to use and manage their lands in ways which are at least compatible with the interests of environmental protection is one of the most intractable problems faced by environmental policy-makers today.
>
> (Farrier et al. 1999: 11)

The argument that Farrier et al. advance against the priority of property rights is that the rights of the public should not be secondary to the rights of private proprietors and leaseholders. It is an argument common to environmentalist critiques of property law and the culture of private proprietorship. It is an argument whose basis seems not to have diminished; on the contrary, it had strengthened, despite the rise of environmental law and environmental awareness in cultural discourse. American legal scholar Joseph Sax laments that even after 40 years of environmental law in the United States:

> [I]t is a chastening fact that the phrase 'rights of the public' . . . is as rare as an endangered species in American environmental jurisprudence, as rare as the phrase 'rights of the private property owner' is commonplace.
>
> (Sax 2008: 16)

The juxtaposition of private and public property, however, seems not to approach people–place relations differently. Rather, their emphases differ only on the appropriate party to the property relation – person or greatest number. Often, environmentalist critiques of legal and cultural discourses of property echo the anthropocentric utilitarian theories of property. Farrier et al., for example, cite Mill in the explication of the public or community rights critique of private property:

> When the 'sacredness of property' is talked of, it should always be remembered, that any such sacredness does not belong in the same degree to landed property. No man made the land. It is the original inheritance of the whole species. Its appropriation is wholly a question of general expediency. When private property in land is not expedient, it is unjust.
>
> (1999: 12)

Mill's notion of people–place relations is expressed in the language of inheritance, appropriation and proprietorship. For Mill, place is a resource that must be enjoyed 'expediently'. The hierarchy of the nature/culture paradigm is unquestioned and indeed a separation of the terms and their realms is implicit in Mill's critique. People are not a part of nature. In drawing from Mill, Farrier et al. indicate how environmental law operates within the same conceptual framework as property law. The discourse of property is fundamentally a discourse of separation and subordination of nature from culture. Environmental law emphasises it according to a different social ideal. The difference of emphasis between them hinges on their definition of human agency. Both laws are constituted by the idea of human agency, but in property law, agency is expressed as entitlement or 'rights', whereas in environmental law it is expressed as duty or 'responsibilities'. Thus when Farrier et al. argue '[W]e cannot leave decisions about land use solely in the hands of landholders claiming the right to do with their land what they please' (1999: 12), they are not arguing against or outside the rights discourse, rather they wish to redistribute those rights and redefine its terms.

The restriction of a property right on environmental grounds is thought to diminish its 'propertyness' and in some cases is described as the 'sterilisation' or 'loss' of the property. Section 51 (xxxi) of the Australian Commonwealth Constitution provides that the acquisition of property affected by government legislation or regulation should be made on 'just terms', which may include compensation. The problem for lawyers, however, is drawing the line between the regulation and the acquisition of property (Gray 2007: 175). Where, in fact, in terms of legal title, no property has been acquired (or 'taken') by the government, lawyers may argue that property has been taken de facto by the restriction of use. Minor and common restrictions of private property rarely form the basis of compensation. However, where the restrictions arguably amount to the same thing as the acquisition or taking of the property then a case may be made. The concepts of 'taking' and 'acquisition' in the American and Australian case law present us not only with a definition of property, but with the reminder of its purpose in contemporary law and culture. The purpose of property is the provision of profit through surplus production, as the case of *Newcrest* reveals: 'For what is land but the profits thereof?' (Coke's *Institutes*, cited in Sax 2008: 14).

The idea that property is sterilised or lost by restriction of its use directly contradicts the notion that property law is not about land use or 'things'. This is precisely the contradiction that *Newcrest* illustrates. In *Newcrest Mining (WA) Limited v Commonwealth*[6] the majority of the Australian High Court upheld the contention of the appellants, the mining company Newcrest, that its property rights (mining leases) at Coronation Hill adjacent to the Kakadu National Park were 'sterilised' by government legislation, the National Parks and Wildlife Conservation Act 1975 (Cth), which prohibited 'operations for the recovery of minerals' in the park. The property right itself had not been acquired by the government. The claim to compensation

6 *Newcrest Mining (WA) Limited v Commonwealth* (1997) 190 CLR 513.

was made out against the regulation of land use that effectively rendered the property right worthless because it was profitless. Kirby J's (majority) judgment equated property rights to human rights saying (at 660):

> Ordinarily, in a civilised society, where private property rights are protected by law, the government, its agencies or those acting under the authority of law may not deprive a person of such rights without a legal process which includes provision for just compensation. While companies such as the appellants may not, as such, be entitled to the benefit of very fundamental human right ... (the Australian Constitution) extends to protect the basic rights of corporations as well as individuals.

Australian legal scholar Karla Sperling argues that this 'preoccupation with property rights . . . limits the ability of the government to act in the public interest through planning and environmental law' (1997: 431). The High Court found in *Newcrest* that the land use restrictions undermined the appellant's property rights, which must be compensated. The fact of compensation reaffirms not only the value of property as a right to a profit, but reaffirms the role of the court in establishing the primacy of property rights and rights holders in legal and cultural discourse:

> It was, almost by definition, the property owners who used courts and it was in the resolution of their disputes that the common law was formed. So the whole climate and ideology of the law stressed private property, its uses and transactions.
>
> (McAuslan, cited in Sperling 1997: 428)

The centrality of property to law explains why environmental and constitutional laws are defined from the perspective of private proprietors. By distancing 'things' from its focus and disavowing the physical, property law implicitly maintains that land use is irrelevant to definitions and determinations of property. Yet by insisting that property is about 'rights' and upholding the rights of landowners to continue using the land as they wish, property law makes possible certain kinds of land use, particularly those that can generate profit. The practice of property law conceals these proscriptions by referring to land only in terms of the land market.

The questions asked in *Newcrest* about the meaning and value of property are debated across the English-speaking world in the same terms of monetary benefits and losses. A Canadian court framed the question as a 'policy issue of how minutely government may control land without buying it'.[7] In the

---

7 *Mariner Real Estate Ltd v Nova Scotia (Attorney-General)* (1999) 177 DLR (4th) 696 at 699 per Cromwell JA, cited in Gray (2002: 220).

United States, Justice Scalia in the Supreme Court held in *Lucas v South Carolina Coastal Council*[8] that the council had denied the landowner 'all economically beneficial or productive options for [the land's] use' (at 1018) and thus awarded compensation. As in *Newcrest* and *Mariner*, *Lucas* was a dispute based on the environmental regulation of land use. *Lucas* is a significant case in the analysis of people–place relations because: '[I]t has played a central role in stimulating a so-called property-rights movement in the United States that has mounted a sustained challenge to environmental protection laws as constitutionally uncompensated expropriations of private property' (Sax 2008: 14).

The claimant, David Lucas, owned two lots of land on the Isle of Palms, a barrier island on the coast of South Carolina, on which he intended to build investment properties: 'Barrier islands are long, narrow bars of sand found just offshore that serve as buffers that protect the mainland against storm-driven waves' (Been 2004: 233). The land was not stable and due to the unpredictable and regular cycles of erosion and accretion of sand on the island, the land was described as 'dynamic'. Expert evidence in the case was that the land on which Lucas' property existed was part of the 'active' part of this dynamic process and had even been submerged for several years (at 1038–1039). In 1988, the South Carolina Coastal Council passed a law to prohibit construction beyond the line of the beach erosion. Consequently, Lucas could not build the structures he had planned to do and he claimed the effect of the law was a 'taking' of his property not by the acquisition of title, but by the erosion of its profitability. The trial court found for Lucas, but the Council won its appeal in the South Carolina Supreme Court in 1991 on the basis that its law was designed, appropriately, 'to prevent serious public harm'.[9] Between the trial and the Council's appeal, in September 1989, the Isle of Palms was hit by a Category 4 hurricane. Hurricane Hugo left 20% of the island's structures destroyed and almost all the remaining houses on the island were flooded, many being condemned (Been 2004: 235). The $215 million cleanup bill was shouldered by the federal government and public commentators bemoaned that taxpayers were effectively subsidising the properties and lifestyles of 'those people who had chosen to settle along South Carolina's hurricane-prone coast' (McAllister, cited in Been 2004: 255).

The 'folly of building on the beach' notwithstanding (Schmich, cited in Been 2004: 235), most of those who had lost their properties to the hurricane rebuilt them. Lucas appealed the decision of the South Carolina Supreme Court. The commercial viability and attractiveness of building on the Isle of Palms, he argued, was unchanged despite the expert evidence about the 'active' and 'dynamic' nature of the specific land in question and despite

---

8 *Lucas v South Carolina Coastal Council* 505 US 1003 (1992).
9 *Lucas v South Carolina Coastal Council* 404 SE2d 895, 898 (1991).

the damage of the most powerful hurricane in the area until that time. As if the questions of erosion, accretion, hurricane and storm damage on the barrier island were irrelevant, a majority in the US Supreme Court ruled that Lucas' property right to develop the land was commercially valuable and the Council's prohibition of the development constituted a taking and thereby attracted the right of compensation. But it wasn't only the majority judgment that articulated a dephysicalised concept of property. The dissenting judgment of Justice Blackmun repeated the technical definition of property as consisting in the twin rights to exclude and to alienate, which he said, had not been 'taken' or diminished. However, although both definitions of property are dephysicalised, the majority, by insisting that the development of 'notoriously unstable coastal area' (Gray 2002: 232) remained commercially viable and attractive the significance of scientific evidence to the contrary notwithstanding and a recent hurricane on the island, extends abstractness to a kind of blindness.

Where *Newcrest* had debated the loss of the property right in terms of sterilisation, the *Lucas* case debated the loss in terms of danger. Significantly, the words used to describe the loss of a property right in both cases, sterilisation and endangerment, were used not in their everyday physical meanings, but in an abstract and hyperbolic sense. The abstraction of language from the context of place in both cases is striking because of the highly contested physical contexts of the relevant land use practices. In *Newcrest*, the mining of land and, in *Lucas*, the commercial development of a sand dune subject to erosion, accretion, hurricane and flooding, were insubstantial aspects of the debate over the property right. The language of *Newcrest* and *Lucas* reveals the way in which the effect of modern property law is concealed from its proponents and beneficiaries. Because place and people are regarded as nature and culture and because property is regarded as a right but not a responsibility, it becomes possible to deny the necessary connection between them. The nature/culture paradigm manifest in the person/thing equation of modern property law creates a strangeness, even an offensiveness in the regulation and proscription of particular land use practices. Because place is irrelevant to property law, the physical capacities and limits of the specific places in dispute are merely meaningless spaces or sites of contest.

In regulatory takings cases, the regulation of land use can be a response to the effects of dephysicalised property law and unilateral people–place relations. For example, the effects of intensive agricultural and pastoral land use activity on the land, such as desertification, have led to various restrictions on land clearing to prevent soil erosion in numerous jurisdictions. Yet these effects, and the responsibilities they place on the proprietor, are conceptually separated from the rights to the profits of the land use activities that created those effects. Accordingly, the experience of many landowners is that environmental regulation and the imposition of responsibilities on them is unfair. The connections between land use and environmental damage and the connections between rights and responsibilities are concealed by the paradigm of modern property law. Environmental regulations are not regarded as responsibilities attached to rights to benefits and profits, but as separate burdens on them. Indigenous Australian legal scholar Irene Watson says that non-Indigenous laws of land ownership and land use 'ignore the laws of reciprocity and obligation' (Watson 2002: 267): 'The non-Indigenous relationship to land is to take more than is needed, depleting ruwi and depleting self. Their way with the land is separate and alien' (Watson 2002: 256).

The separation of people and place, the strangeness and offence taken at the notions of limits of land to 'yield' profits, and of responsibilities accompanying rights of ownership, are evident in the contemporary case law that debates the meaning and value of property. The claimants in these cases do not claim a new right, rather they give expression to their experience of property as a rights holder as defined by modern property law for centuries. The legal practitioners and judges in the cases do not create the concept of dephysicalised property, they merely repeat what they have learned at law school decades before. And their professors claim to have constructed their courses as a response to the practice. This section on placelessness in contemporary legal discourse concludes with a brief exploration of the role of legal education in maintaining the paradigm of modern property law.

6.2.2 Pedagogic practice

> The great ecological issues of our time have to do in one way or another with our failure to see things in their entirety. That failure occurs when minds are taught to think in boxes and not taught to transcend those boxes or to question overly much how they fit with other boxes.
>
> (Orr 2004: 94–95)

The first lecture of a contemporary property law course usually starts with the announcement that property law is in a bad shape, a point echoed in several textbook introductions: 'Property law has a reputation for being a difficult subject' (Chambers 2001: 4). Indeed, a common feature of critiques of legal education is that the law of real property suffers from being 'dauntingly difficult' and intellectually demanding (Castan and Schultz 1997: 75–79), a 'tortuous and ungodly jumble' (Bates 1984: 182) of outdated concepts, rules and vocabulary. Why is property law so regarded? And how is it negotiated? Real property is regarded as a difficult or 'mystifying' (O'Donnell and Johnstone 1997: 65) subject because its 'notorious complexity' (Alexander 1998: 52) is approached via a strategic deployment of history (Alexander 1986: 381–389) and anachronistic grammar (Warrington 1984: 80) that makes any conceptual framework or meaning 'elusive' (Gray 1991: 266). The history and etymology of property law doctrines and its vocabulary are often not situated or rationalised within their varied socioeconomic contexts, but rather are presented as a list of loosely related rules. Such disconnection between topics and doctrines in the subject of real property means that law students learn the 'archaic maxims' as though they were 'mathematical formulae' rather than cultural paradigms (O'Donnell and Johnstone 1997: 16).

Swiftly following the announcement that real property is a hard subject, property law textbooks and lecturers 'disabuse' (Alexander 1986: 382) students of any 'unreflective and naïve' (Gray and Gray 1998: 15) ideas of property, such as those held by 'ordinary non-lawyers' (Alexander 1986: 382), that property is a thing. To the contrary, students are informed that the fundamental prerequisite to understanding real property law is to 'un-learn previous notions' (Castan and Schultz 1997: 79) that property is about physical things. In this way, the pedagogy, or pragmatics of (teaching) property law begins, and indeed exists only through, the absenting of physicality, of place, from law. Gregory Alexander argues that:

> [M]any property teachers would probably consider one of the principal objectives of their course to be just this transformation of consciousness; and so if property is perceived as unintegrated the problem is partially of the teacher's own making.
>
> (1986: 382)

Real property law is not about things, it is about people or interpersonal relations. If the real property curriculum makes little sense, or can be said to be difficult, it is because the very 'thing' or 'property' about which this law speaks does not exist. In other words, the course is meaningless because it merely reflects the meaningless 'state' of real property relations. But does the curriculum really reflect or follow this state in its education of new generations of lawyers? If so, who or what is responsible for changes and developments in legal property relations? And would the law school's decision to follow or reflect existing property relations and structures constitute an abdication or a reverence for the responsibility of the creation of value? Kenneth Vandevelde, who traces the shift in modern property law from Blackstone's person–thing relation to Hohfeld's person–person relation, argues that the values of property ought not to be created by lawyers but by separate political processes. The person–person property relation, however improperly, draws lawyers into that process. To reiterate the idea that property is a person–person relation, or 'bundle of rights' then, as the current pedagogy of real property does, is to involve lawyers in the creation of values. So the law school does not follow or reflect the state of real property law as much as it leads it: by reproducing that state of real property law in its curricula and assessments. It is not adequate then for the law teacher to simultaneously claim that real property is difficult and meaningless while failing to account or question why this may be. The 'disintegration of property' (Grey, cited in Alexander 1986: 383) exists not simply because it is no longer about 'things' but because the cradle of legal thought, the law school, says it *is* so.

Maureen Cain observes the paradox of this situation given that for lawyers 'changing the law is not just their job but the most prestigious part of their job' (1994: 19). The problem with presenting to students the complexity and incoherence of real property law as a fact is that it produces resistance to the very idea of property law reform (Bowrey 1993: 7–10; Warrington 1984: 81). But law students are 'embryonic lawyers' (Warrington 1984: 86) and their education is fundamentally important to the development and improvement of law. It is for this reason that Ronnie Warrington argues in his article subtitled 'Is there any morality in Blackacre?' that real property or 'land law' teachers have a 'moral responsibility' (1984: 87):

> If one thinks that the world can and ought to be improved, and that lawyers have a role to play in fostering the necessary climate which might enable change to be made, and if it is possible to argue that lawyers are uniquely placed in society to help develop 'progressive' changes, then it is incumbent on law teachers to recognise that they ought to perform a role in helping students learn to question.
>
> (Warrington 1984: 87)

Environmental educators would extend Warrington's responsibility to reforming people–place relations: 'But there are better reasons to reform education, which have to do with the rapid decline in the habitability of the earth' (Orr 2004: 2).

One of the most important questions facing modern property law and its practitioners is the intersection of property rights and environmental responsibilities. Legal education plays an important part in prohibiting or enabling 'embryonic lawyers' to question the continued utility and viability of the concept of dephysicalised property. In particular, legal education in England's former colonies have the opportunity to critically reflect on the anthropocentrism of modern property law through learning the alternative perspective of Indigenous laws. The human-centred approach to property law is, some would argue, as necessary as it is clear – we are human. What is missed here, however, is that what it means to be human is culturally specific, as is an anthropocentric worldview. Assumptions about a universal and unilateral relationship between people and place can be identified and questioned from reading the testimony of native title claimants. The anthropocentrism of property law education remains largely unacknowledged, and so the construction of extra-human biota as the 'things' of property relations seems not simply possible, but factual. In this way, the alienation of people from place and the right to alienate land (and in some jurisdictions, water) as a right of property are normalised.

If, as Cain contends, lawyers are 'symbol traders' then law teachers are 'symbol makers'. Property law teachers reflect but also create values of place as well as values of law. The value of place as irrelevant to property law is taught by erasing the complexity and diversity of the very 'things' that constitutes the possibility of property's existence. Teaching *Yanner*, *Newcrest* and *Lucas* without reference to the particular geographical, geological and hydrological contexts of the cases flags to students the irrelevance of those contexts to laws of land use and ownership:

> By what is included or excluded, students are taught that they are part of or apart from the natural world. To teach economics for example, without reference to the laws of thermodynamics or ecology is to teach a fundamentally important ecological lesson: that physics and ecology have nothing to do with the economy. It just happens to be dead wrong.
>
> (Orr 2004: 12)

The dephysicalisation of property over time has been mirrored in discussions about appropriate titles for the courses that teach the subject. In law schools today the subject is increasingly taught as 'property law': 'Law schools which offer land law as a separate course constitute a rapidly dwindling minority' (Mugambwa 1997: 2). This development is also apparent in legal publishers' catalogues of textbook titles and textbook introductions remarking on the significance of the recent shift. The new 'comprehensive' subject that delivers both real and personal property categories in a single course meets 'the demands of legal practice' (Thornton 1991: 1) without increasing the number of compulsory or 'core' subjects in the law programme. Mugambwa relates the 'advantages' of this 'switch' to the anachronism of the categories of real and personal property laws and the increasing similarities between 'real' and 'personal' property relations: 'What are the possible policy or theoretical reasons for treating land and personal property differently? Are the reasons still justified in this day and age?' (1997: 4). Mugambwa accepts as fact that the line between the categories of real and personal property is blurred. Indeed, he argues that by combining the two categories into a single property law course, their diminishing contradistinction can be better understood and theorised:

> Though the concept of property could (indeed should) be covered in land law, the scope for its discussion is likely to be limited to land-related issues. In property law, on the other hand, the scope for discussion of the concept of property is almost limitless.
>
> (Mugambwa 1997: 6)

The 'day and age' of land-related real property law is ending and unhelpful to 'embryonic lawyers' (Warrington 1984: 86) whose trade is in 'symbols' (Cain 1994: 15) rather than 'permanent objects' (Mugambwa 1997: 5). If property law is a subject not directly related to land then what is it about? The shift from land law to real property law to property law suggests that contemporary dephysicalised concepts of property are structured into the law syllabus even before classes begin.

In the law schools of England's former colonies, the questions whether and how Indigenous land laws and their recognition by the non-Indigenous legal system of a jurisdiction are taught can often be regarded as political rather than intellectual questions in the teaching of property law. Depending on the pedagogy of the course designer, the political and intellectual radicalism of place-based Indigenous land law to non-Indigenous and dephysicalised land law is either concealed or paraded. Conventional pedagogical approaches that adopt a doctrinal approach to property law either ignore it completely or add it in as a strange and irrelevant topic at the beginning or end of the course with no necessary connection to the other topics in the course. Critical property law courses use it to demonstrate the relationship between property and politics. The centrality of place or 'country' to Indigenous land law may be referred to in the course, but it is uncommon for either the conventional or the critical approach to use Indigenous land law as a lens through which the placelessness of non-Indigenous property law can be seen.

The practical and theoretical intersections of property and environmental laws in itself suggests that people–place relations are significant and worthy of legal focus. But the presence of a law and form of title based on precisely such a relationship, native title, demands an evaluation of people–place relations within the dominant legal paradigm. The focus or evasion of the political aspects of native title does not prohibit the inclusion of attention to the values of place in non-Indigenous law and culture.

Concepts of land and place are non-existent in contemporary property law education and 'few students have an understanding of Indigenous concepts of property, relationships and "country"' (Castan and Schultz 1997: 81). Indeed, few students have an understanding of *non-Indigenous* concepts of people–place relationships. The difficulty of property law is compounded perhaps by a failure to survey the 'diversity of people's relationship to the earth' (O'Donnell and Johnstone 1997: 66), particularly the relationship codified in the dominant paradigm of property law. The biggest challenge for property teachers is to grasp the opportunity offered by Indigenous perspectives on non-Indigenous property law without allowing the focus of class discussion to narrow to a question of legal and cultural priority and entitlement (Graham 2009b). The loss of place from modern property law makes it possible for students to perceive the discussion of place as relevant only in a cultural sense when it is relevant for life itself: 'The frog's illusion is in not seeing its own vulnerability, that it is the same as all other animals, contained by laws of creation and affected in the same thirsty way when wells run dry' (Watson 2002: 266).

6.3 Cultural practice

> Why do we keep insisting that 'we' are variously disoriented, lost, estranged, and alienated in the face of manifestly contrary cultural and technological dominance?
>
> (O'Carroll 1999: 19)

One answer to O'Carroll's question might be that 'we' talk about the land with a sense of alienation because we, moderns (Latour 2001), are alien to it. Our law and practice of property insistently abstracts land and extra-human biota as things because we are losing our 'battle' to dominate them. This section of the chapter examines cultural discourses of people–place relations and land use practices in two parts. First, 'Battling the land' explores the dominant cultural discourse of property as entitlement and, second, 'Owning the land' explores alternative cultural discourses of property as responsibility and knowledge.

6.3.1 Battling the land

> For farmers and ranchers, for people who make a living on the land, every day is Earth Day. There's no better stewards of the land than people who rely on the productivity of the land.
>
> (President Bush 2002, cited in Ruhl 2002: 408)

In England's colonies, the narrative of struggle between the colonists and the Indigenous peoples and environments was commonplace. Centuries later, the narrative and its characters persist. Doing 'battle' with Indigenous peoples, flora and fauna for control of land is part of the dominant contemporary cultural discourse of property. Yet, the battle of the farmer against the land is framed as being defensive rather than offensive. As J.M. Arthur observed in her lexicographical study of the relationship between people and place in language, the vocabulary of battle allocates agency to place, rather than to people. The language of battle is strategic – it 'sidesteps' the source of the moral and environmental problem over which the battle is fought (Arthur 2003: 87, 125). In other words, the language of battle and the construction of farmers and graziers as 'battlers' does not acknowledge their agency and responsibility for economic and environmental problems. If there is a dysfunctional relationship between people and place; it can be attributed to the land's inadequacy and harshness. Problems associated with intensive land use practices such as overgrazing, salinity, soil erosion and so on, have not arisen from the 'inappropriate responses' of the farmers and graziers to the local geographical and hydrological conditions but from the land itself: 'It puts the onus of any failure of relationship upon the land; the land is difficult, therefore the colonist struggles' (Arthur 2003: 87).

Contemporary land use practices, including especially intensive and often irrigated agriculture and grazing, transform the legal discourse of dephysicalised property into geographical realities. Paradoxically, farmers and graziers define their cultural identity by their relation to the land as battlers, while maintaining a disconnection from it. Consistent with the paradigm of modern property law, rather than a relation of connectivity with and dependence on place, the people–place relation articulated in the dominant cultural discourse of property is a 'battle'. Farmers are 'battlers' in a 'hostile' land or against the 'harsh' elements.[10] They realign their physically dependent cultural identities as farmers with dephysicalised concepts of property by controlling and exploiting the land, thereby asserting human or cultural agency over nature. The image of the farmer as a 'battler' on the land is accurate: '[B]ut there is little evidence to demonstrate that pastoralists have worked within the ecological constraints of arid Australia' (Letnic 2000: 305).

Farmers constitute powerful lobby groups at all levels of politics. Their power is due in part to various electoral and economic conditions, but it is due also to the iconic quality of the 'battler' image. There is a marketability in the image of farmers 'doing it tough on the unforgiving land' (Letnic 2000: 304). But both the economic and iconic power of the notion of farmers as battlers derive from histories of colonisation and improvement of the land legitimised by a particular concept of property: property as a dephysicalised right.

Like David Lucas and the Newcrest Mining Company, many farmers do not welcome environmental regulation of their properties. Environmental regulation is often equated with interference with their property rights. Where property rights are symbols of citizenship and liberty, their diminution through environmental regulation is regarded as a subversion of the rights of citizenship and liberty. In 1972 the US Supreme Court noted that 'a fundamental interdependence exists between the personal right to liberty and the personal right to property. Neither would have meaning without the other'.[11] In 2001 Anna Cronin, the former CEO of the Australian National Farmers' Federation (NFF), made the same point with specific reference to the primary environmental law in the country:

---

10 The analysis of dominant cultural discourse does not, by definition, account for the diversity of people–place relations experienced by all farmers. The political and bureaucratic reasons for the dominance of this discourse are not explored within the scope of the book but it is acknowledged the farming community feels strongly that their understanding of the requirements and purpose of environmental law and regulation that effects their land use practice is based on poor government communication (NFF 2009b: 7).

11 *Lynch v Household Finance Corporation*, 405 US 538, 552 (1972), cited in Olivetti and Worsham 2003: 44.

It is our concern that the function of the *Environment Protection and Biodiversity Conservation Act* is a further step by the Federal Government toward increasing its jurisdiction over land, water and vegetation management.

(Cronin 31 July 2001)

The assumption underlying this concern is that government jurisdiction over place is inappropriate because it is private land where decisions about land use and management should be free from interference. Last year, the submission of the NFF to the interim report on the same Act reiterated a similar point: 'NFF remain extremely concerned that the current construct of the EPBC Act will limit the ability for farmers to be productive and financially viable' (2009b: 6). Environmental regulation, where it requires and/or prohibits specific land use practices, is regarded as antithetical to one of the basic principles or rights of private property, the right of exclusion. It is not simply the right to exclude the physical presence of others, but any interference with the control of the property, including state regulations about land use. The loss of control that environmental regulation presents to landowners is the loss of an entitlement that, being a property right, is sufficiently sacred to invoke claims to the protections afforded by federal constitutions.

The notion of compensation is paramount in the debate about environmental regulation of private land and it reveals not only the continuity between the legal and cultural discourses of property but the normalisation of a particular paradigm of people–place relations – a unilateral and commercially profitable relation. As Kirby J expressed in *Newcrest*, the basic rights of individuals and businesses are property rights. Farms are first and foremost businesses and the land is the economic resource on which those businesses succeed or fail. Farmers work the land to 'yield' its resources and so the prohibition of certain land use practices, such as land clearing for example, directly affects their capacity to profit from the economy of natural resources. Australian environmental historian Libby Robin argues that:

[W]hen elements of nature are selected out as 'natural resources' they are no longer natural. Their local ecological context is replaced by a global economic one. Reading a landscape through the lens of an unnatural economy change the way people see, understand and identify with nature.

(Robin 2007: 186)

Because the places are not seen in their ecological context, but as a source of commercial profit, the paradigm of modern law does not merely prescribe a dephysicalised property relation in an abstract legal sense. The paradigm of modern law prescribes its materialisation through land use practices that have no necessary response to or correlation with their local ecological contexts.

Dephysicalised property is, therefore, not only abstract, it is real. The agricultural and grazing industries, and all that flow from them, depend on the material reproduction of the dephysicalised concept of property.

Commercial profitability is the ultimate function of private property. Accordingly, compensation is claimed by landowners for profits lost through environmental regulation. Yet the power of the cultural discourse of property is sufficient that compensation is also claimed by landowners in the context of drought for profits that were never possible:

> [T]he mind may well boggle at estimates of the cost of a drought calculated to include wool shorn from sheep never conceived and wheat not harvested from crops never sown. Even if it can be admitted that one can in some way lose something which never came into being, the calculation of values of the items becomes very involved.
>
> (Heathcote, citing Butlin 1969: 179)

The notion of compensation used in debates about environmental regulation of private property (and about government response to drought) highlights the absence of intrinsic values of place in the property right. Because the property right in land contains nothing intrinsically valuable, a monetary value for its lost profits can be calculated and paid. In this way, the acknowledgment of the commercial function and objective of property rights in land allows farmers to argue that they have no in principle objection to environmental regulation and conservation. The objection to compulsory acquisition, eminent domain and regulatory takings is economic. The right to alienate one's property is a right to participate in a particular kind of economy. In *Newcrest* and in *Lucas*, both property rights holders claimed they were aggrieved not for the loss of the place (as they had not lost this) but for the loss of its profits. Similarly, statements by powerful lobby groups for farmers and graziers in both Australia and the USA insist that they have no objection to environmental management and conservation, but that where these coincide with consequent commercial burden and loss to their members, they object to that burden and loss and seek relief that is, like that which has been lost, monetary:

> Across the country, farmers are increasingly faced with community/ government expectations that they will deliver nature conservation outcomes for the public good but without due compensation for any loss in production asset value from such actions.
>
> (Cronin 31 July 2001)

The Endangered Species Act (ESA) is one of two federal programs particularly responsible for stoking outrage over violations of people's right to property. The other is federal control of wetlands . . . In each case, the response is to conscript private property to national environmental causes with no compensation.

(DeLong 1997: 91)

Critics of the notion of compensating landowners for restrictions to their land use arising from environmental law argue that 'it would be inequitable to provide these rights to farmers without creating similar rights for other forms of property' (Macintosh and Denniss 2004: vi). The absence of compensation to urban property rights holders, commercial fishing rights holders and the land rights of dispossessed Indigenous communities are used as examples of such inequity (2004: 44–50). Farrier et al. also point out that compensation for interference with private property rights maintains the priority of private property over environmental law and leaves unchallenged the role of farmers in anthropogenic environmental change: 'If landholders are to undertake this responsibility, then they may legitimately expect to be paid for the work that they do. But this is very different from compensating them for interference with so called private property rights' (Farrier et al. 1999: 14).

Even where the vocabulary of the property rights advocates has changed from 'compensation' for profits lost, to 'incentives' to meet the environmental needs of the public, the message is the same: 'The NFF has continually raised the need for incentives . . . for on-farm conservation activities' (NFF 2009b: 29). Incentives are regarded as encouraging 'carrots', rather than punitive 'sticks' of governance (DeLong 1997: 92). As with compensation, incentives for certain prohibited or prescribed land use practices position property rights holders outside the reason of environmental regulation – the protection of place from inappropriate use. The arguments for compensation and incentives reiterate the well-established hierarchical order of property rights over and above other 'rights' and 'interests' including those of the environment on which the profits depend. The calls for compensation and incentives externalise every aspect of people–place relationships that are not commercially profitable. According to this logic, the people–place relationship of modern property law contains no space for reciprocity with place – the benefits flow one way, from things to people. The dephysicalisation of property creates the sense of 'disorientation, estrangement and alienation' from place described by O'Carroll at the opening of this section of the chapter.

The history and philosophy of modern property law suggest that profit is all that property rights are designed to provide and so the claim for compensation for lost profits seems reasonable from within the internal logic of the paradigm. The strangeness of the claims of the 'property rights movement' becomes apparent only once the material conditions of the paradigm no longer support its operation. As Kuhn argued: '[T]he significance of crises is the indication they provide that an occasion for retooling has arrived' (1996: 76). The strangeness and crises of people–place relations prescribed by modern property law are increasingly evident from disputes over property rights where what has been lost has not been the right, but the place. Deemed to be irrelevant to property law for centuries, the places on and over which modern law entitled people to things are in crisis and thus the dependence of law on place is revealed by its own corresponding failure to describe and prescribe viable people–place relations. Specifically, the pressure of the unilateral relationship between people and place on many and diverse places has rendered both the knowledge of and responsibility for place economically imperative. Commercial profit cannot be 'yielded' from geographical and hydrological systems under stress and thus the impossibility of places being only things and resources has become more than a theoretical critique of a paradigm, it has become an experience.

Although the exhaustion of resources and the extinction of species is not a novel experience for any human society's relationship with place, without 'new worlds' and 'frontiers' the battle for control of land, resources and a surplus economy seems to be no longer with land. Unless lands and their systems are restored, the battle with each other for access to and control of remaining viable economic resources is inevitable. But as the need for environmental regulation is increasingly physically apparent, the defence of property rights grows stronger. American scholars Alfred Olivetti and Jeff Worsham argue that the strength and profile of the 'property rights movement' corresponds directly to the strength and profile of the environmental movement. Viewing the former as a reactionary group of 'grass-roots activists, political conservatives, and industry interests' to the latter, Olivetti and Worsham describe the property rights movement as a 'counter-movement' to the environmentalism of the twentieth-century (Olivetti and Worsham 2003: 21). The message of the property rights movement is 'that the public must buy back the right to maintain the remaining elements of biodiversity from owners who have a property right to destroy it' (Sax 2008: 14).

The reason that property rights and environmentalism are adversaries is because modern law has so constructed them. The paradigm of modern law created and maintains the bifurcation of land law into separate and doctrinally detached laws of entitlement and responsibility. Consequently, from the perspective of the property rights holder, the area of law that regulates the environment and attributes responsibility for certain land use practices is different from the area of law by which they are entitled. From the view of a contemporary property rights holder, one area of law remains unchanged while another grows: property rights remain abstract rights of exclusion and alienation, while environmental law increasingly determines the physical limits to the profitability of those property rights. The growth of environmental law has been referred to by a leading advocate of the 'property rights movement' the creation of a 'monster that causes peasants carrying torches and pitchforks to storm your castle' (DeLong 1997: 91). Such a description may seem hyperbolic, but it anticipates and articulates the perception and motivation of a small number of property rights holders whose frustration is enacted on the land itself.

In two recent Australian cases, *Greentree*[12] and *Hudson*[13], two landowners were found to have breached relevant environmental legislation by clearing trees and vegetation from their properties. In the *Greentree* case (a civil proceeding), an inspection of the property found that 100 hectares of Ramsarlisted wetlands had been cleared by the owner, part of the then cleared property dredged and between government inspections of the property, ploughed. When the government department eventually took the matter to court, the Australian Federal Court fined Ronald Greentree and an associated company $450,000. In the *Hudson* case (a criminal proceeding), an inspection of the property found that 486 hectares of land had been cleared by the owner and he was charged with breaching two sections of the relevant native vegetation legislation. Of the various components of his defence, the most striking is his appeal (via his representative agent) to the logic of property rights: 'Mr and Mrs Hudson owned the property in fee simple, the State has no interest in it, and they were thus entitled to do what they did on the land (at 260, para [4]). The trees were their trees.' The court found that Hudson had cleared the property as 'part of the agricultural activities on the land and in that sense the offence was part of a commercial operation – that is, it was motivated by commercial considerations' (Lloyd J at 271, para [86]). While the judge sympathised that Hudson 'no doubt feels a sense of injustice in being unable to use this land as he sees fit' (at 271, para [87]), he was nonetheless fined $408,000 and ordered to pay the prosecution's costs.

The argument made out in both cases that the landowners' property rights were potentially sterilised by environmental regulation was unsuccessful. The dispute in both cases was not over compensation for the loss of the property right but over the cost of exercising it. The outcome in both cases was a monetary penalty, highlighting the crisis of the logic of property law and environmental law. Were the crop yields of the cleared lands sufficiently successful to make the clearing worth the penalty to the landowner, the law could not be said to be effective. While the NFF noted that it 'does not condone the actions of farmers who deliberately seek to contravene' environmental legislation (NFF 2009b: 6), it sympathises that 'there are many cases where whole farms have become totally unviable after the introduction of native vegetation regulations' (Corish 1 September 2005). The sympathy, if not the support of the NFF for contesting environmental legislation, and the tepid concern of the court that proprietors 'may be somewhat misguided as to what [they are] able to do on [their] land' (Lloyd J at 272, para [91]) underline the strength of cultural discourses of property.

---

12 *Minister for the Environment and Heritage v Greentree* (No. 2) [2004] 138 FCR 198.
13 *Director-General of the Department of Environment and Climate Change v Hudson* (2009) 165 LGERA 256.

The strength of this discourse and the attitudes of many pastoralists 'appear to be a product of history and the cultural insularity produced by the isolation of the Australian rangelands' (Letnic 2000: 303). The insularity of cultural attitudes, however, may not be created only by the isolation of farmers from their broader human community but by their isolation from nature itself. Land clearance transforms landscapes dramatically. The removal of trees and vegetation from land physically excludes nature from place, appropriating place as cultured. In this way, it also informs the relationship between people and place because it allows people to regard themselves as alone on the land, 'the sole-occupiers, rights-holders and beneficiaries of nature' (Bartel 2005: 323). It is not possible to experience a connection with place when the complex conditions of that place have been cleared, burnt, drained and ploughed.

Environmental law scholar Andrew Macintosh argues that breaches of environmental legislation are insufficiently monitored and prosecuted by relevant departments and that the willingness of government to negotiate with property rights holders belies the spirit and letter of environmental law (Macintosh 2009). This may be due, in part, to the political and cultural strength of property rights and it is due in part to the conventional legal priority of property law over environmental law. On any analysis, it seems clear that the strength and priority of property rights are waning and the paradigm of people–place relations to which they belong is in crisis occasioned by a crisis in their material conditions:

> Problems like soil erosion, acidification of soils, eutrophication of water ways, soil structure decline and dryland salinity are not unique to Australia, nor are they newly discovered. Like the United States, Australia experienced severe soil erosion problems in the 1930s ... by the 1980s it was not surprising that the effects of settlement on the land-scape were clearly affecting agricultural production itself, not just the aesthetic sensibilities of those who were appalled by the sight of scalded soils, saline paddocks and bare, eroded hills. In financial terms, land degradation costs between $600 million and $1.2 billion annually.
>
> (Williams 2004: 10)

For over three decades, scientists and economists have been publicising the link between land degradation and land use, specifically, agricultural and grazing practices that degrade vast tracts of land:

> We now understand that our European heritage and our forebears' desire to subdue and conquer the land to create a 'useful' landscape were contributing factors. Indeed the mind set was encouraged and demanded by a range of government incentives, standing orders and legislation.
>
> (Goldney and Bauer 1998: 16)

Environmental regulation has developed gradually and to varying degrees of effectiveness against the ubiquitous and prior discourse of private property rights. But the crisis in the paradigm of modern property law was predicted and anticipated by Indigenous people's who witnessed the maladaptation of the colonists' land use practices to local geographical and climatic conditions long before it was recognised by the colonists themselves. Indigenous people's knowledge of the 'countries' of which they were dispossessed was connected to their land laws. The land laws of the colonists were connected neither to their knowledge of local places nor to the knowledge of the local Indigenous custodians. What follows, on cultural discourses of property, explores alternative discourses of property-as-place articulated by non-Indigenous and Indigenous landowners. The emphasis in all but the first of these alternative discourses is the importance to property of the knowledge of place.

6.3.2 More than money

In 2001 American Joy Williams published an article in *Harper's Magazine* entitled 'One acre: on devaluing real estate to keep land priceless' that chronicles the development of a lagoon in Florida, where Williams owned an acre of land. The area, once beyond urbanity and without access to open water became, over a 20-year period, a luxury retreat of large houses and condominiums: 'The condos are investments, mostly, not homes. Like the lands they've consumed, they're cold commodities. When land is developed it ceases being land. It becomes covered, sealed, its own grave' (Williams 2001: 60).

Williams likens the ownership of her land to stewardship, but juxtaposes this notion to the legal reality of the land as private property 'the wildlife didn't know that their world existed only because I owned it' (2001: 63). Compelled to leave her home, Williams sells the land, but simultaneously, radically refuses the core principle of private property – the freedom of enjoyment and the exclusion of others. Like the character Daryl Kerrigan in the Australian film *The Castle*, who claimed he was not interested in compensation for the compulsory acquisition of his property, Williams says 'I wanted more than money for my land'.

Williams made the sale of her property conditional on the conservation of its natural habitat:

> It took eight months to find the right buyer. Leopold's philosophers were in short supply in the world of Florida real estate. But the ideal new owners eventually appeared, and they had no problem with the contract between themselves and the land . . . I had found people with a land ethic too. Their duties as stewards were not onerous to them. They did not consider the additional legal documents they were obliged to sign an insult to their personal freedom.
>
> (2001: 65)

Williams' value and critique of property contains a concept of and relationship in place that, like the placed value of property expressed by the Kerrigan family in *The Castle*, disrupts the dominant discourse of dephysicalised property because it refuses the notion that property is a commodity, always and already exchangeable. Interestingly, Williams does not resist the law from a position of exteriority, rather she manipulates the legal framework and the land market from within its existing framework to reach a compromise, however satisfying that may be.

6.3.3 Adaptive farming

In the Northern Territory of Australia, the dominant form of land use is grazing. This practice is regulated by law, the Pastoral Land Act 1992 (NT). The landscape of the Northern Territory is profoundly shaped by the Act because it prescribes and regulates the land use practices in operation over almost half the land mass of the territory. The arid regions of the territory, where much pastoral (grazing) activity occurs, are subject to high variability of rainfall and thus the long-range perspective required of land use practices to avert substantial land degradation are imperative for enduring and viable property ownership. The Act, however, makes little provision for sustainable farm management approaches. Subsequently, the responsibility of farmers and grazers for the use and management of vast tracts of land beyond immediate commercial profitability of the use is under-acknowledged.

The environmental consequences of pastoralism in the territory are seldom recognised and acknowledged. The 'romantic imagery of Australia's remote, rugged outback' dominates touristic and artistic representations of the 'Red Centre' (Haynes 1998; Letnic 2000: 295). But this imagery of a wild landscape belies the reality of anthropogenically degraded lands. The arid lands of the territory are 'among the most impacted of Australian ecosystems, having had the highest rate of mammal extinctions found anywhere in the world within the last 200 years' (Morton, cited in Letnic 2000: 296). Geographer Mike Letnic argues that pastoralism has been and remains one of the major sources of environmental degradation in Australia. The reason, he says, is one of scale: 'A single pastoral property may cover millions of hectares' (Letnic 2000: 300). Due to the scarcity of water, animals grazed over vast areas of land, consuming any and all available surface water and limited bores (wells) into the artesian basin (groundwater) beneath the surface. Technological advances in the twentieth century provided larger bores. With an increased source of water for livestock, stocking rates increased and 'in many cases degradation from overgrazing' occurred (Letnic 2000: 300). Pastoralism degraded the land not merely because of the numbers of animals that the land supported, but the kind of animals and the kind of land use practices that accompanied grazing. The impact on the fragile soils of the arid lands of the territory of hard-hoofed animals and large-scale clearing of vegetation was profound. Depletion of water resources, soil erosion and the clearing of vegetation that served as the habitat for a range of biota contributed to landscape change that has been called 'desertification' (Mabbut, cited in Letnic 2000: 301).

Non-Indigenous Australian farmer Bob Purvis tells landscape scholar Jim Sinatra his experience of pastoralism as a land use practice and of the paradigm of placelessness in law that facilitates and protects it. His story is a departure from dominant concepts and practices of property as rights, although it retains important aspects of them – the right to profit. The difficulties he encountered as a farmer, the NFF might say, are simple examples of the 'battles' farmers fight. Purvis describes those difficulties, however, in terms of maladaptation, learning and adaptation. His triumph over those difficulties is not a unilateral victory of 'man' over the land; rather, it is a successful adaptation to particular local geographical conditions. Furthermore, compared with the ongoing difficulties of his fellow farmers, Purvis' success is difficult to see as anything other than adaptation. It is important to bear in mind that Purvis is a farmer whose cattle grazing in the desert environment of central Australia remains strange and alien to that environment. Purvis' relation to land is not affecting or pretending an indigenous relation. His relation is simply his personal effort to live a better adapted relation to place than his English forebears.

Atartinga Station (formerly 'Woodgreen') 200km north of Alice Springs, in central Australia, is 2235 square kilometres. Before the English appropriated the land, it had never had been grazed or supported cloven- or hard-footed animals. Purvis inherited the farm from his English-born father in 1960. He also inherited debt in excess of the property's value (Sinatra and Murphy 1999: 70). The debt was due to land degradation and 'near-permanent drought' caused by farming practice based on alien concepts of property: vegetation clearing; the impact of hard-hoofed animals; overgrazing and the introduction of pest plants and animals. Purvis remarks that his father 'didn't really understand this country' (Sinatra and Murphy 1999: 67). The property Purvis inherited suffered extensive soil erosion, pasture decline and the extinction of native plant and animal species (Sinatra and Murphy 1999: 69). Purvis notes that the native plant species, especially the local grasses 'were made for kangaroos and birds; they were not made for cattle' (Sinatra and Murphy 1999: 73). The damage to the land was so extensive that 75% of the land was unusable. Purvis notes that, though his father 'sank the first bore in 1918' (Sinatra and Murphy 1999: 69) and farmed the land until 1960, 'most of the damage was done within five years of first being stocked' (Sinatra and Murphy 1999: 73).

That Purvis' father continued to farm for over 30 years after land degradation had started to appear and affect his productivity demonstrates the power of the 'battler' ideology. He was a farmer whose relation to land, despite being a lessee not an owner, can be likened to the notion of 'full beneficial ownership' expressed by Callinan and McHugh JJ in *Yanner v Eaton*. Any interference with his 'rights' to use his land as he chose, would have been regarded as the 'sterilisation' of property rights and highlighted the importance of compensation. Even in the face of his actual sterilisation of the land, it was the right that mattered, not the thing.

The role of property law in environmental changes to the land is noted by Purvis. His father did not buy the land, he leased it. The conditions of the lease included a requirement about the use of the land:

> The lease states that you have a minimum stocking rate of 3000 head for the property. We reckon that a sustainable number is about 400 . . . In good heart, this country can only support a stocking rate of about 3 per square kilometre. That's what the land can carry, and my father had to stock 23 per square kilometre.
>
> (Sinatra and Murphy 1999: 74)

Purvis' account of the connection between land law and land use demonstrates the way the law materialises the nature/culture paradigm by enforcing the ideology of improvement. His account reflects the power of the paradigm and demonstrates what is maladaptive about it. Along with the land, Purvis inherited the lease and its conditions. Purvis sees the law as politics, for him laws are made and permitted by government. He notes that 'to this day many central Australian farmers retain the government-endorsed grazing philosophy that nearly ruined Atartinga' (Sinatra and Murphy 1999: 71). And again later he says: '[T]he Australian attitude – or this government's attitude – is to plunder that resource, you know, the finite resource, not the infinite resource' (Sinatra and Murphy 1999: 77).

When Bob inherited his father's property, he was not losing the 'battle' to dominate nature. The 'battle', he felt, was already lost. In 1960, when debts exceeded the property's commercial value and 75% of its land was unusable, Purvis decided on a radical change of land use that fundamentally subverted the modern paradigm of people–place relations. Those changes were successful. In 1985 he 'paid off the debt and sold bullocks in the drier than average season while the rest of the pastoral industry in the Alice Springs region was in crisis' (Sinatra and Murphy 1999: 71). Almost 20 years later the crisis continues, many farmers are 'broke', 'their land is going backwards' but 'they don't want to know and they don't want to see' (Sinatra and Murphy 1999: 77–78). Purvis' anecdotal evidence contradicts the claims of the NFF that farmers are interested in environmental conservation because their businesses depend on sustainable productive land use. Farmers' reluctance to change the way they relate to their properties is arguably due to the potent discourse and ideology of property rights. The change and adaptation that Purvis practices and recommends subvert the paradigm that sustains property rights discourse.

So what did Purvis do? Is his use of land fundamentally different from other pastoral farmers and if so, how? Purvis abandoned the notion that culture was active and knowing. He approached the land as its student. He observed what sort of land his property was. He learned that his property was made up of three different sorts of country: '[H]ard Mulga; spinifex sand plain and open woodland; and smaller areas of mixed sweet calcareous country' (Sinatra and Murphy 1999: 69). He examined the soil and learned what caused its erosion and began to restore its former conditions by reintroducing better adapted vegetation and installing ponding banks. He reintroduced fire management. But the most radical change Purvis initiated was reducing the number of stock on the property. The minimum stocking rate set by the conditions of the property lease was 3000. Purvis reduced the number of stock on the land by 30–50% than previous stocking numbers (Pickard 2001: 277) and, in doing so, he was in default of his lease. His account of this process illuminates the vital role of property law in determining land use:

> We've got to convince the bureaucrat that the stocking rate is unrealistic. It took me twenty-odd years to get them to change, and then it changed only for me. Although it did show that there was something seriously wrong with the stocking rate in this area it is difficult to convince that those minimum stocking rates should be maximum stocking rates because the politician, he wants the rent now. He wants it yesterday, and your rent is based on the property's carrying capacity.
>
> (Sinatra and Murphy 1999: 77)

The experience of Purvis is telling. Official environmental audits suggest that '17% of Australia's rangelands are so degraded that they require destocking' (cited in Letnic 2000: 302) yet for Purvis to be able to decrease the stocking rate of his property required protracted negotiation of the lease conditions of his property. It was a radical move because 'how many pastoralists are willing or in a financial position to do this?' (Letnic 2000: 302).

Purvis still uses the land as a resource and he remains a pastoralist in an arid region in a country to which pastoralism was alien. What is radical about Purvis' farming practice is that rather than regarding land as the non-specific thing and rather than 'battling' the land, Purvis transformed his relationship to the land as one of reciprocity and developing knowledge. 'The hardest part was to obtain the expertise', he says, 'because all the landscapes are slightly different, what applies here doesn't necessarily apply somewhere else' (Sinatra and Murphy 1999: 78). Purvis adapted himself to the land rather than trying to force the land to adapt to him. In his experience, the rights of ownership are not restricted externally by government regulation by distant bureaucrats, they are restricted by the capacities and limits of the land itself: 'The land is what limits you' (Sinatra and Murphy 1999: 77).

Another way in which Purvis' property relation is radical is that he disconnects land from profit. Land 'is worth more than money ... it's the thing that drives you' (Sinatra and Murphy 1999: 82–83). Like the character Daryl Kerrigan in the film *The Castle*, Bob Purvis resists the notion that property is alienable and exchangeable: 'If you are completely broke, what do you do about it? The last thing you do is walk off. You just have to get better at looking after the land' (Sinatra and Murphy 1999: 83).

All the changes Purvis' farming practice affected were gradual. Purvis points out that he didn't know and wasn't taught how to care for the land and had to learn from the land itself over a long time, by trial and error. Unlearning the paradigm of nature/culture and departing from conventional property relations was slow. The time it took, Purvis says, was unnecessary and particular to the cultural ignorance of colonial Australians:

> 450 ponding banks in twenty-odd years doesn't seem many, but five or six or eight years of that was learning how to do it. Whenever you are teaching yourself it takes a long time. If somebody had the knowledge they could maybe teach you in one week that which took me five years to learn.
>
> (Sinatra and Murphy 1999: 81)

When talking about the use of fire as part of his management strategy, Bob complains that people *had* learned over time and did know and practise better adapted land use. The loss of their knowledge and their dispossession he attributes to the paradigm of property that colonised the country:

> The blackfella burned, but my father's generation stopped the blackfella from burning and the blackfella has another generation that is not taught how to burn. And then there's my generation ... comes along and has to learn what the blackfellas knew three generations back.
>
> (Sinatra and Murphy 1999: 82)

Purvis laments the loss of this knowledge of place, but he perceives it to be an irreversible loss. The interview does not record a discussion about the dispossession of the local original owners or about the link between their loss, and his proprietorship. Without resuming a discussion of property as a simple matter of contested 'rights' between 'persons' or cultures, it is interesting to consider that Purvis talks about their dispossession only in terms of their knowledge of the land and not of the land itself. The connection he himself feels to the land is felt despite, rather than because of, his cultural heritage. And while he recognises the importance of his connection to the land to its careful management, he does not discuss the possibility of deprivatising his right and returning the land to the dispossessed Aboriginal community of the area: 'An easy acceptance of non-Indigenous rural attachment to land runs the danger of perpetuating the erasure of Aboriginal relationships to land' (Gill 1999: 59).

Non-Indigenous Australian farmer Peter Andrews is another dissident voice against the paradigm of placelessness in modern law, whose model of people–place relations is also based on knowledge of place. His farming methods attract criticism, fines (his practices breach several environmental regulations) and condemnation from government, departments, environmentalists and conservative landowners. His methods are controversial because they go against mainstream wisdom about land management. Andrews believes that sustainable farming begins with the restoration of the various local natural systems (soil, vegetation, hydrological) of the land to prefarming functionality.

Restoration, Andrews says, begins with the stabilisation and fertility of the soil. For Andrews, weeds are not pests but key players in the restorative process. His perspective on weeds is part of his broader and unconventional perception of the landscape, 'whether a plant is a weed depends entirely on how farmers perceive it; there's no hard-and-fast definition' (Andrews 2006: 128). Weeds, he argues, are 'soil revitalisers' that aggressively and opportunistically grow in degraded soils where other plants struggle to grow. The advantage of using weeds to stabilise soils, he says, is that they grow rapidly, add organic bulk to the soil and deter animals from grazing around it 'thus enabling the surrounding soil and vegetation to recover' (Andrews 2006: 128). The main advantage of weeds, he says, is that weeds restore fertility to the soil. Unlike grass, which extracts carbon from the soil, weeds add it. Grass, he says 'is a debtor, as far as fertility is concerned. Weeds . . . [are] donors in terms of fertility. Weeds are the plants that repair the environment, so if they were edible how would the environment ever get repaired?' (Andrews 2006: 132). Allaying concerns of farmers sceptical about his advice on weeds Andrews says: '[T]he farmer should be aware that the presence of nodding thistles is a sign that the land is crying out for a repair cycle' (Andrews 2006: 129) and that 'once you raise the fertility of the soil to a critical level, grass will take over. The weeds won't be able to compete' (Andrews 2006: 131). Andrews' view on the use of weeds does not sit well with many farmers (or the producers of herbicides). His restorative method of weed use also breaches environmental regulations regarding noxious weed control. Like Greentree and Hudson, Andrews' land use practices breach environmental laws (for which he has been penalised). But whereas Greentree and Hudson both cleared the land for profitable agricultural land use productivity, Andrews re-vegetates the land for landscape restoration and later sustainable land use productivity where the objective is not profit.

Conscious of the controversy of his approach to landscape management and to weed use in particular, Andrews qualifies his position on weeds by linking it to the practical and material function of weeds. It is not, he stresses, an ideological position that he takes, it is a pragmatic position that is situated in place and 'evidence-based' rather than ad hoc and short range in vision:

I'm not in favour of weeds for their own sake. I'm not suggesting we should go out and spread weeds over the entire landscape. If there were other plants that performed the essential functions that weeds perform and were more acceptable to farmers, then sure, I'd be all in favour of using them instead of weeds.

(Andrews 2006: 127)

Not surprisingly, then, the centrepiece of knowledge of place, according to Andrews, is the knowledge of the function of plants in the landscape: 'I once said to a Landcare person, "Who cares for the land?" She said, "We do." "No you don't," I said. "Plants do." Plants are the only thing that can look after the land' (Andrews 2006: 140). Andrews' approach to farming and landscape management begins with a rejection a one-size-fits-all style of farming where land use practices are activated independently of the particular local geographical and hydrological conditions of the property such as the carrying capacity of the land, the waterways, the types of existing vegetation and condition of the soil etc. He rejects ideologies of landscape management, preferring practice-based knowledge that is inherently specific to particular landscapes.

John Williams, former Chief of CSIRO Land and Water, writes that Andrews':

[A]bility to read the country, in part derived from his respect for and engagement with Aboriginal people, is in my experience consistent with and informs modern geomorphology, although Peter has done this without formal scientific education.

(Williams' *Foreword* in Andrews 2006: ix)

Andrews developed his approach to farming and landscape management by observing, reading and listening to the land over several decades. Understanding his approach to farming, Williams says, would not be comprehensible without a willingness 'to think outside the box, and try thinking in ways that are . . . not burdened by traditional perspectives' (Williams, in Andrews 2006: x). Andrews' perspective on the contemporary legal and cultural discourses of property developed from an acknowledgment of the crisis of the material conditions of its overarching paradigm of placelessness:

Can farming survive as a viable industry in a landscape that's becoming increasingly degraded and afflicted by salinity? Can farmers somehow keep their land productive without spending more on chemical fertilizers and herbicides?

(Andrews 2006: 1)

Rather than encounter these concerns and questions with anxiety, Andrews reminded himself and reminds others that the 'environment had survived and flourished for millions of years without anyone spending a cent on it'. The reassurance he found in this fact encouraged him to pursue the reasons for its recent and dramatic decline and to ascertain whether they were irreversible processes of decline or whether there was reason to hope. Andrews describes in detail maladaptive land use practices that led to the disappearance of numerous wetlands. The problem with the practices and the values that support them is that they are not physically viable. Wetlands, he says, are as 'vital as our liver and kidneys are to our own health. If you lost 90 per cent of your liver and kidneys, you wouldn't be feeling very well. Our landscape isn't well either' (Andrews 2006: 6). By anthropomorphising the landscape he encourages his readers to connect to the land as another living creature of multiple and networked systems. Rather than seeing the land as a blank slate or undynamic state, his view of place is not inherently different to his view of people. This creates the possibility of empathetic, communicative and reciprocal relationships with place. The important thing for farmers, Andrews' says, is 'a change of mindset' (Andrews 2006: 138).

Whether his principles of land use practice, called 'natural sequence farming' prove helpful, in scientific and agricultural terms, is beyond the scope of this book. What is relevant to the question of the relationship between law and the land is that Andrews' critique of the status quo emphasises relationships and connectivity between people and place based on knowledge of the Earth's systems. Consequently, he presents a departure from dephysicalised concepts of property and the paradigm of placelessness not only in intellectual but also practical terms. His curiosity about the possibility of lessons from the consequences of past land use practices also creates room for change (Andrews 2006: 7). Most importantly, his observation of contemporary land use practices leads him to an unequivocal conclusion that change is necessary and urgent. The crisis is as undeniable as the reasons for it, he argues. And he would agree with geographer David Harvey that 'the only interesting question is what we make of it and what we do with it' (Harvey 2000: 149).

6.3.4 Custodians

Obligations and responsibilities are regarded in modern law as fiduciary duties. Trusts and similar creatures of equity are the source of increasing interest by legal scholars interested in notions of bilateral people–place relations whereby people give, as well as take, from the land. In addition to recycling old legal categories in rethinking property relations, alternative discourses of 'land ethics' and 'stewardship' in environmentalist scholarship also draw considerably from Indigenous laws and models of people–place relations. And these constitute an obvious and sensible source of reflection on modern property relations because in addition to containing concepts of responsibility, Indigenous land laws are demonstrably successful regulatory systems over a long period of time. There are many reasons for their success, some of which relate to geography itself of course, but others relate, importantly, to the worldview or paradigm that supports the laws: 'Our future lies not in the stars, but in our models' (Nordhaus, cited in Brown 1998: 11).

However, there is a limit to models with atopic application and it is precisely the importance of place to knowledge that constitutes the basis of many Indigenous land laws. Because of the complexity of places with networks of systems that are particular to those places, Indigenous land laws are correspondingly complex and particular rather than one-size-fits-all. The contextual and holistic character of Indigenous land law (Weir 2009: 11) contrasts greatly to the paradigm of non-Indigenous property law to which place is irrelevant. The difference between them also makes it difficult for some 'moderns' to see Indigenous knowledge of country as 'more than the sum of its parts' (Weir 2009: 11). Australian geographer Jessica Weir's study of Indigenous people–place relations in the Murray River Country of southeastern Australia draws out the complexity of both Indigenous relations to place and the miscognisance of those relations by non-Indigenous society. In particular, she observes the way in which the conceptual binaries within the paradigm of modern people–place relations blind the 'moderns' to non-binary connections and relations. Consequently, she notes there are patterns of reductive and essentialising analysis in modern legal and cultural discourse that either 'collapse' Indigenous people 'into the landscape, or if their identities profoundly confound this collapse, they are perceived as not really being Indigenous' (Weir 2009: 23).

The contemporary dominant cultural discourse of dephysicalised property regards Indigenous people as either natural or cultural. Consequently, depending on the value attributed to the category, Indigenous knowledge of place is racialised as primitive or noble. In his study of representations of Native American peoples, anthropologist Shepard Krech argues that both European and Native Americans mythologise Indigenous relationships with land. Critiquing a famous 1971 ad campaign for Keep America Beautiful, Inc., that used a photograph of 'Iron Eyes Cody' with tears in his eyes, Krech says the campaign: '[M]ade unfamiliar American Indians familiar by using customary taxonomic categories, but in the process often reduced them simplistically to one of two stereotypes or images, one noble and the other not' (Krech 1999: 16).

One of the problems with the racialisation of Indigenous knowledge is that, as Weir points out, 'important information about how to live in the world persists in being confounded by binary thinking at a time when life-sustaining ecological ethics are really needed' (Weir 2009: 23). This part of the section on cultural discourses of property presents Indigenous knowledge of place not as a homogenous body of static information but as laws that challenge the paradigmatic categories of landscapes: natural or cultural, pristine or spoiled, wild or improved. Indigenous knowledge of place was not intuited, but learned and experienced within specific places over long periods of time. The knowledge of place that is central to Indigenous law 'comes through the living of it' (Watson 2002: 255). What makes any law succeed is not whether it is somehow, inherently good or bad, right or wrong, but whether it meaningfully and practically describes, explains and prescribes activities in the context of local and dynamic material conditions. Where laws exceed their material contexts their authority flounders as the economies they facilitate collapse.

The consequences of losing knowledge of country deeply concerns Nyikina man Paddy Roe, lawman and guardian of the Lurujarri Trail in Broome, Western Australia. His work is to pass on that knowledge, in an effort to arrest what he calls a process of 'killing the country', through the sort of environmentally degrading land use practices that farmers like Purvis inherited from his father. Roe was 'the first Aboriginal child of a white father in that region [and] worked much of his life in the cattle industry' (Healy 1999: 67). The arrival of pastoralists in 1865 'resulted in great changes to land use patterns' in their country. The changes, led by introduced diseases, war and abduction of women and children meant that by the time Roe visited their 'traditional' country in 1931, 'only the elderly members of the tribe remained' (Sinatra and Murphy 1999: 13). The elders 'walked him through the country' teaching its stories, names and sacred sites.

Roe was 'entrusted with the custodianship of the three countries held by the Jabirr Jabirr elders' (Sinatra and Murphy 1999: 13). Roe was concerned that the knowledge of country that the Jabirr Jabirr elders had passed onto him would be lost unless he too could teach it: 'I must look after the country, that's what the old people told me' (Sinatra and Murphy 1999: 15). The contrast between the property relations of the Aboriginal communities of the Kimberley and the property relations of colonial Australians like Purvis' father is indicated by the different vocabulary used to describe Aboriginal property relations. Roe was 'entrusted' with the 'custodianship' of 'country' rather than 'entitled' to the 'profits' of 'property'. Roe's identity as custodian emphasises the importance of knowledge of and kinship with the land and responsibility for its care.

In the 1980s Roe developed the Lurujarri heritage trail to teach people 'to respect' the country and 'return home to become caretakers of their own country' (Sinatra and Murphy 1999: 15). The country, Roe says, is 'waiting for people' (Sinatra and Murphy 1999: 18). He taught his children tribal knowledge that:

> You are the land, and the land is you. There's no difference . . . We have separated from it because we are told it is separate . . . we have people and everything else. So people got separated from nature and don't see themselves as part of it anymore. But we are part of it. Like the

fish, like the birds, like the rocks, we all have our function. We put birds into a box – they are birds. We put trees into a box – they are trees. But they are one and we part of it. We all make up the *living country*.

(Sinatra and Murphy 1999: 19)

The Jabirr Jabirr knowledge of country learned by Roe and its connection to law and to life confounds the conceptual separation of people and place in the paradigm of modern property law. The idea that people are in, and part of, a particular place or country is fundamentally different to the paradigm of nature/culture in the dominant cultural and legal discourses of property. Indigenous relations to place unsettle the dominant cultural and legal discourses and practices of property. The relation they express is not different and compatible with property law, it undermines the law: 'Our relationship to land is as irreconcilable to the western legal property law system, as it is to fit a sphere on top of a pyramid' (Watson 2002: 257).

The importance of Roe's knowledge is not that it is subversive or that Roe himself is a static 'repository of knowledge' or a 'living archive' (Healy 1999: 67). The importance of Roe's knowledge is that it comes from and responds to a living and changing place and the knowledge connects him with that place. Knowledge of place supports life not only in an important economic sense, it 'goes beyond food web dependencies to include stories, histories, feelings, shared responsibilities and respect' (Weir 2009: 50). The poem 'Spiritual song of the Aborigine' written by Hyllus Maris, a Yorta Yortan woman may better express the point:

I am a child of the Dreamtime People
Part of this Land, like the gnarled gumtree
I am the river, softly singing
Chanting our songs on my way to the sea
My spirit is the dust-devils
Mirages, that dance on the plain
I'm the snow, the wind and the falling rain
I'm part of the rocks and the red desert earth
Red as the blood that flows in my veins
I am eagle, crow and snake that glides
Through the rain-forest that clings to the mountainside
I awakened here when the earth was new
There was emu, wombat, kangaroo
No other man of a different hue
I am this land
And this land is me
I am Australia.

(Maris, cited in Gilbert 1988: 60)

Modern property law excludes such dynamic people–place relations preferring them to be fixed as either natural or cultural. In the 1999 *Yorta Yorta*[14] native title case, the Federal Court ruled that the relation between the Yorta Yorta people and their land was severed by colonisation. Justice Olney argued that it was not possible to 're-establish' a connection with the land and that having not 'survived' colonisation and was 'not capable of revival' (at 129). He expressed a familiar ideal of Aboriginal people as being somehow more 'natural' than their cultural, colonial counterparts. Justice Olney imagines Indigenous land use practices to be untouched by culture. Native title, he says, protects relationships that remain 'natural'. When the Yorta Yorta's ways of living changed because of colonisation, Justice Olney regarded them as having now become denatured. In legal discourse this idea is expressed by the concept of 'unbroken' relationships between people and place. One of the most significant aspects of the case in regard to the notion of an 'unbroken' connection between the Yorta Yorta and their country was the interpretation of a piece of evidence submitted by the claimants in support of their claim to have an 'ongoing connection to country as an identifiable people' (Weir 2009: 74). The document, written in 1881, was a petition from the Yorta Yorta to the governor of New South Wales, for the return of some of their country to use for commercial farming. Justice Olney interpreted the petition as evidence of the break in the traditional connection between the Yorta Yorta and the land because farming was not an Indigenous land use 'pre-contact' (Strelein 2009: 75).

Watson argues that native title is 'a further erosion and subversion of Nunga identities, and not a recognition of Nunga rights to land . . . Native title does nothing to help us care for country' (Watson 2002: 260). The relationship between people and place is not based on 'rights' but on connectivity: 'We believe the land is all life. So it comes to us that we are part of the land and the land is part of us. It cannot be one or the other. It cannot be separated by anything or anybody' (Yunupingu 1997: 2–3).

Like the concept of nature and the concept of *terra nullius*, the notion of an 'unbroken' connection between people and place in native title law is fixed. It 'freezes' Indigenous land use practices in time and avoids the fact of adaptation. The subversive perspectives and practices of custodianship are neutralised by abstracting their physical conditions into transcendental cultural traditions. But traditions are not simply inherited; they are *made* in response to the particularity of lands and waters, seasons and global climatic rhythms such as El Niño and La Niña, for example. Traditions are traditions because the reason for them is materially apparent.

---

14 *The Members of the Yorta Yorta Aboriginal Community v State of Victoria and Others* (1998) 1606 FCA 130, upheld by the 2002 High Court decision *The Members of the Yorta Yorta Aboriginal Community v State of Victoria and Others* (2002) 214 CLR 422.

The responsive knowledge of Bob Purvis to the specificity of the three sorts of land he leased is something he wishes to pass on to his children not simply as a fixed family tradition, but as a successful practice of living with those lands. If Purvis' practices do become traditions, if they survive, it is partly because they are made in response to physical conditions that are inescapable and unfixed. The accumulation of knowledge of place that native title law refers to as 'tradition' is as material as it is cultural. It is not because Indigenous land use practices are intrinsically 'more ecologically sound than those of non-Indigenous people' (Gill 1999: 63) that their traditions of property are important. It is not because Indigenous land use practices are natural rather than cultural that these traditions are important to listen to and understand. It is because these traditions are practices have specifically adapted over a long period of time to specific places. This is how they are laws and why they are authoritative.

6.4 Conclusion

This chapter examined contemporary legal and cultural practices of property and their facilitation and subversion of the paradigm of placelessness that supports them. Definitions of property in court judgments, in the speeches and reports of property rights advocates and in university lecture theatres perpetuate both the legal discourse of dephysicalised property and its cultural authority and priority over different kinds of people–place relation. The placeless paradigm of modern property law is maintained not only in theory, but in practice. Contemporary dominant people–place relationships have not departed from their colonial histories and economies. The legal and cultural practices of property interact with the earth's systems and in so doing, shape the landscape itself. But the paradigm of modern property law is subverted not only by alternative paradigms and traditions of people–place relations but by the crises in the material conditions that it has, itself, created.

Chapter 7

Epilogue
Placing property

The land is neither prison nor palace, but a decent home.

(Morris 1984: 96)

Property law today is a tapestry of concepts of possession, ownership and title. Its threads are of different lengths and colours and some of the images it embroiders are fading with time. It is not adequate to an understanding of law to approach these central concepts believing they come from nowhere. The vocabulary and discourse of property does not transcend place and culture; it is not universal. Law has origins in time and in place. Property law is spoken of today in abstract terms. Property theorists have even contended that property is an illusion. In such an illusory relationship, how real can 'real property' be? What is the proper place for it? We are at a distance today from the time and place of origin of our contemporary property law, but we must interrogate the conditions of this history and geography to adequately grasp whether these conditions sufficiently reside here and now to warrant the residue of this past in our words today. Because we 'cannot be concerned with the law, or with the law of laws, either at close range or at a distance without asking where it has its place and whence it comes' (Derrida 1992a: 191).

Thomas Kuhn argued that paradigms succeed because they are simultaneously ideological and practical, that is, they are able to make sense of the world and they are physically possible. In Kuhn's theory, a paradigm reaches crisis not only because other ideas or frameworks of meaning seem more plausible than the current paradigm, but because other practices seem more viable. The crisis of one paradigm and the 'shift' to another are, to Kuhn, not instances of progress, but a matter of adaptation. A paradigm is not part of the imagined teleological movement from the primitive to the civilised, a process of perfection (Kuhn 1996: 170–171). Rather a paradigm is a function of time and place; it succeeds only within particular cultural and natural conditions. Importantly, Kuhn makes this point by reference to Darwin's theory of evolution, which he says:

[R]ecognised no goal set either by God or by nature. Instead, natural selection, operating in the given environment and with the actual organisms presently at hand, was responsible for the gradual but steady emergence of more elaborate, further articulated, and vastly more specialised organisms.

(1996: 172)

Following the metaphor of evolution, Kuhn argues that paradigms result, like organisms in any given environment, 'from mere competition ... for survival'. It is difficult to accept that change and development are not part of a progress toward a specific goal because we are more familiar with the notion of *telos* than with the notion of *habitus*. Kuhn concludes that it is important to regard the specialisation and development of ideas not as paths to truths or predetermined goals, but as products of particular historic and geographic circumstances.

Kuhn's theory is helpful to an understanding of the emergence and crisis of the paradigm of modern property law because it allows us to regard its origins and traditions not as lesser or better than they are, as more or less progressed, but as particular to their time and place. The paradigm of modern property law derives from an anthropocentric model of the world, in which humans are the first of two categories, the second being reductively 'everything else' in the world. The dichotomous logic and the hierarchical dynamic governing the relation between the realms of nature/culture belong to a particular time and place – modern Europe. Property law and its parallel paradigm of people/things were established by increasingly exclusive interests in land as private property. The dispossession and diaspora of the English extended the regime of private property in England across the globe via colonisation. The logic, its dynamic and practice are universalising, but they are not universal.

Debates about the dispossession of Indigenous peoples, the experience and possibility of connectivity with place, and environmental critiques of contemporary people–place relations allow us to reconsider the myths and traditions of modern property law. Instrumentalist views of nature and the discourse and practice of 'improvement' were made real, by very particular forms of land use, agriculture and pastoralism. These practices not only evidenced and measured cultural progress, they provided entitlement to property. Property law was defined by an abstract relation to place, rather than by the possibilities and limits of local environmental conditions. The result of the inability of an alien regime of property to adapt the regulation of land ownership and land use to the conditions on the ground was the degradation of the land on a large scale over a long period of time.

The land itself demonstrates the limits of the relationship between people and place institutionalised by modern property law. The paradigm of property law constitutes the abstraction and removal of place and replaces relationships to places with a relationship between 'persons'. Yet, while lessons from the past and from contemporary landscapes are available, modern property law and theory cling to the paradigm that in part created the circumstances that the law is increasingly unable to address. Currently, according to property law, the only 'thing' of which we are in possession is the right itself. Because property law emphasises a 'right' over the 'thing', it bases its legitimacy in power rather than place. The emphasis on 'rights' discourse in defining modern property law maintains the notion that place is irrelevant. This discursive emphasis is materialised by land use. Although the deteriorating condition of landscapes around the world signal an environmental crisis, addressing that crisis has not yet been linked to a crisis of property law: 'Habitat not considered to be "lost" may nonetheless no longer be able to sustain either the abundance or the variety of species that it formerly did' (Sax 2001: 1003).

It is not a coincidence that modern property law says place is irrelevant, that 'things' are immaterial to law and that landscapes are in crisis. The unimportance of 'things', the insignificance of their particularity and diversity in property relations, creates a lack of care for the particularity and diversity of land, when and where it is the 'thing' of property. The values and work of land custodians demonstrates the difference a land ethic makes to sustainable people–place relations. Nevertheless, their land ethic remains marginal and subversive. In the semiology of modern property law, the possession of land means power over it. An owner might say 'it belongs to me'. For custodians, possession of land means connection with it. A custodian might say 'I belong to the land'.

Reading the differences in theories of property as diversities in time and place collapses the possibility of their transcendence. Thus, rather than accepting the theory of dephysicalised property, it becomes possible to ask where and when that theory emerged and whether its validity is related, if not limited to those historical and geographical conditions. Despite its claims, law cannot refer outside itself to an unmediated reality (Ryan 1996: 4); rather it shapes and partly creates that reality – as landscape. The point is not to construe human agency in the environment as inherently destructive or to valorise different cultural forms of human agency, as if they were inherently less destructive or somehow 'natural'. That would reverse the privileged term in the dyad of nature/culture, but at the same time maintain the paradigm that articulates these two distinct and all-encompassing terms. The point is that adaptation achieves a sustainable economy in its environment.

Adaptation is necessarily a process of becoming local. Presently, modern property law is part of a process not of *being* or *becoming*, but of *having*. Things are had, not for their particularity, but for their general value in a global sense. Where adaptation requires connection with all things at a local level, property law disconnects people from 'everything else'. Therefore, the question is not whether environmental change is natural or anthropogenic, as if humans were not part of nature; neither is the question whether some cultural groups have a better entitlement to the land. The question is to what extent we recognise that our economy or ecology is historically and geographically specific and, then, to what extent and for how long it can endure in a different time and place. The question of place in property law is thus disruptive.

Property law is an ideology and practice of a relationship between people and place. The practice and the ideology work together, they are part of a paradigm. The paradigm of modern property law is, like other paradigms, particular to specific cultural and natural conditions. Where those conditions are not truly local conditions, the people–place relations that property law enables and prohibits, have adverse consequences. In this way, it is possible to think of property law as maladapted. *Lawscape* has not attempted to redefine the law of property, rather it has unpicked the paradigmatic components and consequences of legal definitions of property in order to evaluate how they inform and are informed by relationships between people and place. The paradigm of modern law, a paradigm of placelessness, is not meaningful or viable as a prescriptive theory and practice of relationships between people and place.

Jared Diamond argues that the reason the human societies of the eastern Mediterranean and Fertile Crescent weakened after centuries of socioeconomic success is because the material conditions that supported them existed in an 'ecologically fragile environment' (Diamond 1997: 411). Whether they lacked the knowledge or the normative paradigms to adapt to their fragile environment, these regions that once covered in 'fertile woodland' eventually 'eroded to scrub or desert' (Diamond 1997: 410). Diamond's conclusion is that 'they committed ecological suicide by destroying their own resource base' (1997: 411). The role of law in prescribing and regulating people–place relations is central to the success or failure of any society. *Lawscape* has explored the extent to which the concept of dephysicalised property law is successful in prescribing people–place relations. Integrating the material conditions and consequences of law into law's logic and operation are not only helpful, but vital, to authoritative and sustainable people–place regulation. If we want to know how to reshape our property law, we have to look no further than the landscape because it is the landscape that reveals our place in the world and the opportunities and limits of our connection with it.

Bibliography

Cases and Legislation

Attorney-General v Brown 1 Legge 313

Commonwealth of Australia Constitution Act 1900 (UK)

Director-General of the Department of Environment and Climate Change v Hudson (2009) 165 LGERA 256

Fejo (on behalf of the Larrakia People) v Northern Territory (1998) 156 ALR 721

Johnson v McIntosh (1823) 21 US 543

Lien of Wool and Mortgage of Live Stock Act 1843 (NSW)

Lucas v South Carolina Coastal Council 404 SE2d 895 (1991)

Lucas v South Carolina Coastal Council 505 US 1003 (1992)

Mabo v Queensland (No. 2) (1992) 175 CLR 1

Mariner Real Estate Ltd v Nova Scotia (Attorney-General) (1999) 177 DLR (4th) 696

Members of the Yorta Yorta Aboriginal Community v State of Victoria and Others (1998) 1606 FCA 130

Members of the Yorta Yorta Aboriginal Community v State of Victoria and Others (2002) 214 CLR 422

Milirrpum v Nabalco Pty Ltd (1971) 17 FLR 141

Minister for the Environment and Heritage v Greentree (No 2) (2004) 138 FCR 198

National Parks and Wildlife Conservation Act 1975 (Cth)

Native Title Act 1993 (Cth)

Native Title Amendment Act 1998 (Cth)

Newcrest Mining (WA) Limited v Commonwealth (1997) 190 CLR 513

Pastoral Land Act 1992 (NT)

Randwick Municipal Council v Rutledge (1959) 102 CLR 54

St Catherine's Milling and Lumber Company v R (1888) 14 App Cas 6

Steel v Houghton 1 BHH 51, 126 ER 32

Victoria Park Racing and Recreation Grounds Co. Ltd v Taylor (1937) 58 CLR 479

Walsinghams' Case (1573) 75 ER 805

Waste Lands Occupation Act 1846 (UK)

Wik Peoples v State of Queensland (1996) 187 CLR 1

Williams v Attorney-General (NSW) (1913) 16 CLR 404

Yanner v Eaton (1999) 201 CLR 351

Historical Records

Watson, F. (ed.) (1925) *Historical records of Australia*, Ser. 1, Vol. 1, Sydney: Government Printer.

Unpublished Materials

Bowrey, K. (ed.) (1993) 'Law of property', course materials, Macquarie University.
Carney, T. (2001a) 'Real property law', course outline, University of Sydney.
Carney, T. (2001b) 'Real Property', unpublished lectures, University of Sydney.
Kerruish, V. (1999) 'Property and equity', unpublished lectures, Macquarie University.
Kerruish, V. and Bowrey, K. (eds) (1999) 'Property law and equity', unpublished course materials, Macquarie University.
McCoy, D. (1997) 'From hotel to home: immigration resettlement and community: the ethnic Vietnamese in Australia 1975–1995', unpublished thesis, University of New South Wales.
Skapinker, D. (2001) 'Real property', unpublished lectures, University of Sydney.

Film

The Castle (1997) videorecording, Village Roadshow Pictures, Australia.

Media and Internet Sources

Australian Bureau of Statistics on Land Ownership and Land Use from Yearbook Australia (2002). Available http://www.abs.gov.au/ (accessed December 2009).
Canadian Encyclopaedia (2009). Available http://www.thecanadianencyclopedia.com (accessed December 2009).
Cordery, A. (2010) 'Pursuing his case through courts with zeal', *Sydney Morning Herald*, 5 January 2010. Available http://www.smh.com.au (accessed January 2010).
Corish, P. (2005) 'The impact of native vegetation legislation on farmers,' address of the President of the National Farmers' Federation at the Tasmanian Farmers and Graziers' Association Annual Conference, 1 September. Available http://www. nff. org.au/media-files/2428470953.html (accessed July 2009).
Cronin, A. (2001) 'A better deal for farmers', address of the Chief Executive Officer of the National Farmers' Federation at the AgForce Annual Conference, Mackay, Queensland, 31 July. Available http://www.nff.org.au/pages/speeches/speech_old/2001_AgForce_AGM.htm (accessed July 2002).
Donges, I. (2001) 'Salinity a landholder's view', address of the President of the National Farmers' Federation at the National Local Government Salinity Summit, Echucha, Victoria, 18 June. Available http://www.nff.org.au/pages/speeches/speech_old/2001_Salinity.html (accessed July 2002).
Harrison, D. and Cubby, B. (2010) 'Hunger strike drives further wedge into coalition', *Sydney Morning Herald*, 5 January. Available http://www.smh.com.au (accessed January 2010).
Kumar, S. (2007) 'Cutting carbon is a rich fool's errand', *The Guardian*, 29 August. Available http://www.guardian.co.uk/society/2007/aug/29/guardiansociety supplement. comment1 (accessed January 2008).

National Farmer's Federation (2009a) 'Farm, facts'. Available http://www.nff.org.au (accessed September 2009).

National Farmer's Federation (2009b) 'Submission to the interim report for the independent review of the Environment Protection and Biodiversity Act 1999 (EPBC Act)', 10 August. Available http://www.nff.org.au (accessed November 2009).

Books, Reports and Articles

Alexander, G. (1986) 'History as ideology in the basic property course', *Journal of Legal Education*, 36(3): 381–389.

Alexander, G. (1997) *Commodity & propriety: competing visions of property in American legal thought 1776–1970*, Chicago: University of Chicago Press.

Alexander, G. (1998) 'Critical land law', in S. Bright and J. Dewar (eds), *Land law: themes and perspectives*, New York: Oxford University Press.

Allen, R. (1992) *Enclosure and the yeoman*, Oxford: Clarendon Press.

Andrews, P. (2006) *Back from the brink: how Australia's landscape can be saved*, Sydney: ABC Books.

Aplin, G., Beggs, P., Brierley, G., Cleugh, H., Curson, P., Mitchell, P. et al. (1999) *Global environmental crises: an Australian perspective*, 2nd edn, Melbourne: Oxford University Press.

Arendt, H. (1958) *The human condition*, Chicago: University of Chicago Press.

Arendt, H. (1992) 'Introduction', in W. Benjamin, *Illuminations* (trans. H. Zohn), London: Fontana Press.

Arneil, B. (1994) 'Trade, plantations and property: John Locke and the economic defence of colonialism', *Journal of the History of Ideas*, 55(4): 591–609.

Arthur, J.M. (2003) *The default country: a lexical cartography of 20th century Australia*, Sydney: University of New South Wales Press.

Ashton, P. (1987) *On the land: a photographic history of farming in Australia*, Kenthurst, NSW: Kangaroo Press.

Austen, J. (1970) *Pride and prejudice*, London: Oxford University Press.

Ayto, J. (ed.) (1991) *Dictionary of word origins*, New York: Arcade Publishing.

Bacon, F. (1990) [1626] *The new Atlantis*, Cambridge: Cambridge University Press.

Baker, J. (1979) *An introduction to English legal history*, London: Butterworths.

Ball, D.E. and Walton, G.M. (1976) 'Agricultural productivity change in eighteenth century Pennsylvania', *Journal of Economic History*, 36(1): 102–117.

Banner, S. (1997) 'The political function of the commons: changing conceptions of property and sovereignty in Missouri, 1750–1850', *American Journal of Legal History*, 4: 161–193.

Barcan, R. and Buchanan, I. (eds) (1999) *Imagining Australian space: cultural studies and spatial inquiry*, Nedlands: University of Western Australia Press.

Barnhart, Robert K. (ed.) (2000) *Chambers dictionary of etymology*, Edinburgh: Chambers Harrap Publishers.

Barrell, J. (1972) *The idea of landscape and the sense of place 1730–1840*, Cambridge: Cambridge University Press.

Barrell, J. (1986) *The political theory of painting from Reynolds to Hazlitt: 'the body of the public'*, New Haven, CT: Yale University Press.

Bartel, R.L. (2005) 'When the heavenly gaze criminalises: satellite surveillance, land clearance regulation and the human–nature relationship', *Current Issues in Criminal Justice*, 16: 322–339.

Bate, J. (1991) *Romantic ecology: Wordsworth and the environmental tradition*, London: Routledge.

Bates, F. (1984) 'Like an unwelcome guest: the moral crisis in modern legal education', *Law Teacher: Journal of the Association of Law Teachers*, 18(3): 181–202.

Baudrillard, J. (1994) *Baudrillard: a critical reader* (ed. and trans. D. Kellner), Oxford: Blackwell.

Been, V. (2004) 'Lucas v. the green machine: using the takings clause to promote more Efficient regulation?', in G. Korngold and A. Moriss (eds) *Property stories*, New York: Foundation Press.

Beilharz, P. (2002) *Imagining the Antipodes: culture, theory and the visual in the work of Bernard Smith*, Cambridge: Cambridge University Press.

Bellamy, L. and Williamson, T. (1987) *Property and landscape: a social history of land ownership and the English countryside*, London: George Phillip.

Benjamin, W. (1992) *Illuminations* (trans. H. Zohn), London: Fontana.

Bentham, J. (1838) *The works of Jeremy Bentham*, Vol. I. (ed. J. Bowring), Edinburgh: William Tate.

Bentham, J. (1978) [1864] 'A theory of legislation', in C.B. Macpherson (ed.) (1978) *Property: mainstream and critical positions*, Toronto: University of Toronto Press.

Benton, T. (1995) 'Adam Smith and the limits to growth', in S. Copley and K. Sutherland (eds) *Adam Smith's wealth of nations*, New York: Manchester University Press.

Berman, M. (1981) *The reenchantment of the world*, Ithaca, NY: Cornell University Press.

Best, S. (1994) 'The commodification of reality and the reality of commodification', in D. Kellner (ed.) *Baudrillard: a critical reader*, Oxford: Blackwell.

Blackstone, W. (1966) [1765–1766] *The commentaries on the laws of England, Books 1 & 2*, London: Dawsons.

Blaisdell, B. (ed.) (2000) *Great speeches by Native Americans*, Mineola, NY: Dover Publications.

Blake, W. (1972) *Complete writings* (ed. G. Keynes), Oxford: Oxford University Press.

Blomley, N. (1994) *Law, space, and the geographies of power*, New York: Guilford Press.

Blomley, N. (1998) 'Landscapes of property', *Law & Society Review*, 32(3): 567–612.

Blomley, N., Delaney, D. and Ford, R. (eds) (2001) *The legal geographies reader: law, power and space*, San Francisco: Wiley-Blackwell.

Bolton, G. (1981) *Spoils and spoilers: Australians make their environment 1788–1980*, Sydney: Allen & Unwin.

Bonyhady, T. (ed.) (1992) 'Property rights', in *Environmental protection and legal change*, Sydney: Federation Press.

Bonyhady, T. (2000) *The sacred earth*, Carlton South: Melbourne University Press.

Bonyhady, T. and Griffiths, T. (2002) *Words for country: landscape and language*, Kensington: University of New South Wales Press.

Bourdieu, P. (1990) *In other words: essays towards a reflexive sociology* (trans. M. Adamson), Cambridge: Polity Press.

Boyce, J. (2009) *Van Diemen's Land*, Melbourne: Black Inc.

Boyd White, J. (1990) *Justice as translation: an essay in cultural and legal criticism*, Chicago: University of Chicago Press.

Brace, L. (1998) *The idea of property in seventeenth century England*, Manchester: Manchester University Press.

Brace, L. (2001) 'Husbanding the earth and hedging out the poor', in A. Buck, J. McLaren and N. Wright (eds), *Land and freedom: law, property rights and the English diaspora*, Aldershot: Ashgate.

Brace, L. and Hoffman, J. (eds) (1997) *Reclaiming sovereignty*, London: Pinter.

Bradbrook, A.J., MacCallum, S.V. and Moore, A.P. (1997) *Australian real property law*, 2nd edn, North Ryde, NSW: Law Book Company Information Services.

Brady, V. (1991) 'The possibilities of order', in M. Dugan (ed.) *Furious agreement*, Melbourne: Penguin (in association with the Australian Institute of Management).

Brewer, J. and Staves, S. (eds) (1995) *Early modern conceptions of property*, London: Routledge.

Briggs, A. (2000) *The age of improvement 1783–1867*, 2nd edn, Harlow: Longman.

Bright, S. and Dewar, J. (eds) (1998) *Land law: themes and perspectives*, New York: Oxford University Press.

Brown, D. and Sharman, F. (1994) 'Enclosure: agreement and acts', *Journal of Legal History*, 15(3): 267–286.

Brown, P.G. (1998) 'Toward an economics of stewardship: the case of climate', *Ecological Economics*, 26: 11–21.

Buck, A. (1990) 'The politics of land law in Tudor England 1529–1540', *Journal of Legal History*, 11(2): 200–217.

Buck, A. (1994) '*Attorney-General v Brown* and the development of property law', *Australian Property Law Journal*, 2(1): 128–138.

Buck, A. (1995) 'Property law and the origins of Australian egalitarianism', *Australian Journal of Legal History*, 1(2): 145–166.

Buck, A. (1996) 'Torrens title, intestate estates and the origins of Australian property law', *Australian Property Law Journal*, 4: 89–98.

Buck, A. (2001) 'Strangers in their own land: capitalism, dispossession and the law', in A. Buck, J. McLaren and N. Wright (eds) *Land and freedom: law, property rights and the British diaspora*, Aldershot: Ashgate.

Buck, A. and Wright, N. (2001) 'Property rights and the discourse of improvement in nineteenth century New South Wales', in A. Buck, J. McLaren and N. Wright (eds) *Land and freedom: law, property rights and the British diaspora*, Aldershot: Ashgate.

Burroughs, P. (1967) *Britain and Australia 1831–1855*, Oxford: Clarendon Press.

Burt, R. and Archer, J. (eds) (1994) *Enclosure acts: sexuality, property, and culture in early modern England*, Ithaca, NY: Cornell University Press.

Butlin, N.G. (1993) *Economics and the Dreamtime: a hypothetical history*, Cambridge: Cambridge University Press.

Butt, P. (1998) *Land law*, 2nd edn, Sydney: Law Book Company.

Butt, P. (2001) *Land law*, 4th edn, Sydney: Law Book Company.

Cain, M. (1994) 'The symbol traders', in M. Cain and C.B. Harrington (eds) *Lawyers in a postmodern world: translation and transgression*, Buckingham: Open University Press.

Campbell, E. (1994) 'Promises of land from the Crown', *University of Tasmania Law Review*, 13(1): 1–42.

Capra, F. (1992) *The tao of physics: an exploration of the parallels between modern physics and eastern mysticism*, London: Flamingo.

Carr, L.G. (1992) 'Emigration and the standard of living: the seventeenth century Chesapeake', *Journal of Economic History*, 52(2): 271–291.

Carter, E., Donald, J. and Squires, J. (1993) *Space and place: theories of identity and location*, London: Lawrence & Wishart.

Carter, P. (1996) *The lie of the land*, London: Faber & Faber.

Casey, E.S. (2002) *Representing Place: Landscape Painting and Maps*, Minneapolis: University of Minnesota Press.

Castan, M. and Schultz, J. (1997) 'Teaching native title', *Legal Education Review*, 8(1): 75–98.

Chambers, R. (2001) *An introduction to property law in Australia*, Sydney: Law Book Company Information Services.

Charlesworth, H. (1988/1989) 'Critical legal education', *Australian Journal of Law and Society*, 5: 27–34.

Cixous, H. (1986) *The newly born woman* (trans. B. Wing), Minneapolis: University of Minnesota Press.

Clare, J. (1984) *John Clare (the Oxford authors)* (eds E. Robinson and D. Powell), Oxford: Oxford University Press.

Clare, J. (2000) *A champion for the poor: political verse and prose* (eds P.M.S. Dawson, E. Robinson and D. Powell), Manchester: Carcanet Press.

Copley, S. and Sutherland, K. (eds) (1995) *Adam Smith's wealth of nations*, New York: Manchester University Press.

Cotterrell, R. (1986) 'The law of property and legal theory', in W. Twining (ed.) *Legal theory and common law*, Oxford: Blackwell.

Coyle, S. and Morrow, K. (2004) *The philosophical foundations of environmental law: property, rights and nature*, Oxford: Hart Publishing.

Cushing, N. (2002) 'The Pacific Highway and Australian modernity', in X. Pons (ed.) *Departures: how Australia reinvents itself*, Carlton South: Melbourne University Press.

Daniels, S. (1993) *Fields of vision: landscape imagery and national identity in England and the United States*, Princeton, NJ: Princeton University Press.

Daniels, S. and Cosgrove, D. (eds) (1988) *The iconography of landscape: essays on the symbolic representation, design and use of past environments*, Cambridge: Cambridge University Press.

Davies, M. (2007) *Property: meanings, histories, theories*, Abingdon: Routledge-Cavendish.

Davies, N. (2000) *The Isles: a history*, London: Papermac.

Dawson, P.M.S., Robinson, E. and Powell, D. (eds) (2000) *A champion for the poor: political verse and prose*, Manchester: Carcanet Press.

Deimann, S. and Dyssli, B. (eds) (1995) *Environmental rights: law, litigation and access to justice*, London: Cameron May.

DeLong, J.V. (1997) *Property matters: how property rights are under assault and why you should care*, New York: Free Press.

Demsetz, H. (1967) 'Toward a theory of property rights', *American Economic Review*, 57(2): 347–359.

Derrida, J. (1978) *Writing and difference* (trans. A. Bass), Chicago: University of Chicago Press.

Derrida, J. (1992a) 'Before the law', in D. Attridge (ed.), *Acts of Literature* (trans. C. Roulston), New York: Routledge.

Derrida, J. (1992b) 'The law of genre', in D. Attridge (ed.), *Acts of Literature*, New York: Routledge.

Descartes, R. (1978) *Discourse on method and the meditations*, Harmondsworth: Penguin.

Diamond, J. (1997) *Guns, germs and steel*, London: Vintage.

Dick, S. (1996) *The biological universe*, New York: Cambridge University Press.

Dickens, P. (1996) *Reconstructing nature: alienation, emancipation and the division of labour*, London: Routledge.

Dodds, S. (1994) 'Property rights and the environment', in L. Cosgrove, D. Evans and D. Yencken (eds) *Restoring the land: environmental values, knowledge and action*, Carlton South: Melbourne University Press.

Dorsett, S. (2002) 'Since time immemorial': a story of common law jurisdiction, native title and the Case of Tanistry', *Melbourne University Law Review*, 26: 32–59.

Dorsett, S. and McVeigh, S. (2002) 'Just so: the law which governs Australia is Australian law', *Law and Critique*, 13: 289–309.

Dorsett, S. and McVeigh, S. (2005) 'An essay on jurisdiction, jurisprudence, and authority: the High Court of Australia in Yorta Yorta (2001)', *Northern Ireland Legal Quarterly*, 56(1): 1–20.

Drew, P. (1994) *The coast dwellers*, Ringwood: Penguin.

Dunlap, T. (1999) *Nature and the English diaspora: environment and history in the United States, Canada, Australia and New Zealand*, Cambridge: Cambridge University Press.

Edgeworth, B. (1994) 'Tenure, allodialism and indigenous rights at common law: English, United States and Australian land law compared after *Mabo v. Queensland*', *Anglo-American Law Review*, 23(3): 397–434.

Elton G.R. (1982) *The Tudor constitution: documents and commentary*, Cambridge: Cambridge University Press.

Estabrook, C.B. (1998) *Urbane and rustic England: cultural ties and social spheres in the provinces 1660–1780*, Manchester: Manchester University Press.

Farrier, D., Lyster, R. and Pearson, L. (eds) (1999) *The environmental law handbook: planning and land use in New South Wales*, 3rd edn, Redfern: Redfern Legal Centre Publishing.

Ferry, L. (1995) *The new ecological order* (trans. C. Volk), Chicago: University of Chicago Press.

Fitter, C. (1995) *Poetry, space, landscape: toward a new theory*, Cambridge: Cambridge University Press.

Fitzpatrick, P. (1992) *The mythology of modern law*, London: Routledge.

Flannery, T. (1994) *The future eaters: an ecological history of Australasian lands and people*, Kew, VIC: Reed.

Foucault, M. (1973) *The order of things: an archaeology of the human sciences*, New York: Vintage.

Foucault, M. (1990) *The history of sexuality*, Vol. I, New York: Vintage.

Fraser, D. (1988/1989) 'What a long, strange trip it's been: deconstructing law from legal realism to critical legal studies', *Australian Journal of Law and Society*, 5: 35–43.

Freud, S. (1990) *Penguin Freud library*, Vol: 14, *Art and literature* (ed. and trans. J. Strachey), London: Penguin.

Freud, S. (1991) *The standard edition of the complete works of Sigmund Freud*, Vol. XIX, London: Penguin.

Freyfogle, E. (2003) *The land we share: private property and the common good*, Washington, DC: Island Press.

Garner, R. (1997) 'Ecology and animal rights: is sovereignty anthropocentric?', in L. Brace and J. Hoffman (eds) *Reclaiming sovereignty*, London: Pinter.

Gascoigne, J. (2002) *The enlightenment and the origins of European Australia*, Cambridge: Cambridge University Press.

Gava, J. (1988/1989) 'Introductory essay – current controversies in legal education', *Australian Journal of Law and Society*, 5: 1–10.

Gelder, K. and Jacobs, J. (1998) *Uncanny Australia: sacredness and identity in a post-colonial nation*, Melbourne: Melbourne University Press.

George, R. (1996) *The politics of home*, Cambridge: University of Cambridge Press.

Gilbert, K. (ed.) (1988) *Inside black Australia*, Ringwood: Penguin.

Gill, N. (1999) 'The ambiguities of wilderness', in E. Stratford (ed.) *Australian cultural geographies*, Melbourne: Oxford University Press.

Girard, P. (2005) 'Land law, liberalism and the agrarian ideal: British North America, 1750–1920', in J., McLaren, A., Buck and N. Wright (eds) *Despotic dominions: property rights in British settler societies*, Vancouver: UBC Press.

Godden, L. (1998) 'Preserving natural heritage: nature as other', *Melbourne University Law Review*, 22: 719–743.

Goldney, D. and Bauer, J. (1998) 'Integrating conservation and agricultural production: fantasy or imperative?', in J. Pratley and A. Robertson (eds) *Agriculture and the environmental imperative*, Collingwood: CSIRO Publishing.

Goot, M. (1998) 'Hanson's heartland: who's for one nation and why?', in R. Manne and T. Abbott (eds), *Two nations: the causes and effects of the rise of the One Nation Party in Australia*, Melbourne: Bookman Press.

Graham, N. (2002) 'Ec-centric places: departures in property law', in X. Pons (ed.) *Departures: how Australia reinvents itself*, Carlton South: Melbourne University Press.

Graham, N. (2009a) 'Restoring the "real" to real property law,' in W. Prest (ed.) *Blackstone and his commentaries: biography, law, history*, Oxford: Hart Publishing.

Graham, N. (2009b) 'Indigenous property matters in real property courses at Australian universities', *Legal Education Review*, 19(2): 5–20.

Grant, D. (ed.) (1950) *Alexander Pope: poems*, Harmondsworth: Penguin.

Grattan, S. and McNamara, L. (1999) 'The common law construct of native title: a "refeudalisation" of Australian land law', *Griffith Law Review*, 8(1): 50–85.

Gray, K. (1991) 'Property in thin air', *Cambridge Law Journal*, 50(2): 252–307.

Gray, K. (1993) *Elements of land law*, 2nd edn, London: Butterworths.

Gray, K. (2002) 'Land law and human rights', in L. Tee (ed.) *Land law: issues, debates, policy*, Cullompton: Willan Publishing.

Gray, K. (2007) 'Can environmental regulation constitute a taking at common law?', *Environmental and Planning Law Journal*, 24: 161–181.

Gray, K. and Gray, S.F. (1998) 'The idea of property in land', in S. Bright and J. Dewar (eds) *Land law: themes and perspectives*, New York: Oxford University Press.

Greenfield, S. (2000) *The private life of the brain*, London: Penguin.

Griggs, L. and Snell, R. (1997) 'The curriculum and teaching of property law in Australian law schools', *Australian Property Law Journal*, 5: 213–226.

Grigg-Spall, I. and Ireland, P. (1992) *The critical lawyers handbook*, London: Pluto.

Grosz, E. (1993) 'Judaism and exile: the ethics of otherness', in E. Carter, J. Donald and J. Squires, *Space and place: theories of identity and location*, London: Lawrence & Wishart.

Grundmann, R. (1991) *Marxism and ecology*, Oxford: Oxford University Press.

Guillory, J. (1995) 'Literary capital: Gray and Barbauld', in J. Brewer and S. Staves (eds) *Early modern conceptions of property*, London: Routledge.

Guy, J.A. (1985) *Christopher St. German on chancery and statute*, London: Selden Society.

Hage, G. (1998) *White nation: fantasies of white supremacy in a multicultural society*, Annandale: Pluto Press.

Harris, J.W. (1996) *Property and justice*, Oxford: Clarendon Press.

Harvey, A.D. (1980) *English poetry in a changing society, 1780–1825*, London: Allison & Busby.

Harvey, D. (2000) *Justice, nature and the geography of difference*, San Francisco: Wiley-Blackwell.

Hay, P. (2002) *Main currents in western environmental thought*, Sydney: University of NSW Press.

Hayman, R. (2003) *Trees: woodlands and western civilization*, London: Continuum.

Haynes, R. (1998) *Seeking the centre: the Australian desert in literature, art and film*, Cambridge: Cambridge University Press.

Hayward, T. and O'Neill, J. (eds) (1997) *Justice, property and the environment*, Aldershot: Ashgate.

Head, L. (2000) *Second nature: the history and implications of Australia as Aboriginal landscape*, New York: Syracuse University Press.

Healy, C. (1999) 'White feet and black trails: travelling cultures at the Lurujarri Trail', *Postcolonial Studies*, 2(1): 55–73.

Heathcote, R.L. (1969) 'Drought in Australia: a problem of perception', *Geographical Review*, 59(2): 175–194.

Hegel (1977) *The phenomenology of spirit* (trans. A. Miller), Oxford: Oxford University Press.

Hepburn, S.J. (1998) *Principles of property law*, Avalon, NSW: Cavendish Publishing.

Hodge, B. (1999) 'White Australia and the Aboriginal invention of space', in R. Barcan and I. Buchanan (eds) *Imagining Australian space: cultural studies and spatial inquiry*, Nedlands: University of Western Australia Press.

Hohfeld, W.N. (1913) 'Some fundamental legal conceptions as applied in legal reasoning', *Yale Law Journal*, 23: 16–59.

Hohfeld, W.N. (1917) 'Fundamental legal conceptions as applied to judicial reasoning', *Yale Law Journal*, 26: 710–770.

Holt-Jensen, A. (1999) *Geography: history and concepts*, 3rd edn, London: Sage.

Horton, D. (2000) *The pure state of nature: sacred cows, destructive myths and the environment*, St Leonards: Allen & Unwin.

Hoskins W.G. (1988) *The making of the English landscape*, London: Hodder & Stoughton.

Hoskins, W.G. and Stamp, L.D. (1963) *The common lands of England and Wales*, London: Collins.

Hughes, R. (1987) *The fatal shore. A history of the transportation of convicts to Australia 1788–1868*, London: Collins Harville.

Hundert, E.J. (1972) 'The making of homo faber: John Locke between ideology and history', *Journal of the History of Ideas*, 33(1): 3–22.

Kamenka, E. and Neale, R.S. (eds) (1975) *Feudalism, capitalism and beyond*, London: Edward Arnold.

Karsten, P. (2002) *Between law and custom 'high' and 'low' legal cultures in the lands of the British diaspora – the United States, Canada, Australia, and New Zealand, 1600–1900*, Cambridge: Cambridge University Press.

Kellner, D. (ed.) (1994) *Baudrillard: a critical reader*, Oxford: Blackwell.

Kercher, B. (1995) *An unruly child: a history of law in Australia*, Sydney: Allen & Unwin.

Kerruish, V. (2002) 'At the court of the strange god', *Law and Critique*, 13: 271–287.

Klingaman, D. (1971) 'Food surpluses and deficits in the American colonies, 1768–1772', *Journal of Economic History*, 31(3): 553–569.

Kohen, J. L. (1995) *Aboriginal environmental impacts*, Sydney: UNSW Press.

Krech, S. (1999) *The ecological Indian: myth and history*, New York: Norton & Co.

Kristeva, J. (1991) *Strangers to ourselves*, New York: University of Columbia Press.

Kuhn, T. (1996) *The structure of scientific revolutions*, 3rd edn, Chicago: University of Chicago Press.

Lacan, J. (1992) *The ethics of psychoanalysis*, London: Routledge.

Lachapelle, P.R. and McCool, S.F. (2005) 'Exploring the concept of "ownership" in natural resource planning', *Society and Natural Resources*, 18: 279–285.

Lametti, D. (2003) 'The concept of property: relations through objects of social wealth', *University of Toronto Law Review*, 325: 325–378.

Lane, P. (2000) 'Native title – the end of property as we know it?', *Australian Property Law Journal*, 8: 1–37.

Langford, P. (1989) *A polite and commercial people: England 1727–1783*, Oxford: Clarendon Press.

Langford, P. (1991) *Public life and the propertied Englishman 1689–1798*, Oxford: Clarendon Press.

Large, D. (1973) 'This land is whose land? Changing concepts of land as property', *Wisconsin Law Review*, 4: 1039–1083.

Latour, B. (2001) *We have never been modern*, Cambridge, MA: Harvard University Press.

Leopold, A. (1966) *A sand county almanac*, New York: Ballantyne.

Letnic, M. (2000) 'Dispossession, degradation and extinction: environmental history in arid Australia', *Biodiversity and Conservation*, 9: 295–308.

Lines, W.J. (1991) *Taming the Great South Land: a history of the conquest of nature in Australia*, Athens: University of Georgia Press.

Linn, R. (1999) *Battling the land: two hundred years of rural Australia*, St Leonards: Allen & Unwin.

Locke, J. (1988) [1689] *Two treatises on government* (ed. P. Laslett), Cambridge: Cambridge University Press.

Lubowski, R.N., Vesterby, M., Bucholtz, S., Baez, A. and Roberts, M.J. (2006) *Major uses of land in the United States, 2002*. Economic Information Bulletin No. 14 Economic Research Service/USDA.

McConnochie, K. (2002) 'Desert departures: isolation, innovation and introversion in ice-age Australia', in X. Pons (ed.) *Departures: how Australia reinvents itself*, Carlton South: Melbourne University Press.

McDowell, L. (1999) *Gender identity and place: understanding feminist geographies*, Minneapolis: University of Minnesota Press.

Macintosh, A. (2009) 'Australia's national environmental legislation: a response to early', *Journal of International Wildlife Law & Policy*, 12(3): 166–179.

Macintosh, A. and Denniss, R. (2004) *Property rights and the environment: should farmers have a right to compensation?* Discussion Paper No. 74, Canberra: Australia Institute.

McLaren, J., Buck, A., and Wright, N., (2005) *Despotic dominion: property rights in British settler societies*, Vancouver: UBC Press.

McLeod, B. (1999) *The geography of empire in English literature 1580–1745*, Cambridge: Cambridge University Press.

McMichael, P. (1984) *Settlers and the agrarian question*, Cambridge: Cambridge University Press.

Macpherson, C.B. (1962) *The political theory of possessive individualism: Hobbes to Locke*, Oxford: Oxford University Press.

Macpherson, C.B. (1973) *Democratic theory: essays in retrieval*, Oxford: Clarendon Press.

Macpherson, C.B. (1975) 'Capitalism and the changing concept of property', in E. Kamenka and R.S. Neale (eds) *Feudalism, capitalism and beyond*, London: Edward Arnold.

Macpherson, C.B. (ed.) (1978) *Theory of legislation in property: mainstream and critical positions*, Toronto: University of Toronto Press.

McRae, A. (1992) 'Husbandry manuals and the language of agrarian improvement', in M. Leslie and T. Raylor (eds), *Culture and cultivation in early modern England: writing and the land*, London: Leicester University Press.

McRae, H., Nettheim, G. and Beacroft, L. (1991) *Aboriginal legal issues: commentary and materials*, Sydney: Law Book Company.

Mancall, P.C., and Weiss, T. (1999) 'Was economic growth likely in colonial British North America?', *Journal of Economic History*, 59(1): 17–40.

Manne, R. and Abbott, T. (1998) *Two nations: the causes and effects of the rise of the One Nation Party in Australia*, Melbourne: Bookman Press.

Marshall, P. (1994) *Nature's web: rethinking our place on earth*, New York: Paragon.

Marx, K. (1975a) [1844] 'Paris manuscripts', in *Marx, Engels: collected works III*, London: Lawrence & Wishart.

Marx, K. (1975b) [1847] *The poverty of philosophy*, Moscow: Progress Publishers.

Marx, K. (1978) *The Marx-Engels reader* (ed. R. Tucker), New York: Norton.

Massey, D. and Jess, P. (1995) *A place in the world?: places, cultures and globalisation*, New York: Oxford University Press.

Maurer, B. (1999) 'Forget Locke? From proprietor to risk-bearer in new logics of finance', *Public Culture*, 11: 365–385.

Mazoyer, M. and Roudart, L. (2006) *A history of world agriculture: from the Neolithic age to the current crisis* (trans. J.H. Membrez), London: Earthscan.

Merchant, C. (1980) *The death of nature: women, ecology, and the scientific revolution*, San Francisco: Harper & Row.

Midgley, M. (1996) *Utopias, dolphins and computers: problems of philosophical plumbing*, London: Routledge.

Mill, J.S. (1978) [1878] *Principles of political economy*, in C.B. Macpherson (ed.) (1978), *Property: mainstream and critical positions*, Toronto: University of Toronto Press.

Milsom, S.F.C. (1969) *Historical foundations of the common law*, London: Butterworths.

Milsom, S.F.C. (2003) *A natural history of the common law*, New York: Columbia University Press.

Mohanram, R. (1999) *Black body: women, colonialism and space*, St Leonards: Allen & Unwin.

Morris, W. (1984) *New from nowhere and selected writings and designs* (ed. A. Briggs), Harmondsworth: Penguin.

Muecke, S. (1992) *Textual spaces: Aboriginality and cultural studies*, Kensington: University of New South Wales Press.

Mugambwa, J. (1997) 'From teaching the law of real property to teaching property law in Australasian law schools', *James Cook University Law Review*, 4: 4–12.

Neave, M.A., Rossiter, C.J. and Stone, M.A. (eds) (1999) *Sackville and Neave property law: cases and materials*, 6th edn, Sydney: Butterworths.

Neave, M.A., Sackville, R. and Stone, M.A. (eds) (1994) *Sackville and Neave property law: cases and materials*, 5th edn, Sydney: Butterworths.

Neeson, J.M. (1993) *Commoners: common right, enclosure and social change in England, 1700–1820*, Cambridge: Cambridge University Press.

Neidjie, B. (1989) *Story about feeling* (ed. K. Taylor), Broome, WA: Magabala Books.

Neumann, K., Thomas, N. and Eriksen, H. (eds) (1999) *Quicksands: foundational histories in Australia and Aotearoa New Zealand*, Kensington: University of New South Wales Press.

Nightingale, P. (ed.) (1986) *A sense of place*, St Lucia: University of Queensland Press.

O'Carroll, J. (1999) 'Upside down and inside out: notes on the Australian unconscious', in R. Barcan and I. Buchanan (eds) *Imagining Australian space: cultural studies and spatial inquiry*, Nedlands: University of Western Australia Press.

O'Donnell, A. and Johnstone, R. (1997) *Developing a cross-cultural law curriculum*, Sydney: Cavendish Publishing.

Olivetti, A.M. and Worsham, J. (2003) *This land is your land, this land is my land: the property rights movement and regulatory takings*, New York: LFB Scholarly Publishing LLC.

Orr, D.W. (2004) *Earth in mind: on education, environment and the human prospect*, Washington, DC: Island Press.

Pearce, D., Campbell, E. and Harding, D. (1987) *Australian law schools: a discipline assessment for the Commonwealth Tertiary Education Commission* (*the Pearce Report*), Canberra: Australian Government Publishing Service.

Penner, J.E. (1997) *The idea of property in law*, New York: Oxford University Press.

Pickard, J. (2001) 'Safe carrying capacity and sustainable grazing: how much have we learnt in semi-arid Australia in the last 170 years?', in A. Conacher (ed.) *Land degradation*, Amsterdam: Kluwer Academic Publishers.

Plato (1951) *The symposium*, London: Penguin.

Pope, A. (1950) [1711] 'An essay on criticism', in D. Grant (ed.) *Poems*, Harmondsworth: Penguin.

Postema, G.J. (1986) *Bentham and the common law tradition*, Oxford: Clarendon Press.

Pottage, A. (1990) 'Property: re-appropriating Hegel', *Modern Law Review*, 53(2): 259–270.

Pottage, A. (1993) 'Review of *The mythology of modern law*', *Modern Law Review*, 56: 615–619.

Pottage, A. (1994) 'The measure of land', *Modern Law Review*, 57(3): 361–384.

Pottage, A. (1998a) 'Evidencing land ownership', in S. Bright and J. Dewar (eds) *Land law: themes and perspectives*, New York: Oxford University Press.

Pottage, A. (1998b) 'Instituting property', *Oxford Journal of Legal Studies*, 18: 331–344.

Pottage, A. (2001) 'Persons and things: an ethnographic analogy', *Economy and Society*, 30(1): 112–138.

Pottage, A. and Mundy, M. (eds) (2004) *Law, anthropology, and the constitution of the social: making persons and things*, Cambridge: Cambridge University Press.

Rapoport, A. (ed.) (1972) *Australia as human setting: approaches to the designed environment*, Sydney: Angus & Robertson.

Read, P. (1996) *Returning to nothing: the meaning of lost places*, Cambridge: Cambridge University Press.

Read, P. (2000) *Belonging: Australians, place and Aboriginal ownership*, Oakleigh, VIC: Cambridge University Press.

Redclift, M. and Benton, T. (eds) (1994) *Social theory and the global environment*, London: Routledge.

Reed, M. (1990) *The landscape of Britain: from the beginnings to 1914*, London: Routledge.

Reynolds, H. (1987) *The law of the land*, Ringwood: Penguin.

Richter B.D. and Redford K.H. (1999) 'Conservation of biodiversity in a world of use', *Conservation Biology*, 13: 6.

Ricoeur, P. (1977) *The rule of the metaphor* (trans. R. Czerny), Toronto: University of Toronto Press.

Robin, L. (2007) *How a continent created a nation*, Sydney: University of New South Wales Press.

Rose, C. (1994) *Property and persuasion: essays on the history, theory and rhetoric of property*, Boulder, CO: West View Press.

Rose, D.B. (1988) 'Exploring an Aboriginal land ethic', *Meanjin*, 2: 379.

Rowley, C.D. (1972) *The destruction of Aboriginal society*, Melbourne: Penguin.

Ruhl, J.B. (2002) 'Three questions for agriculture about the environment', *Journal of Land Use and Environmental Law*, 17: 395–408.

Russ, D.J. (1993) 'How the "property rights" movement threatens property values in Florida', *Journal of Land use and Environmental Law*, 9(2): 395–436.

Ryan, S. (1996) *The cartographic eye: how explorers saw Australia*, Cambridge: Cambridge University Press.

Said, E.W. (1994) *Culture and imperialism*, London: Vintage.

Sax, J. (2001) 'Comment on John Harte's paper, "Land use, biodiversity, and ecosystem integrity: the challenge of preserving the earth's life support system",' *Ecology Law Quarterly*, 27: 1003–1014.

Sax, J. (2008) 'Environmental law forty years later: looking back and looking ahead', in M. Jeffery, J. Firestone and K. Bubna-Litic (eds) *Biodiversity conservation, law and livelihoods*, New York: Cambridge University Press.

Schama, S. (1995) *Landscape and memory*, London: Fontana.

Seddon, G. (1997) *Landprints: reflections on place and landscape*, Cambridge: Cambridge University Press.

Seipp, D.J. (1994) 'The concept of property in the early common law', *Law and History Review*, 12(1): 29–91.

Serres, M. (1995) *The natural contract* (trans. E. MacArthur and W. Paulson), Ann Arbor: University of Michigan Press.

Sessions, G. (ed.) (1995) *Deep ecology for the 21st century: readings on the philosophy and practice of the new environmentalism*, Boston, MA: Shambhala.

Shaffer, K. (1987) 'Landscape representation and Australian national identity', *Australian Journal of Cultural Studies*, 4(2): 47–60.

Shaw, A.G.L. (1990) 'Colonial settlement 1788–1945', in D.B. Williams (ed.) *Agriculture in the Australian economy*, South Melbourne: Sydney University Press.

Sherman, B. (2008) 'Taxonomic property', *Cambridge Law Journal*, 67(3): 560–584.

Shields, R. (1991) *Places on the margin: alternative geographies of modernity*, New York: Routledge.

Siemon, J. (1994) 'Landlord not king: agrarian change and interarticulation', in R. Burt and J. Archer (eds) *Enclosure acts: sexuality, property, and culture in early modern England*, Ithaca, NY: Cornell University Press.

Simmons, I.G. (1989) *Changing the face of the earth: culture, environment, history*, New York: Blackwell.

Simmons, I.G. (1993) *Interpreting nature: cultural constructions of the environment*, London: Routledge.

Sinatra, J. and Murphy, P. (1999) *Listen to the people listen to the land*, Carlton South: Melbourne University Press.

Sinclair, P. (2001) *The Murray: a river and its people*, Carlton South: Melbourne University Press.

Smith, A. (1976) 'An inquiry into the nature and causes of the wealth of nations', in R.H. Campbell and A.S. Skinner (eds) *Of the experience of justice*, Oxford: Clarendon Press.

Smith, M. (1998) *Ecologism: toward ecological citizenship*, Minneapolis: University of Minnesota Press.

Sokol, M. (1994) 'Bentham and Blackstone on incorporeal hereditaments', *Journal of Legal History*, 15(3): 287–305.

Sperling, K. (1997) 'Going down the takings path: private property rights and public interest in land use decision-making', *Environmental and Planning Law Journal*, 14: 427–436.

Springer, J.W. (1986) 'American Indians and the law of real property in colonial New England', *American Journal of Legal History*, 30: 25–58.

Sterba, J. (1998) *Justice for here and now*, Cambridge: Cambridge University Press.

Stone, C. (1972) 'Should trees have standing?: toward legal rights for natural objects', *Southern Californian Law Review*, 45: 450–501.

Strelein, L. (2009) *Compromised jurisprudence: native title cases since Mabo*, 2nd edn, Canberra: Aboriginal Studies Press.

Stuckey, M. and Kelly, G. (2000) *Property law*, Sydney: Butterworths.

Sugarman, D. (1994) 'Blurred boundaries: the overlapping worlds of law, business and politics', in M. Cain and C.B. Harrington (eds), *Lawyers in a postmodern world: translation and transgression*, Buckingham: Open University Press.

Sugarman, D. and Warrington, R. (1995) 'Land law, citizenship, and the invention of

"Englishness": the strange world of the equity of redemption', in J. Brewer and S. Staves (eds), *Early modern conceptions of property*, London: Routledge.

Sveiby, K. and Skuthorpe, T. (2006) *Treading lightly: the hidden wisdom of the world's oldest people*, Crows Nest, NSW: Allen & Unwin.

Swann, B. (ed.) (1996) *Native American songs and poems: an anthology*, Mineola, NY: Dover Publications.

Takacs, D. (1996) *The idea of biodiversity: philosophies of paradise*, Baltimore, MA: Johns Hopkins University Press.

Teh, G.L. and Dwyer, B.M. (1992) *Introduction to property law*, 2nd edn, Sydney: Butterworths.

Thompson, E.P. (1991) *Customs in common*, London: Merlin Press.

Thornton, M. (1991) 'Portia lost in the groves of academe wondering what to do about legal education', inaugural lecture, La Trobe University, Melbourne, June.

Tooher, J.G. and Dwyer, B. (1997) *Introduction to property law*, 3rd edn, Sydney: LexisButterworths.

Tudge, C. (2003) *So shall we reap: what's gone wrong with the world's food and how to fix it*, London: Penguin.

Tully, J. (1993) *An approach to political philosophy: Locke in contexts*, Cambridge: Cambridge University Press.

Turner, J. (1979) *The politics of landscape*, Oxford: Blackwell.

Twining, W. (ed.) (1986) *Legal theory and common law*, Oxford: Blackwell.

Unger, R. (1976) *Law in modern society*, New York: Free Press.

Vandevelde, K. (1980) 'The new property of the nineteenth century: the development of the modern concept of property', *Buffalo Law Review*, 29: 325–367.

Vidler, A. (1992) *The architectural uncanny: essays in the modern unhomely*, Minneapolis: University of Minnesota Press.

Wadham, S. and Wood, J. (1957) *Land utilization in Australia*, 3rd edn, Melbourne: Melbourne University Press.

Warrington, R. (1984) 'Land law and legal education: is there any justice or morality in Blackacre?', *The Law Teacher: Journal of the Association of Law Teachers*, 18(2): 77–94.

Watson, I. (2002) 'Buried alive', in *Law and Critique*, 13: 253–269.

Weaver, J.C. (1996) 'Beyond the fatal shore: pastoral squatting and the occupation of Australia 1826–1852', *American Historical Review*, 101(4): 980–1007.

Weaver, J.C. (2003) *The great land rush and the making of the modern world 1650–1900*, Montreal: McGill-Queens University Press.

Weir, J.K. (2009) *Murray River Country: an ecological dialogue with traditional owners*, Canberra: Aboriginal Studies Press.

Williams, C. (2004) *Old land, new landscapes: a story of farmers, conservation and the Landcare movement*, Carlton South: Melbourne University Press.

Williams, J. (2001) 'One acre: devaluing real estate to keep land priceless', *Harper's Magazine*, 302(1808): 59–65.

Williams, R. (1973) *The country and the city*, New York: Oxford University Press.

Williams, R. (1976) *Keywords*, Glasgow: Fontana.

Williams, R. (2005) *Culture and materialism*, Verso: London.

Winikoff, T. (ed.) (1995) *Places not spaces: place making in Australia*, Sydney: Envirobook.

Young, A. (2000) *Environmental change in Australia since 1788*, 2nd edn, Melbourne: Oxford University Press.

Young, S. (2008) *The trouble with tradition: native title and cultural change*, Annandale: Federation Press.

Yunupingu, G. (1997) *Our land is our life*, St Lucia: Queensland University Press.

Ziff, B. (2005) 'Warm reception in a cold climate: English property law and the suppression of the Canadian legal identity', in J. McLaren, A. Buck and N. Wright (eds) *Despotic dominion: property rights in British settler societies*, UBC Press: Vancouver.

Index